The

MALIGN HAND

of the

MARKETS

The

MALIGN HAND
of the
MARKETS

**The Insidious Forces on Wall Street
that are Destroying Financial Markets
—and What We Can Do About it**

JOHN STADDON

Mc
Graw
Hill

New York   Chicago   San Francisco   Lisbon   London
Madrid   Mexico City   Milan   New Delhi   San Juan
Seoul   Singapore   Sydney   Toronto

1 2 3 4 5 6 7 8 9 0   DOC/DOC   1 8 7 6 5 4 3 2

ISBN: 978-0-07-179740-5
MHID: 0-07-179740-8

e-book ISBN: 978-0-07-179741-2
e-book MHID: 0-07-179741-6

McGraw-Hill books are available at special quantity discounts to use as premiums and sales promotions, or for use in corporate training programs. To contact a representative please e-mail us at bulksales@mcgraw-hill.com.

This book is printed on acid-free paper.

To
Lucinda

Contents

Acknowledgements

I thank first, Duke University, for research support and for providing an atmosphere conducive to interdisciplinary research over many years. I am also grateful to York University, UK, for a research home during several summers. I thank libraries—The British Library, the University of York Library, the City of York Public Library and, especially, the libraries of Duke University. The internet has been indispensable. Without it, getting up to speed in many areas of knowledge novel to me five years ago would have been nearly impossible. For comments on the manuscript and on talks I have given about this topic I thank Jérémie Jozefowiez, Armando Machado, Jessica Staddon and Knox Huston. I thank my agent, Don Fehr, for cutting my original draft down to a more focused form. I am grateful to NSF and NIH for research support over many years.

As this book was going to press, I became aware of a couple of others, by writers more expert than I in the arcana of finance, making very many of the same points: British finance experts Kevin Dowd and Martin Hutchinson's *Alchemists of Loss: How Modern Finance and Government Intervention Crashed the Financial System* (Wiley, 2010) and Australian economist Steve Keen's *Debunking Economics – Revised and Expanded Edition: The Naked Emperor Dethroned?* (Zed Books, 2011). We differ to some extent on the cures, but the diagnoses are similar.

Preface

A runner-up for the title of this book was "Alice in Finance-Land." I'm not a financial professional or an academic economist. When I came to look at how modern finance is organized, I felt more than a little like Alice, encountering alien structures, strange "products" and disturbing belief systems. But, "Veeery interesting..." as the old *Laugh-In* guy used to say. He would usually add "...but stupid!" which echoes my own puzzlement: Why are they doing this? Why is it legal? What on earth do they think will happen in the long term? To a financial innocent, financial markets look more than a little crazy.

Perhaps it's just ignorance? I have a background in experimental psychology, behavioral economics, and in the concepts and mathematics of dynamical systems—like markets. But I have never traded financial products for a living nor published much in economics or at all in finance journals. I do have some relevant technical knowledge. Still, does that really qualify me to write a book centered on the economics of financial markets? Well, as Ms. Palin might say, "How's conventional economics doin' for ya?" The answer, of course, is "not very well." Most professional economists failed to predict the "dislocation" (as it is now euphemized) of 2008–9 and don't agree now on the best way to deal with it. There is, in the words of my high-school report cards, room for improvement. Unlike physicists or engineers, economists can't afford to be too snooty about interlopers.

Polls show that most Americans feel that something is wrong with their country, that the system is broken, or at least damaged. Bestsellers with names like *Broke, House of Cards, Crisis Economics, Meltdown* and *Freefall* proliferate. These books are often riveting blow-by-blow accounts of an unfolding financial crisis involving powerful people and large sums of money—fun to read but not always helpful in understanding problems or finding solutions. Something *is* wrong, but a page-turner may not provide the answer. This book is not about people, although including a few strong characters cannot be avoided. It isn't really a page-turner. It is as close as I can make it to a readable and disinterested scientific analysis of a set of economic problems that is complex but more comprehensible than you might think.

The book ends with suggestions for reform. People usually react to any such suggestion in two ways. First, they look at where it comes from: is it from my guys (left vs. right, Democrat vs. Republican) or the other guys? If it's from their team they are likely to support it, if from the other, not. After a little thought, they may actually look at the proposal to see if it supports their values: is it for "working families," or against big government, or "green," or whatever? They rarely ask about the long-term effects of a proposal: how will it actually work out over time? British economist John Maynard Keynes, quotable as always, had something to say about this issue. Fanning the flames of short-termism, although this was not his intention, he famously wrote: "The long run is a misleading guide to current affairs. In the long run we are all dead."[1] Well, yes, but if the survival of the American experiment in anything like its present form is important, the long run is in fact *all* that matters.

In this book I look at long-term effects, at whether the current system, or proposed fixes for it, can yield a sustainable outcome. How do financial markets actually work? How and why do they break down? And what might be done to remedy these problems? A realistic account must involve not just economics but psychology, evolutionary biology, philosophy, both moral and conceptual, and some understanding of dynamical systems. Experiment—the only valid way to identify cause and effect in science—is for the most part impossible. The government can't mess about with fiscal and monetary policy in a controlled way to look at their effects on employment and national wealth. Even if it could, an uncontrolled world environment means that the effects of an experiment at one period might not hold for a later period. No one is smart and knowledgeable enough to study and understand every aspect of a modern society in depth. My excuses for taking another bite at the apple are two: the current crop of experts has not done well; and I have a sufficiently odd mix of interests and expertise that something new may emerge from my own efforts to understand what has been happening. You can judge whether or not I have succeeded.

Introduction

The idea of the *efficient free market* dominates modern economic thought. The free market is a kind of Platonic arrangement where traders buy and sell subject only to the most minimal rules. "Efficiency" is an idea I will look at in much more detail later. Suffice it to say now that many believe this ideal market always tends to the common good. But this idea is utterly false, as recent events indicate and the arguments of this book will show.

The ideal free market supposedly has only two rules: the right to property and the sanctity of contracts. Wikipedia describes it as "a market in which there is no economic intervention and regulation by the state, except to enforce private contracts and the ownership of property. It is the opposite of a controlled market, in which the state directly regulates how goods, services and labor may be used, priced, or distributed, rather than relying on the mechanism of private ownership."

A naïve student might be forgiven for answering on the exam, "There are two kinds of market, free and controlled." False, of course: all markets must follow some rules if they are not to degenerate into a Hobbesian war of all against all. The differences among them are the amount and type of regulation, not its presence or absence. There is nothing magical about just these two rules. There is no perfect "free" market. I will show in a moment that rules in addition to contracts and property rights are essential if financial markets are to work as advertised.

If our student wants a good grade, he might go on to laud the free market and perhaps even quote Scottish Enlightenment psychologist, philosopher, and father of modern economics Adam Smith. When the merchant sells you something, said Smith, in the most famous line in the credo of capitalism, "he intends only his own gain, and he is in this, as in many other cases, led by an *invisible hand* to promote an end which was no part of his intention"—that end being, of course, the public good. The baker hopes to make a profit, but in the course of that pursuit, you get bread. This is the magic of the free market.

But Smith was no dope. He knew that the pursuit of self-interest did not always lead to good results for the community. He pointed out that "People of the same trade seldom meet together, even for merriment and diversion, but the conversation ends in a conspiracy against the public, or in some contrivance to raise prices." Smith would certainly have agreed that to make a market work for the common good, some regulations against monopoly and price fixing are necessary. So there are laws in the U.S. and most other developed nations against both of these things—although, as we'll see, they are utterly inadequate to deal with monopolies in financial markets. But are monopoly and price fixing the only ways the invisible hand can fail to work as advertised? Emphatically, no, especially in financial markets. These other "failure modes" are even less visible than the invisible hand. Consequently, they are widely neglected. This book is about them.

Conventional economics says little about what is actually going on in markets, about the real-time processes that drive prices up or down. The reason is obvious. Markets usually involve thousands of people each with his or her own set of likes and dislikes and financial constraints. Economists love mathematical models but it's hard to apply them to the behavior of thousands of idiosyncratic individuals. Science must simplify. Economists have simplified by concentrating on *equilibria* and steady states, and by largely ignoring the process by which an equilibrium is reached. Following are a couple of examples of how this is supposed to work.

If you assume that, as the price of something goes up, more of it will be produced, and also that, as price goes down, more of it will be bought—the "law" of supply and demand—then it seems to follow there will be an *equilibrium price* at which these two tendencies, increasing for supply and decreasing for demand, cross. At that price, amount produced just equals amount bought. The amount produced and the price will both be stable, not showing any systematic change over time. By making assumptions about how things like the cost of production or changes in wages affect the supply and demand curves, conventional economics can make predictions that can be used to guide (for example) tax policy.

This simple picture tells us little or nothing about exactly how these supply and demand curves come about. Static curves say nothing about the real-time processes that allow producers to arrive at their prices and—even more uncertain—consumers to arrive at their preferences. The foundational assumption of all equilibrium models is that *whatever these processes are*, in the absence of any external shock like a natural disaster or a spontaneous change in fashion, they lead to a stable equilibrium. If this assumption is not true, if the underlying processes are *not* stabilizing, then all the conceptual elegance in the world cannot save these static models from irrelevance. I will show later that even the very simplest dynamic supply–demand processes can be highly unstable.

Standard supply–demand analysis allows the invisible hand to work pretty well. Producers' self-interest moves them to reduce costs; consumers seek lower price. Supply and demand curves ensure that a high-cost producer will lose out to a lower-cost one and consumers will benefit. But there are some well-studied situations where pursuit of self-interest fails to lead to the best result for the common good. The best-known example is something called the *prisoner's dilemma*, from the economics-Nobel-rich discipline of game theory. The basic idea is pretty simple, although the situation seems rather artificial, and the idea is not always easy to grasp at first. Imagine two suspects, partners in crime, captured by the police. The prosecutor has enough evidence to convict but wants a confession. He offers each prisoner separately the same deal in hopes of getting at least one to confess. The deal is this: if neither confesses they will both get light sentences. If one confesses and the other does not, the "defector" will get off scot-free and the other will get a heavy sentence. If both confess, both get an intermediate sentence. Obviously, it is best for the pair if they cooperate and stay silent, since both are then assured of a light sentence. If they could communicate, doubtless they would cooperate. But, deciding in isolation, they cannot. Numerous laboratory experiments with payoffs along these lines have shown that in fact both "prisoners" usually confess, leading to a medium sentence for both, a sub-optimal result for the group. And this is "rational" according the standard models of economic behavior.[1]

What might this rather artificial situation, the prisoner's dilemma, have to do with real markets? Well, it turns out to be only one of many ways that the pursuit of self-interest can fail to benefit the common good. Here is another one, similar to the prisoner's dilemma but easier to understand, from ecology. In medieval times in England, and more recently in the American West, farmers grazed their flocks on common land, land owned by no one and open to all. Under these conditions, putting an additional sheep on the moor always adds something to the income of shepherd Gawain. In other words, individual self-interest always favors adding another animal to your herd. Eventually, of course, as the collective herd increases, Gawain's gain from each new sheep is reduced as the fertility of the common land is reduced by overgrazing. But the basic *contingency* (more on contingencies in a moment) remains the same: for each farmer, adding one more is always a gain, because the loss from each new grazer is shared but the benefit goes to the owner alone. The commons is a sort of free market, but it's one where *after a certain point*, self interest leads not to public good, as in the invisible hand, but to public harm. Fishing in the open sea obviously suffers from the same problem. Fishing and grazing on common land are examples of the *tragedy of the commons*, made famous by biologist Garrett Hardin in a *Science* article in 1968.[2]

Neither supply–demand nor game theory models take into account the critical dimension of *time*. The prisoners in the dilemma are presumed to know the outcome of their actions immediately and so also with the producers and consumers in supply–demand analysis. But the tragedy of the commons arises partly because the ill-effects of overgrazing are delayed. Indeed, the first few sheep put on the moor increase the common stock of wealth. It takes time before the accumulation of grazing animals begins to damage the common land on which all depend.

Delayed effects like this are a consistent feature of financial markets. Here is an example where the invisible hand is a minor player with the malign hand in the lead. Supply–demand theory tells us that when supply lags behind demand, prices will rise, though it obviously doesn't say exactly when or by how much. Now consider the housing market, which is largely financed not by a fixed store of savings but by debt. (If modern financial markets are good at anything it is the creation of debt!) Suppose some financial innovator, or a succession of them, in collusion with the Federal Reserve, which can literally make money, comes up with new "products," new ways of increasing the supply of mortgage money. Demand for houses will increase, and it will increase faster than new homes can be supplied because building a house takes longer than coming up with new money. The result is that housing prices will rise, at least in the short term. Because housing prices are now rising, people who own homes can make a profit by selling the one they bought just a few months ago. What is more, buying a house is the only way that the average citizen can exert financial *leverage*. He may have to pony up only $1,000 to get a mortgage on a $100,000 property. His $1,000 has bought him $100,000 to play with, leverage of a 100, larger even than the 20 to 40 to 1 that allows so many investment bankers to grow rich. With this leverage, if the property increases in value by a mere $2000—not unusual in a lively market—the property owner has doubled his money in a couple of months.[3]

With profits like this, more mortgages are given to weaker and weaker borrowers, so more borrowers enter the housing market, driving up prices, and profits, still further—in an apparently virtuous cycle. For a while, everybody wins and free-market fans can cheer. Just like the shepherds on the commons: at first, everybody wins. Eventually, of course, supply increases, as more houses are built, and demand begins to fall as over-extended borrowers, tempted by ever-slacker credit criteria and ever-trickier mortgage products, begin to default. The rise in house prices slows, stops and begins to go the other way. The same process that drove prices up now drives them down, the bubble collapses and thousands of people suffer financial devastation. Like the tragedy of the commons, a multitude of individuals, each acting in his own interest, has eventually caused collective harm.

Why do we let these things happen? There are many reasons, some of which I will get into later. An important one is that policy makers are not omniscient. They see the immediate good effects (profits) that benefit a few; they fail to foresee the bad effects that are delayed and affect many. In real markets, effects often lag their causes by days, months or even years. But foresight alone is not enough. Even if you know the market will crash on a date uncertain, it is very often best to follow the crowd. In the infamous words of soon-to-be-bailed-out Citigroup's Chuck Prince in July 2007, just before the crash of 2008: "When the music stops, in terms of liquidity, things will be complicated. But as long as the music is playing, you've got to get up and dance. We're still dancing." And as long as everybody is dancing, regulators don't want to turn off the music.

Silence about temporal factors is a huge problem for static economic models. But most economists don't worry because the real economic world is pretty stable for much of the time. They are also unfazed by the fact that they can rarely tell in advance when it will become unstable. The fact of local stability, and people's short memories and even shorter *time horizons* (how far they are willing to look ahead), have made static models acceptable to economists even though they cannot predict when they will break down. But even if static models work in the short term, we need at least to understand whether the real world corresponds to standard supply–demand economics, where the invisible hand reigns and individual self-interest promotes the common good, or to the prisoner's dilemma and similar situations, where self-interest injures the common good. Better still, we need to incorporate *time* into our analysis of market economics so delayed bad effects can be foreseen and forestalled.

In this book I look at how financial markets have evolved in ways that very often cause general harm: booms and busts and the suffering that comes from them. In these situations the invisible hand fails to work as Adam Smith suggested. By pursuing "rational" self-interest, market actors promote their own good but cost everyone else. I call these effects collectively the *malign hand*, by contrast with the benign invisible hand of Smith. The malign hand can appear whenever benefits are immediate and targeted—to an individual or a group—but costs are delayed and/or dispersed. The idea of the malign hand is not new. As we have just seen, in decision science, it shows up as the prisoner's dilemma, in ecology as the tragedy of the commons. Economists use terms like "external costs" or "externalities," "systemic risk," "the free-rider problem", "misaligned incentives," "information asymmetry," "rent-seeking," the "agency (conflict-of-interest) problem" or "moral hazard." Because it has different names in many different contexts, because it is harder to understand and to see operating around us than the invisible hand (and perhaps because it offers no comfort to the greedy!), it is not as widely appreciated as Adam Smith's great insight. The malign hand is important not just because it causes harm but also because it is so often ignored. The argument of this book is that by understanding something of the underlying psychological and social processes, it is possible to get a better idea of the real causes of the disasters that are a too-regular feature of financial markets. Knowing the causes, solutions—simpler and more realistic than the hand-waving, well-intentioned-but-ultimately-ineffectual "regulation" that is currently on offer—realistic solutions can be devised.

REINFORCEMENT CONTINGENCIES

The right kind of psychology can help. There are many "psychologies," unfortunately. Most psychology textbooks, aiming for the largest possible readership and not wanting to offend any potential adopter, deal with the problem by presenting all of them—a veritable rainbow of "perspectives." So the many conflicts and contradictions between, say, cognitive and behaviorist psychology, go unmentioned. But surely there are some unquestioned psychological facts and laws that we might apply to these economic problems? Certainly there is a fashionable field of behavioral economics that proposes to do just that. I will have something to say about behavioral economics later on. For now, suffice it to say that the main task of behavioral economists has been to show that human decision makers are not always "rational" in the sense of maximizing personal gain. But this misses the point that most of the problems of financial markets are due not to a failure of individual rationality but to a failure of rational behavior by individuals to promote the common good—the malign hand. If there is a failure of rationality, it is on the part of politicians and market regulators who promise to control something they do not understand.

There is one simple psychological idea that does seem to apply to financial markets. It is generally accepted in the psychology of learning in animals, and perhaps for this reason seems to have been missed in all the market analyses that I have seen. That is the idea of *reinforcement*. *Reinforcement contingencies* (schedules), the rules according to which reward or punishment is given or withheld, affect the behavior of laboratory animals in beautifully orderly and predictable ways. Two simple examples, familiar to every Psych 101 student, are interval and ratio schedules of reinforcement. On a ratio schedule, a bit of food is intermittently delivered to a hungry rat who has learned to press a lever. On a fixed-ratio 10, for example, the rat gets the food pellet after every tenth lever press. Rats, pigeons and many other animal species, respond predictably to this contingency by waiting briefly after each pellet and then pressing at a high rate until the next one is delivered. Notice that this behavior is rational—the faster you press the sooner you get the food—but only partially: the brief pause before pressing the lever after receiving each pellet delays the next food unnecessarily. Perhaps the rat is fatigued or satiated after each bit of food, and that's why he waits before returning to work? Well, no. If the number of presses per pellet *averages* ten but varies randomly from pellet to pellet (a *variable*-ratio schedule, just like the Las-Vegas-style one-armed bandit), the high response rate remains, but the pause after food goes away. The post-food pause is an automatic effect of the regularity of the time between pellets on a fixed-ratio schedule.

On a fixed-*interval* schedule, only the first lever press after a fixed time has elapsed since the preceding food is reinforced. When regularity is enforced, the rat also waits to respond after each food delivery. The source of the post-food pause is obvious because it is proportional to the interval over quite a wide range of interval values.

These results are typical of behavior on reinforcement schedules: broadly "rational," but with quirks that reflect either automatic processes, like the timing effect shown by the post-food pause on fixed ratio, or cognitive limitations—rats and pigeons cannot learn complicated sequences, for example. A rat can learn to alternate between two levers to get a pellet, but even rudimentary left-right Morse code is well beyond him! Human beings have a similar problem with complex financial instruments.

Burrhus Frederick ("Fred") Skinner (1904–1990) was the most influential American psychologist in the second half of the 20ᵗʰ century. Trained in the Harvard laboratory of the physiologist William Crozier, he taught at Minnesota and Indiana before returning in 1948 to Harvard, where he remained for the rest of his life. Although mostly an animal-lab researcher himself, his legacy is an active international group of mostly clinical psychologists,[4] a radical behaviorist philosophy that animates them, as well as a set of experimental methods and data that has become standard in behavioral neuroscience.

Skinner's greatest contributions to science were undoubtedly the discovery of reinforcement schedules and invention of the technology for studying learning in individual organisms in real time. Unfortunately he is much better known for his ambitious extrapolations from an infant science to human society at large. He wrote simple, persuasive prose and for a while books like *Walden Two* (a lightweight utopian novel) and his best-seller *Beyond Freedom and Dignity* (a provocative attack on free will) strongly affected both public sentiment and educational policy. See, for example, the *Time* magazine for September 20, 1971, which features Skinner on the cover.[5] Skinner thought that all important human behavior could be explained by reinforcement. Like the standard economist, he thought that incentives, reward and punishment, could explain everything—although, unlike many economists, he knew that money is not the only reinforcer for human beings. He applied reinforcement ideas to human behavior in ways that are sometimes persuasive but often naïve. He proposed that gambling could be explained as an example of ratio-schedule behavior. Well, yes and no. Yes, a one-armed bandit is just like a variable-ratio schedule, but no that's not all you need to explain gambling. Why are some people susceptible and others not, for example? Why do some people prefer roulette and others poker?

Skinner also pointed out that *piecework*, payment for each item produced by a worker rather than by a fixed wage, is also a ratio schedule and should produce high rates of work. Usually it does, especially if the rewards are very large—surgeons, lawyers and investment bankers, pieceworkers all, come to mind. The high pressure on stock traders and their long hours have become famous since the first *Wall Street* movie. But if the rewards are *not* large, both animals and humans quit. The rats stop lever-pressing if the ratio between number of responses required and size of each reinforcer obtained is too large; if the piecework rate is too low, human factory workers object and form unions to jack up wages or change work arrangements.

Reinforcement theory works for human beings when the reinforcement or punishment is strong and can be clearly identified, and the contingencies are well defined. This is the case for the clinical treatment of severely autistic children, for example. Unreachable by any other means, they can often be taught minimal skills by behavioristic methods using potent reinforcers like food and even, in treating severe cases of self-harm, electric shock. Reinforcement theory works much less well in explaining normal human interactions. What is the reinforcer or reinforcers? What are the contingencies? Who is reinforcing whom? Meaningful experiments cannot be done with people because delivering strong reinforcers—something substantial like a lottery prize or food for the hungry, not points on a computer screen—is impossible for practical and ethical reasons.

But there is one area of human life where the reinforcers are strong and contingencies are very well defined indeed, namely financial markets. In financial markets, unlike other kinds of markets, the only reinforcer is *money*. Sure, every seller in every market wants to make money, but there are usually other motives as well. A restaurateur is likely to enjoy cooking and exploring new foods; a furniture maker likes woodwork and a boat builder likes boats—Apple's Steve Jobs loved digital devices and, according to Walter Isaacson's official biography, disdained business people motivated only by profit. But financial people have no motivation other than making money. Not that it has always been that way. Many of the "old" financial houses emphasized things like client relationships and responsible stewardship: Goldman Sachs' motto is "Our client's interests always come first." But in recent years the word "client's" seems to have been grayed out.[6] In the words of a current notoriety, "winning" has become the only thing for Wall Street.[7]

So we know the reinforcer in financial markets and we know it is effective. We also know the reinforcement contingencies, which are of course much more complex than the simple procedures used with animals. The reinforcement contingencies are those misleadingly named financial "products" like securitized mortgage bonds, swaps and insurance. These things are not products at all, in the conventional sense. They are not for "end use" like a TV or a pair of shoes. They are reinforcement contingencies that permit certain financial actions by buyer and seller with more or less certain money returns (reinforcement) to each. They constrain the buyer and seller in well-defined but almost invariably complex, and often only partially understood, ways. If we understand the contingency, and understand how people might adapt to it, we can begin to understand the market. But it is vital *not* to treat these financial creations as regular products. They are a set of rules and constraints that favor some kinds of behavior over others. Regulating them as products rather than as reinforcement schedules is unlikely to work well. The periodic crises that affect financial markets are a living proof of this profound misunderstanding of what they are and what they involve.

The word *product* is just one example of the misleading language used in the financial community. Another is "liquidity," which sounds just like the scientific term "viscosity." Viscosity is an objectively measurable property of a fluid, like water or oil. "Liquidity" sounds much the same doesn't it? So is a "liquid asset" something whose "liquidity" can be measured objectively? Well, no, not at all. A "liquid asset" is one that people are willing to buy *now* for a reasonable price. An illiquid asset is something they are not willing to buy now and indeed may not be willing to buy at all unless the price is set much below what the owner would like. In other words, "liquidity" is not a property of the asset itself, but of people's willingness to buy it at a price the seller would like—a three-term relation among buyer, seller and asset. Liquidity is not a "thing"—certainly not something that is objectively measurable in any easy way.

Another suspect term is *risk*, as in "selling risk." Risk is treated again as a thing, an independent, stable property of a financial asset like a bond or a mortgage. The problem is that the risk associated with an asset type is not independent of how it is bought and sold. If we sell a mortgage, is the risk it will default unaffected? Well, yes, for *this* particular mortgage. But not perhaps for the next one sold-on in this way, as the risk-taker is increasingly separated from the risk-holder, the buyer of the CDO or other such bundle of mortgage bits, in the process misleadingly called *securitization*.

Treating financial instruments as reinforcement contingencies to which market actors adapt also avoids the messy philosophical issue of whether or not players are *rational*. The issue is no longer rationality but *adaptation*: how do people adapt to a set of well-defined costs and benefits? As I've already pointed out, looking for the "optimal" behavior can sometimes be illuminating—it clarifies the selfish and apparently dumb behavior of players in the prisoner's dilemma game and accounts for high response rates on ratio schedules. But as the tragedy of the commons, and the pause after reinforcement in fixed ratio, showed, you cannot ignore the reinforcement contingency and *time* and processes that occur in time. To understand how people adapt to financial contingencies we need to have some inkling, imperfect though it is likely to be, of the processes that are operating.

Adaptation to reinforcement contingencies is a real-time Darwinian process of variation and selection. The subject, animal or human, has a repertoire of actions induced by a given situation. The repertoire is rather limited for a rat or a pigeon, not so limited (but not *un*limited) in the case of a human being. From this repertoire, the best, most effective behavior is selected according to relatively simple principles of immediate gain. The repertoire is more complex for humans than for rats but the reinforcement is pretty simple. It is often surprisingly easy, therefore, to predict the usual adaptations.

The book has twelve chapters and this Introduction. Chapter 1 is intended to fix the idea of the malign hand in your mind. It describes the malign hand in three different contexts: bureaucracy and politics, economic globalization, and scientific research.

Chapter 2 opens the main theme of the book. It explains how the malign hand in financial markets works to undercut democracy. The underlying problem is excessive income inequality. Gross inequality is perceived as unjust and, in a democracy, leads to a progressive tax regime in which fewer and fewer people wind up paying a larger and larger fraction of government expenses. Those who receive more than they pay soon become a majority able to dominate the political process. They adapt by behaving less and less responsibly. The poorer majority are in a position to vote themselves more and more at the expense of the richer minority—a process that never ends well. The underlying problem is not the tax system but the extreme income inequality it was created to mitigate.

Income inequality has grown mightily in the last three decades. In 1980 the top 1 percent of taxpayers took in 8.5 percent of total national income and the bottom 50 percent took in 17.7 percent. But in 2009, the top one percent earned 17 percent of total income—double—whereas the bottom 50 percent earned just 13.5 percent, a *decrease* of 24 percent.[8] Where does this inequality come from? Is it simply just desserts, fairly awarded to people of varying interests and abilities? The smart and energetic get rich, the dumb and indolent do not. Or does the huge inequality we see now come from some malfunction of our economic system that has little to do with equal opportunity and unequal ability? The facts suggest that the source of our current huge inequality is the operation of the malign hand in the financial system. It's not justice or injustice, it's an out-of-control, ill-designed financial system that is the culprit. The rest of the book explains how this works.

Chapter 3 looks at some of the assumptions that underlie the structure of our present financial system. Of the seven I list, six are clearly wrong. Chapter 3 dissects two of them, the idea of real value and the concept of rationality. Later chapters deal with the idea of the efficient market and market equilibrium, the supposed virtues of financial innovation and the role of financial markets in the allocation of scarce resources. Chapter 4 is a critique of the efficient-market hypothesis, the Apostles' Creed for many free-market fundamentalists. Chapter 5, a relief from theory, discusses the housing bubble. Cheap money plus financial ingenuity led to a pyramiding of debt in a positive feedback loop in which prices first increased and then collapsed as demand increased and then decreased and supply lagged behind. Chapter 6 looks at the fundamentals of static economics and shows how easily even the simplest market can become unstable. Static economics is inadequate. Chapters 7 and 8 show how the creation of money by a central bank violates elementary conservation principles which are essential to the stability of any dynamic system. Chapter 9 is about John Maynard Keynes, a fascinating figure in his own right and a fountain of both good and bad economic ideas. Unfortunately, economies in recent times have followed the bad ones rather than the good.

The last three chapters summarize the problems with financial markets and suggest some solutions to them. Chapter 10 looks again at the Federal Reserve and how it might be restrained; at leverage and the misguided politics of home ownership; at Glass-Steagall and other useful regulations that have been abolished; and at the real inefficiency of the financial industry. Chapter 11 is about different kinds of risk, the difference between voluntary and involuntary risk, the fact that Wall Street is much less competitive than it pretends to be, and the effectiveness or otherwise of the massive bailouts that have been delivered to the financial sector over the past three years. Chapter 12 is about what can be done. I distinguish between "regulation by scrutiny" and "regulation by rule." "Scrutiny" is what is offered by the embarrassing Dodd-Frank regulatory bill of 2010. The bill enjoins the regulators to discover "systemic risk" and do something, *something*, about it—Fed Chairman Ben Bernanke as Carnac the Magnificent, Johnny Carson's humorous soothsayer, as the *Wall Street Journal* put it. The alternative is regulation by rule, which attends to the reinforcement schedule under which financial players operate. I propose four simple rules designed simply to make sure that the person who takes a voluntary risk bears its full cost. Speculators tirelessly work to evade this principle. It is up to regulators to thwart them. It is an obligation they continue to shirk.

PART

I

1

The Malign Hand

This book is mainly about financial markets, where the malign hand has its most dramatic and hard-to-detect effects. But it may help to fix ideas if in this chapter and the next I begin with some examples from other areas of human social life. The malign hand is rarely the only process at work. There are usually factors such as Smith's invisible hand that counteract its destabilizing effects. There must be, or else society would have collapsed long ago. But, because malign-hand effects are usually both hard to see and delayed, there are certainly many other fuses smoldering all around U.S. Here are a few places to look.

Bureaucracy and Politics Bureaucracy is the "operating system" of any organization, from individual firms to the whole economies. Ever since the wonderful work of English naval historian C. Northcote Parkinson[1]—a very serious satirist—everyone knows that bureaucracies have a natural tendency to expand beyond the size necessary to perform their original function. Parkinson's most memorable data was a table showing that between 1924 and 1928 the number of capital ships in commission in the Royal Navy declined by 68 percent while the number of Admiralty officials *increased* by 78 percent. Much the same happened in the British Colonial Office: as the colonies shrank almost to zero from 1935 to 1954, the number of Colonial Office officials increased more than fourfold. Parkinson even proposed mathematical formulas to describe these increases. A relatively recent example that has attracted surprisingly little attention, so used have we become to the disconnect between a bureaucracy and its intended function, is the North Atlantic Treaty Organization. Founded in 1949 as a collective defense effort against possible attacks from the Soviet Union, its raison d'être vanished when the Soviet Union collapsed in 1989 and the Warsaw Pact ended in 1991. Was NATO disbanded? No, expanded.

Austrian economists and the public choice movement[2] in the U.S. have shown, more or less, why bureaucracies increase in this way: because the incentives for the bureaucrats are never perfectly aligned with those of the organization of which they are a part. Short-term gain for the bureaucrat often means long-term problems for the rest of us—the malign hand. Every bureaucrat wants to hire more people and expand his role. Budget rules that encourage a department to spend all its allocation every year—lest its next-year budget be cut—are a ratchet that allows only upward growth. Salary scales that give largest weight to the number of employees an individual supervises, encourage hiring. Each new hire creates work to justify still more hires, and so on.

Competition is the natural antidote to the malign hand. The bureaucratic dynamic may not matter too much in a competitive environment. The firm whose bureaucracy gets out of hand will lose in competition with more efficient firms—so long as the expansionist tendency intrinsic to all bureaucracies does not infect all firms equally.

But government bureaucracies are different because there are fewer checks on their growth. The government can therefore swell with little restraint—until a crisis forces change. The 2009 economic crisis in the UK, for example, is clearly associated with a massive increase in public-sector employment in preceding years. In response to the crisis, the 2010 coalition government apparently intends to actually reduce the number of public-sector employees by 11 percent to a still large 4.92M and has made noises about even more severe cuts.[3]

Public-sector growth in the U.S. is probably worse and forces to reduce it much weaker. Public-sector unions have been growing in recent decades while private-sector unions have declined substantially. The private sector is generally subject to competitive restraint, the public, not so much. Current statistics are hard to evaluate; but recent small drops in U.S. unemployment have all been dominated by Federal hires. The pain of the recession is already being borne almost entirely by state governments, most subject to balanced-budget laws, and the private sector. There are proposals to both cut the public sector and freeze salaries in the UK. As of the end of 2010, no such proposals had been made in the U.S.

Government growth is promoted by both internal and external forces. I've already said something about internal forces. Here is an example of how external forces work. In 2010 the State of North Carolina decided, in its wisdom and following recent tradition, to pass a law targeting substantial tax breaks at the company Microsoft. The purpose? To induce Microsoft to open a new facility in the state which, it was hoped, would create new jobs and generate new tax revenue in excess of the concessions. Alas, NC's generosity was exceeded by Virginia's. The Old Dominion upped the ante and Microsoft opted to open its facility there.[4]

Rather to my surprise, a conservative friend thought the original NC plan a good thing—because it promised to turn a profit for the state. Maybe so, if profit is the only motive by which state governments should be guided. But the malign-hand possibilities are pretty obvious—a bidding war between states, a diversion of the state's attention from the needs of its citizens to profit flowing to the government, not necessarily to the people, potential for conflict of interest and corruption, distortion of priorities, creation of a new incentive-administration bureaucracy, and so on. Nevertheless, the case against subsidies of this sort is far from open-and-shut.

Much, much stronger is the case against that accepted staple of U.S. democracy: pork. Recently deceased Alaskan[5] Ted Stevens, longest-ever serving Republican senator, is an iconic figure in this. Stevens was much loved in Alaska for his capacity to attract Federal funds to the state. Citizens Against Government Waste reports that "Sen. Stevens has helped bring home a total of 1,452 projects worth $3.4 billion between 1995 and 2008."[6] His efforts peaked in 2005 when he got the Hogzilla Award for bringing home $646 million of U.S. taxpayers' money to Alaska.

But why is pork bad? Is it really wasteful? Wasn't Stevens just doing what he was elected to do, helping his state? Individual projects may be wasteful, but even if all are carried out with exemplary efficiency, there is an inevitable bad result of a very different kind. The problem isn't waste but the malign hand. It works like this. Recall the tragedy of the commons: each farmer gains from adding cattle to the common land, but the result eventually is overgrazing and a general loss. Just as every farmer gains from adding to his herd on the common land, every representative gains from each diversion of Federal funds to his own district. The general loss is shared by each individual, but only after a delay, and only in small measure. Concentration of benefits, but delay and dispersion of costs, is always a problem if those who pay the cost have less influence than those who incur it. So it is with pork and with many government programs that don't look particularly local—defense projects, intentionally spread over many states, for example. Legislators are voted in by the people of their states, who see the immediate benefits of pork. But the pork is paid for—if it is paid for at all—by residents of all states, who have little voice in projects other than their own. Because all feed off resources of the central government, central resources are either depleted, like the commons, or, more likely, they increase to meet demands that grow without limit.

"Increase"—that's the problem. Unlike the land commons, the Federal government is not limited. Central government not only ensures that each individual expenditure is shared by all, but, without some kind of balanced-budget constraint, it can in effect add more land. As demands from elected representatives increase, the Feds "add land" by creating debt—which must be paid for either by taxing directly, or creating a deficit—which, in turn, must be paid off either by tax increases, now or later, or by inflating the currency (i.e., taxing the thrifty). It's not hard to figure out which of these options is usually easier politically. Either way, government takes a bigger chunk of the collective pie. Estimates vary, but Federal spending, i.e., the size of the Federal government, has grown from about 10 percent of total GDP in 1910 to over 35 percent now, with spikes up to 15 percent and 45 percent during the two world wars. The Federal government has swelled mightily, as the malign hand suggests it will.

But is it really *too* big? Hard to say—how big is "too big"? But what we can say is that its present size is the outcome of a runaway, unstable process that is not subject to those competitive restraints that discipline well-functioning markets. At the same time, the healthy competitive interactions among the states are slowly over-shadowed as they dispose of a smaller and smaller part of the national wealth. And don't forget that when the Feds send money to a state they can legally override state decisions over things such as the legal drinking age or highway speed limits. ("You want Federal highway money? Well, then...") The less independent states become, the less they are subject to the discipline of competition. Not "experiments in democracy" so much as lab rats with the Federal government as experimenter.

The growth of the public sector shows itself in another way in the enormous growth in the number of megabytes of regulations, rules—from the government—and compliance documentation—from everyone else—in recent years. The reason is simple: Each legislator benefits from a law he supports, but the cost of the growing legal corpus is shared by everybody—the malign hand. The standard measure is the size of the *Federal Register*, which publishes government rules and regulations. The *Register* was around 13,000 pages in 1965 (already too large, one might think), but by 2008 it had swelled to over 79,000 pages and, by 2010, to 81,405 pages.[7] Another example is the tax code. The size of the U.S. tax code is a matter of dispute. One website in 2006 gave estimates based on quotes from members of Congress.[8] Here is a sample:

U.S. Representative Rob Portman (R-OH):

> The income tax code and its associated regulations contain almost 5.6 million words—seven times as many words as the Bible. Taxpayers now spend about 5.4 billion hours a year trying to comply with 2,500 pages of tax laws....

U.S. Representative J.C. Watts, Jr. (R-OK):

The heart of IRS abuse lies in the existing tax code. Most of the folks who work for the IRS are good people just trying to do their job, but they are caught in a bad, overextended tax system. At 3,458 pages, twice the length of the Bible, it's impossible for the average taxpayer to know, understand, and accurately apply its provisions. The length is twice that of the Bible! Even tax experts cannot do so reliably.

U.S. Representative Nick Smith (R-MI):

The Federal tax code has about four times as many words as the Bible. Accompanying the law are a staggering two-and-a-half million pages of regulations. A recent count is 3.8 million words.[9]

No exact agreement, but clearly the U.S. Federal Tax Code is very large indeed—"Ten times longer than the Bible without the good news" as Congressman Dave Camp put it.[10] J. C. Watts is certainly right that no one knows exactly how to comply with these rules. From time to time, financial publications will submit identical, "typical" moderately complicated tax returns to several experts to see how much tax is owed. Invariably, they all come up with different estimates.

The tax code reflects tax legislation, which has also grown vastly in recent years. Bills in Congress are now quite routinely 1,000 or more pages long—far too long to be read by the congressmen and women who vote on them. Speaker of the House Nancy Pelosi, speaking about the two-thousand-plus-page 2010 health bill,[11] notoriously blurted out "But we have to pass the bill so that you can find out what is in it…"!

Why are these bills so long? The reasons are many and not well understood, at least by me. But among them are surely growth of bureaucracy and the value to legislators of complexity itself. Each member of Congress now has a staff upwards of 20 people who do most of the work of creating and reading bills. If members of Congress don't need to write, or even read, the bills they vote for, there is little limit to how long and complex those bills can become. The technology of word processing and digital documents allows Congress, just like the financial industry (as I will show later), to use the length and complexity of legislation as a protective shield to hide, or at least delay, public discovery of special-interest favors, strengthening the malign hand. The possibility of longer, more complex bills allows for increased influence of special interests, which need to tweak draft legislation either to protect themselves or to gain special advantage. (I recognize that a lot of lobbying, at least initially, is done as much for self-protection as for special favors.) The downside of these changes, all giving immediate advantage to some group—members of Congress, lobbyists—is not just special-interest-favoring provisions, a few of which may actually benefit the public, but a serious loss of transparency and public access to laws that govern the lives of everyone.

The Dodd-Frank financial regulation bill of 2010, of which more later, shows just how out of control the legislation/regulation process has become. The bill itself has been variously sized at between 1,300 and 2,600 pages (depending on the font and stage of the legislative process, I suppose). But that's only step one. The bill contains few actual well-specified rules. These must be written by a bureaucracy, in response to "comments" (i.e., requests from lobbyists) that numbered in the *tens of thousands* by October 2011. When the process ends, if it ever does, the *Federal Register* will be tens of thousands of pages longer, thousands of man-hours will have been wasted and thousands more will be spent on compliance in the future—and the financial system will be no safer.[12]

Just how bad are these malign-hand effects and what should be done about them? Libraries need to be "pruned" regularly; we all need to throw out stuff from the attic from time to time; even your hard disk needs attention to delete damaged or irrelevant files every now and then. Perhaps something similar is needed to deal with the apparently unrestrained growth of legislation, not just of tax legislation but every kind of legislation. Coincidentally, the British coalition government announced in 2010 a plan to repeal as many redundant laws as possible and has asked the public for suggestions. How successful this will be remains to be seen.

I have a simpler suggestion: Since there is probably general agreement that the existing body of law is already too long, the simplest expedient would be one more law requiring that for any and all subsequent legislation, for every word added, at least one word of existing legislation must be repealed. What a bracing exercise it would be if our representatives had to actually go back and study what they and their predecessors have wrought over the years, and do it with sufficient care to figure out what to repeal or rewrite!

Economic Globalization is the continuing integration of national economies through trade, foreign investment, capital flows, migration, and technology. It has many opponents, some of them violent. Most opposition to globalization is ideological and far from coherent. Opponents share dislike of capitalism, of large corporations (small ones are usually OK), of "exploitation" of workers in poor countries, and of inequality. They are pro-environment (not that anyone is actually against the environment) and for "fair" trade. They regard employees of companies in developing nations that serve consumers in the rich nations as "exploited" almost by definition, even though such employment is usually a free choice by workers who find it preferable to the alternatives. Most of these claims do not withstand careful scrutiny.

On the other hand, almost all economists are in favor of globalization. Even those who are critical see problems with it as primarily political in nature, not economic. For example, Nobelist Joseph Stiglitz writes:

> The great hope of globalization is that it will raise living standards throughout the world: give poor countries access to overseas markets so that they can sell their goods, allow in foreign investment that will make new products at cheaper prices, and open borders so that people can travel abroad to be educated, work, and send home earnings to help their families and fund new businesses.
>
> I believe that globalization has the potential to bring enormous benefits to those in both the developing and the developed world. But the evidence is overwhelming that it has failed to live up to this potential ... the problem is not with globalization itself but in the

way globalization has been managed. Economics has been driving
globalization... But politics has shaped it.[13]

Economists generally agree on the economic arguments in favor of
globalization—division of labor, comparative advantage and the like,
all those things you learned in Econ. 101. Global economic integration should lead to great increases in efficiency, hence to more wealth
for all. Globalization seems to mean swift gain for everyone.

But no one seems to have noticed that there is a huge contradiction between economists' faith in increased international global integration and the general economic consensus on the "too-big-to-fail"
problem revealed by the great crash of 2008. Now most economists
agree that if large financial institutions like Merrill Lynch or insurance giant AIG are too big to fail, they are also "too big to exist."
Essentially nothing has been done in the U.S. to implement this
insight, but most economists seem to agree with it. No one is suggesting that large institutions should combine and become even larger
and more integrated as a way of stabilizing the financial system. Yet
this is precisely what is being proposed for the international economic
system. If Greece has failed, then she needs to be even more tightly
integrated into the European Union and the EU must be strengthened. If the U.S. or France wants to tighten banking regulations, the
critics object: "No, there must be international coordination. The U.S.
should not act unilaterally!"

It should be obvious that there is a tradeoff between efficiency
and stability, between immediate gain and long-term benefit. This
is apparent to common sense, and there are even a few mathematical models that make the same point. For example, one analysis
concludes that "... chaotic fluctuations are much stronger in single
large economies, or a single completely globalized economy, than in
the world economy consisting of national economies that are to a
degree separated."[14] As the global system becomes more integrated
and more efficient, it also becomes in the long term more unstable.
It is the malign hand again: immediate gains in wealth associated
with increased globalization leading to long-term cost in the form of
increased instability of the whole system.

Why should pulling back on globalization make the world economy more stable? One reason is just statistical. A number of independent economies, each with some tendency to instability, are less likely to fail all at once than a single world economy. A fully globalized international system would see each nation specializing in particular products or functions. Competition would therefore tend to be between producers within each nation rather than among nations. But competition among nations aids stability, preventing any one nation from developing those inefficiencies endemic to monopolies. And if one of many independent economies fails, there will be others still able to function. When a unified global system fails, unlike the happy outcomes for AIG and Merrill Lynch, there will be no U.S. government to step in and rescue it.

If we value stability, therefore, nations should be willing to accept some inefficiency in order to attain a degree of economic independence. Exactly how this independence should be achieved—by increased tariffs, reduced capital flows, subsidies for local industries—all of which are deplored by most economists—or in some other way remains to be worked out.

Scientific Research is what has given Western civilization its edge in the world in recent centuries. Science is vital to every aspect of modern life and is the main counterweight to some of the malign-hand effects I discussed earlier in the chapter. Yet despite the incredible advances in science and technology in recent decades, there are some signs that our ability to do creative science is being undermined by the very institutions we have set up to promote it.

Basic and applied scientific research use the same methods. The difference between them is not the methods they use, but where the questions they try to answer come from. In applied research the questions are posed by some outside source: a practical problem or some crisis to be resolved. How do you make a more efficient jet engine? How do you make a cheaper, more energetic battery? What makes a traffic-accident "black spot"? Basic research, on the other hand, is motivated by sheer, even idle, curiosity. The aim is to understand something—a phenomenon, like magnetism, say, or pea heredity or the spots on butterfly wings. Basic researchers don't usually worry much about the financial implications of their discoveries. Not that they are totally unaware—*viz.* electrical pioneer Michael Faraday's famous response to English Prime Minister Gladstone's query about the usefulness of his work with wires and magnets: "Why, sir, there is every possibility that you will soon be able to tax it!" Many advances in basic science eventually lead to something of general use. But with basic research you can't be sure. Since uncertainty is abhorred by bureaucrats, this leads to trouble.

The two strands, applied and basic, of course intermingle from time to time. To figure out the causes of traffic accidents it may be necessary to draw on basic psychological research on attention.[15] Designing turbine blades for a jet engine may require basic research in materials science.

The conventional wisdom is that because the benefits of basic research are necessarily shared, it cannot be funded privately, but must be supported by the government. If he who pays for the research is not to get especial benefit from it, it will not pay him to support it. This is the well-known malign-hand "free-rider problem" in economics. The conclusion is that if left to the private sector, there will not be "enough" basic research.

But there turn out to be many problems with this apparently self-evident conclusion. The most obvious, perhaps, is how can we know just what is "enough"? Where is it written that X or Y or Z percent of GDP should be devoted to basic research? Not that this kind of uncertainty has ever troubled the political class. I recall UK Prime Minister Tony Blair setting a national target of 50 percent for college attendance and, amazingly, President Obama recently announced the same percentage as a target for an increase in U.S. exports. What a coincidence—what nonsense! Their calculations might more plausibly have arrived at 43 percent or 71 percent, but no, 50 percent is just right! The answer, of course, is that we really don't know how much is "enough" research or college attendance or level of exports. The politicians are just trying to gain credibility for a reasonable claim—let's have *more* exports, or higher university attendance rates or whatever—by stating a meaningless number as a goal.

So how essential is government support for science? Well, how essential was it in the past? All the great leaps of classical science— Newtonian physics, relativity, the atomic theory, thermodynamics, electromagnetism, evolution by natural selection, genetics, the theory of the circulation of the blood, and many others—occurred with no government aid whatever. The fact that Albert Einstein was employed by the Swiss Patent Office when he made his first great discoveries hardly counts as government support for science. Few are troubled by this contradiction between past history and present presumption, because everyone assumes that science and the world have somehow changed in ways that make government science funding vital. We now know how to do science in an organized way that is more efficient than the old haphazard method and requires governmental programs, or so it is assumed. Science is more expensive now, so private funding is insufficient. Science is more necessary to economic competitiveness now, so its support is a matter of national urgency.

These and many other arguments for government support for science have been effectively demolished in two brilliant books by Britain's Terence Kealey, a biochemical scientist and currently Vice-Chancellor (President) of the University of Buckingham,[16] Britain's only private university. It is possible to quarrel with some of the details of Kealey's analysis, but his case against a common-good argument for government support of basic science is substantial.

Unfortunately, rational argument is often impotent against contrary social forces, and most basic research in the U.S.—and almost all such research in the biomedical sciences—is now supported by the government. A tipping point was reached some time ago. The case for government support was initially boosted by the huge growth of U.S. government intervention during World War II. Persuasive pronouncements by senior bureaucrats such as Vannevar Bush in his influential *Science: The Endless Frontier* (1945)[17] carried this forward into peacetime, leading to the formation of the National Science Foundation and a much expanded National Institutes of Health. Government funding reached a critical mass and soon crowded out all but a handful of private sources of support for biomedicine, for example. In particular, what are called "research universities," now feel little obligation to pay for research by their own faculty. With government in effect the only buyer for basic research in many fields, arguments against government funding for science lost their main audience some time ago.

It is conventional in behavioral psychology to divide reinforcement into two types: positive and negative. A schedule of positive reinforcement delivers something good for the appropriate action— food for lever pressing, wages for work, etc. In a schedule of negative reinforcement, on the other hand, the appropriate action puts off or avoids something bad—turns off a stimulus signaling electric shock or causes those enhanced interrogators to stop waterboarding. "Your money or your life!" is a schedule of negative reinforcement. It will come as no surprise that people and animals, if allowed to choose freely, will seek out situations associated with positive reinforcement but avoid those with negative reinforcement.

When the U.S. government first began funding research in universities, in the 1950s and 1960s, a successful grant application was a positive reinforcer. The minority of faculty who got research grants got a nice little boost to their efforts. A grant was not essential to most non-military research ("big science"—cyclotrons, radio astronomy, experimental nuclear reactors and the like—was the exception). But as both government research funds and the number of researchers grew massively during the last decades of the twentieth century, private research funds diminished and competition increased. Grants even took over much of the salary bill for many biomedical researchers, a dangerous practice in itself because of the malign incentives it creates. In short, a research grant shifted from being a bonus to a necessity. The reinforcement schedule changed decisively from positive to negative. More and more able young people are deterred from going into science because … who likes a schedule of negative reinforcement?

Grants are now essential not just for promotion and tenure, but also because research has become much more expensive. Why? One reason is the development of new, expensive technologies. These increases are probably unavoidable, but they are easily matched by cost reductions made possible by ever-cheaper computing and other technology. So why have research costs gone up anyway? The most obvious cause is a metastasizing regulatory burden. More elaborate time-accounting, conflict-of-interest and result-reporting procedures, institutional review boards, animal-care-and-use committees, ethics committees and the training, housing and reporting requirements they generate. These rules, in turn, are administered by a growing, interlocking bureaucracy inside and outside the university that is almost impossible to disassemble or even disentangle. I can personally attest to these increases.

This massive dependence on external, largely governmental, funds has had many effects on the structure, governance and development of universities, and on the opinions and interests of faculty. Not all these effects are benign.

Amazingly, U.S. science has done pretty well despite obvious handicaps, partly because the situation in competing countries is generally much worse. But I believe that, now, the malign hand is beginning to emerge. There are two related problems: bureaucracy and monopsony (a single buyer). Bureaucracy seeks accountability. If funds are to be given out, some specified outcome must result, else the bureaucrats are unhappy. If you're buying some tangible product like bricks or military aircraft this makes perfect sense. Order 10 dozen bricks, get 10 dozen bricks, order 10 Ospreys, get 10 aircraft. But when the product involves applied research, as in the case of the tilt-rotor Osprey, then uncertainty cannot be avoided and the contract must allow for Mr. Rumsfeld's "unk-unks" (more on these later). Most military contracts therefore permit cost overruns—after a long and troubled development period, the Osprey program wound up costing more than 10 times the original estimate, for example.[18] The military got a lot of criticism for this, because of the size of the Osprey overrun. But the need to allow *some* overrun when the contract is for a product that goes well beyond current technology can hardly be disputed.

Although the amounts of money involved are smaller, the situation in basic research is much worse because the outcome cannot be specified in advance, even in outline. In the case of the trouble-prone Osprey, the military knew what it wanted: a tilt-rotor plane with the speed and range of a fixed-wing aircraft and the VTOL capacities of a helicopter. They just didn't know quite how to get there, and they didn't really know how just much they didn't know, hence the exploding cost of development. But the outlines of the desired final product were clear. Basic research is completely different. In the mid-nineteenth century, Augustinian monk Gregor Mendel was simply curious about what seemed to be regularities in numbers of types of hybrid pea plants. No one at the time could have foreseen the revolutionary implications of the field of genetics which Mendel kicked off. Basic research is like a dictionary in the sense that most of what is part of it—most research—amounts to little or nothing, and some of the things that do work out are accidents spotted by an alert researcher (penicillin, X-rays). But you don't discard a dictionary because you don't look up every word; so a science program should not be abandoned because most studies fail.

These limitations were pretty well understood when Federal agencies began funding university basic research after the World War II. The aim was, and presumably still is, to distribute money in a way that is most likely to promote the best research. A rational approach would begin by asking: What is the best predictor of good research? And the answer would be at once: A good researcher. In other words, the best predictor, at least for relatively senior scientists who have accumulated a "track record," *is* the track record. A less reliable predictor, because of the inherent unpredictability of basic research, is the project proposal—but it is almost the only predictor for young researchers, who have had no opportunity to generate a track record.

The Feds responded to these constraints at the outset by creating both individual awards and project awards. Initially, these "K" awards to individuals were wonderfully generous[19]—a lifetime of salary support, freeing awardees from all teaching obligations, for example. Project-proposal requirements were at first modest. Only a very general, relatively short account of the intended research was required. My first, and successful, National Institutes of Health "RO1" proposal, written from a Canadian university several decades ago, was just ten double-spaced pages. But soon bureaucratic imperatives began to assert their baleful influence. A few of the lifetime awardees rested on their oars and produced very little. The obviously elitist nature of the program upset a few people—even though science, like sport and every other competitive enterprise, is unavoidably elitist: not everyone can be a Darwin or an Einstein—or a David Beckham.

The reinforcement contingencies for administrators were, and are, asymmetrical in a way that devalues creativity. Grant bureaucrats are not punished for creative research that has *not* occurred as a consequence of their policies, how could they be? On the other hand, they may be punished for obvious idlers, apparently unproductive grantees who are quiescent for extended periods. Of course, some apparent idlers may be thinking productively, or experimenting hard but failing to find anything; but the grant administrator will be judged on finished product—publications—not on missed opportunities. These contingencies drive the process continually in the direction of more review, more accountability, more emphasis on "product"—both from grantees and from those who are tasked with reviewing them.

So, the time period for hard-to-evaluate and even harder-to-justify lifetime K-awards was reduced, first to five years, renewable, then to five years, not renewable, and finally these awards were abolished for most PhD researchers. The project awards, on the other hand, grew in size and importance. Forty years ago, a few double-spaced pages with a minimal budget sufficed. This grew to a maximum (somehow every proposal reached this maximum!) of 25 single-spaced pages in almost the smallest font, with many additional pages of budget, budget justification, conflict of interest and other "compliance" certifications, usually adding up to fifty pages or more.

Proposals are always "peer reviewed" by a committee of a dozen or more. The decisive influence on the fate of a proposal will usually be the two or three committee members most expert in the relevant area. As proposals grew in length and number, committee members began to ask more detailed questions. Peer reviewers—working scientists who do this for minimal compensation—had the unpleasant task of turning down an increasing number of proposals. Early in the game, funds were generous in relation to applications, so the "hit" rate was 50 percent or more. But as the growth of funds failed to keep pace with the growth in number and cost of applications, a point was reached in the 1990s where reviewers were basically looking for reasons to reject proposals. Hit rates dropped to 10 percent or less and reviewers began to ask questions at a level of detail that literally required the applicant to have already done (but not published!) the "proposed" work. Since basic research cannot in fact be predicted in detail, "good" proposals were—are—either accounts of work that has already been done, or a rather boring sort of science fiction.

In the best case, awardees would go on and do creative work very likely only loosely related to what they had proposed. In the worst case, awardees would blindly follow their own science fiction, usually some pedestrian variation on previous research. I say "pedestrian" because such is now the level of scrutiny, nothing really creative, no research of the form, "let's just see what will happen if we try X," where X is based not on a modest extension of previous work but on a hunch or whim—no research like that will get funded. An even worse outcome is that research support may be terminated because the researcher has strayed too far. A brilliant colleague of mine was recently in serious trouble not because he had ceased to be productive or had changed his research objective beyond the limits of his grant, but because he had begun to use a *new experimental technique* not specified—three years earlier—in the original proposal. The bureaucrat in charge, showing a misunderstanding of basic science that should have been grounds for dismissal, could not grasp the idea that research in many areas depends on the continual evolution of technique.

What has been the effect of this bureaucratic stranglehold on the scientific community? The malign hand has begun to show itself in three main ways. First, because the hit rate is now so low in most areas, researchers, particularly the biomedical researcher whose very job may depend on grant support and thus on finding something exciting (think "moral hazard"), have had to spend more and more time submitting more and more proposals—so doing less and less actual research. A typical full-time biomedical researcher may write six or eight of these 50-page monsters every year, spending perhaps 50 percent of his time on proposal preparation. A positive-feedback "bubble" has developed in which low hit rates have produced more proposals, which has further reduced hit rates, provoking a further increase in proposals, and so on.

The second and third effects are more sinister. They affect more the "softer" fields of science—science where experiments simply cannot be done and an established theoretical framework is lacking. This includes fields like economics, political science, sociology, and many aspects of psychology, toxicology, epidemiology, and climate science. So-called "hard" science—physics, chemistry, materials science, etc.—is less affected by politics and fashion, not because physicists are more virtuous than sociologists, but because the truth of any proposition is much easier to establish in such fields. But in all fields, to a greater or lesser degree, funding pressures have led researchers to look for their own niche, a sub-area in which they can be an acknowledged authority. The battle to win turf can get quite ugly, not to say amusing. The weapons are selective citation (omitting your competitors), choosing sympathetic reviewers for journal articles, trashing your rivals in anonymous peer reviews, and doubtless others I have not thought of. The malign-hand aspect to this is that encroachments on alien turf are severely punished. The pressure to be really, really good in a tiny, tiny area has much increased as competition for research grants has grown over the years. Consequently, grant support for the kind of broad-gauge, synthetic research that in the past has led to major advances has become almost impossible to get.[20]

The third effect is perhaps the worst. Public criticism of science by working scientists has become muted to the point of silence. The reason is simple. Working scientists are totally dependent on their colleagues' goodwill for the support of their work. If they make too many enemies, their papers will not be published in "high-impact" journals and their grant applications will not be funded. If they miss the high-impact journals, at least they can usually get published in a less-prestigious place. But, and here is the monopsony problem, for most researchers there is really only one place to get funded. It is the National Institutes of Health for most biomedicals. If they make enemies among the peer reviewers there, they are lost. And since the hit rates have been so low in recent years, all that's necessary to doom a proposal is simply to be "not enthusiastic" about it. So, as in the Wild West, when everyone is armed, people are real polite!

There are fixes for some of these problems. Basic science is a Darwinian trial-and-error business. Most experiments fail; most hypotheses are wrong. As Darwin himself commented, "I cannot remember a single first-formed hypothesis which had not after a time to be given up or greatly modified." Science funding needs therefore to attend more to the overall success rate of a *program* than to individual failures. The fact that a few lifetime awardees in the original NIH K-award fellowship program flamed out should not have been sufficient reason to abandon it.

Science-support agencies are necessarily organized by discipline. But all applications within a given sub-area then go to the same review committee, which is tidier bureaucratically and seems more "fair." But this means there is no competition *between* committees to fund the best research—only competition within each committee to favor your own area. It also means that any given area is likely to be dominated by a particular point of view—the "niche" problem I just discussed. One solution is to have at least two review committees in any sub-area and let them compete: which one has produced the most important findings? Reward it with increased funding taken from the other group. This is not a proposal likely to gladden the heart of any science bureaucrat, but it would surely be better for science. And finally, pork!—those "earmarked" funds that members of congress like to bring home to their districts. Research projects so funded are not, for the most part, peer reviewed in the usual way, so are scorned by many critics. But from the point of view of intellectual diversity an almost random set of selection criteria for at least a few projects may not be a bad thing. A silver lining, perhaps?

These three areas—Bureaucracy and Politics, Economic Globalization, and Scientific Research—do not exhaust the activities of the malign hand. I leave, as an exercise for the reader, applications of it to foreign aid, health and safety, health care, modernity and multiculturalism, "green" technology, regulatory agencies, tort law and class action, education, both higher and lower—and much, much more on bureaucracy!

My final topic in this survey of the malign hand is its destructive effects on democracy. This is a natural prelude to the main topic of this book, which is the workings of the malign hand in financial markets, but it needs a separate chapter.

Democracy, Fairness and the Tytler Dilemma

Democracies are not very stable (that is, sustainable) and the closer they are to one-person, one-vote, the less stable they seem to be. Monarchies, tyrannies, and oligarchies, from Ancient Egypt and China to classical Rome, have all lasted much longer than the oldest living democracy, which is often identified as the U.S., young as it is. A comment attributed to eighteenth-century Scottish aristocrat Alexander Tytler lays out one reason:

> A democracy is always temporary in nature; it simply cannot exist as a permanent form of government. A democracy will continue to exist up until the time that voters discover that they can vote themselves generous gifts from the public treasury. From that moment on, the majority always votes for the candidates who promise the most benefits from the public treasury, with the result that every democracy will finally collapse due to loose fiscal policy...[1]

Tytler is describing the malign hand: private good—immediate benefit from the public treasury—followed by collective bad—public bankruptcy. Obviously, as soon as a majority discover that they can gain more from government largesse than it costs them in taxes, there is a danger they will so vote.

But this is only true so long as taxes are progressive—take a larger fraction of higher incomes—and incomes are unequal. Given enough income inequality, social forces I will describe in a moment almost guarantee the Tytler problem. In other words, after income inequality reaches a certain point, forces come into play that will inevitably erode any democratic system. In the rest of this chapter, I will show how this works and provide some evidence that runaway financial markets are the root cause of the substantial growth in income inequality in recent decades.

Income inequality in 2011 is greater than at any earlier time in the U.S. Although the economy grew robustly during the 1950s and '60s, top salaries were pretty stable. But, after 1975 or so, executive compensation soared, even though the economy grew more slowly than in the previous decade. The money paid to top executives—in finance, especially, but also in many multinationals—has skyrocketed. In 1980, average executive compensation was about fifty times the average wage; by the year 2000 it was closer to three-hundred and fifty times.[2] The mind-numbing compensation of the Lloyd Blankfeins (Goldman Sachs – $54M in 2006) and Chuck O'Neills (Merrill Lynch, $48M)—not to mention hedge fund titan Ray Dalio ($3.9 *billion* in 2011)—of the financial world has become legendary. But what about income inequality overall? Blankfein, Dalio and their ilk are the "peak performers." A few people might get very rich without affecting income inequality in general. Not in this case, though: a general rise in income inequality has gone right along with grotesque increases in compensation for the winners. In 1980 the top 1% of taxpayers took in 8.5% of total national income and the bottom 50% took in 17.7%. But in 2009, the top one percent earned 17% of total income—double—whereas the bottom 50% earned just 13.5%, a *decrease* of 24%.[3] The Gini coefficient,[4] a broad measure of income inequality (0 is perfect equality, 100 all income goes to one person, everybody else has zero) changed from 40 in 1980 to 47 in 2009. By any measure, income inequality in the US has grown over the last three decades.

Here is an example of how income inequality combined with progressive taxation leads to the Tytler dilemma. Imagine a hundred citizens. Let's suppose all have the same income. Any income tax will then hit everyone in the same way, and any income-based "welfare benefit" will be applied to all equally. Everyone will be paying himself from his own money, so no one benefits. Under these conditions, no one will vote for transfer payments. People will prefer to spend all their own money rather than pay it to the government just to have some of it returned to them.

But now let's see what happens as incomes become more unequal and tax a bit more progressive. Suppose that our 100 incomes now range from 10 to 43 (arbitrary currency), with a median (middle-ranking) income of 19 and an average income of 21.5.[5] Suppose we levy a 10 percent income tax on everybody. A proportional tax like this is usually regarded as "regressive," i.e., favoring the rich. To make things more progressive, suppose we give every "poor" person, with income less than 20, say, an "earned-income tax credit" of, say, 4. This example amounts to a negative income tax of the sort recommended years ago by Milton Friedman as a simple alternative to welfare. (Nevertheless, as I will show, it does not avoid the Tytler dilemma.) Now everyone who gets the tax credit—and it turns out there are 53 out of the total population of 100—is making more in credit (4) than they pay in taxes (2 or less). The minority who make more than the 20 threshold just pay the flat tax. In other words, a majority of this population of taxpayers gets more from the system than they actually pay in tax. There is nothing special about these numbers. The point is that all you need to arrive at a situation where a minority pay and a majority benefit is a certain degree of income inequality plus a progressive tax system.

Under conditions like this, argues Tytler, what is to prevent the majority from voting themselves—or, more precisely, voting for representatives who will vote them—still larger tax credits, at the expense of the wealthier minority? If unchecked, this process will obviously at some point lead either to higher tax rates, or a budget deficit, as credits spent by the government grow to exceed taxes received. Or, more usually, both, because political pressures against raising taxes beyond a certain point are also strong, so that an increasing government deficit will often be the easiest escape route. The "Micawber option" is likely to be the only outcome: "Income, twenty shillings a week, expenditure, twenty shillings and sixpence; result, misery…"

The benefits to the "poor" majority need not be in form of a tax credit. The same result can come about because of progressive (disproportional) tax brackets or an increase in public sector employment and wages. In the U.S., for example, in 2006, 41 percent of the population paid no Federal income tax at all[6] because their incomes either fell below the personal-exemption threshold or they had sufficient deductions to reduce their liability to zero. Not yet a majority, but if you add to this percentage other low-income benefits, 50 percent may soon be exceeded. As a British writer recently noted about a similar situation in Britain, "[The Labour leader] quietly but skillfully enmeshed large sections of the middle class in a gladiator's net of state dependency."[7] Not that it takes much skill given the complementary reinforcement schedules under which legislators and the populace operate. Legislators want to get re-elected, the people want benefits. Given enough income inequality, generous welfare and a progressive tax regime satisfies both needs. A recent UK Liberal-Democrat proposal in 2010 is to advance the process still further by completely excluding the first £10,000 in income from tax. The Tytler process seems to be well advanced in most Western countries, where the proportion of people who actually pay income tax has been declining steadily in recent decades.

Benefits can be given in other ways than tax credits and relief—early retirement, say, or long holidays, large retirement pensions, or free health care. But the problem is the same in every case: the benefit received is paid by others and is not linked to the behavior of the recipient. The logic is the same, but the more complex the benefit structure, the harder it is to detect the malign hand. It seems to be well advanced in all the developed nations, where a majority profit more than they pay and a minority pay more than they benefit.

Another process which diverts national income into the public sector is public-sector employment, whose cost has much increased as a percentage of GDP in most Western nations in the past few decades. Public-sector wages, which used be lower than private-sector wages, with greater job security as the presumed counterweight, have now risen above the private sector. In the U.S., for example, "The typical Federal worker is paid 20 percent more than a private-sector worker in the same occupation."[8] Other sources contend that the disproportion is even greater, with government workers now getting as much as twice the compensation of comparable workers in the private sector. In the UK the compensation of government employees, like head teachers and police chiefs, whose wages and bonuses[9] are set via bureaucratic process and are not widely known or much constrained by public opinion, often exceeds the compensation of the Prime Minister. Why this disparity? The malign-hand explanation is the absence of competition for government resources. A private company that gives in to wage demands will soon lose to more resistant, hence lower-cost, competitors. But a government, especially a central government, which can print money, is subject to less restraint. The voters may throw out the spendthrift politicians, but only after a delay and the failure of union-financed election campaigns on their behalf. And the new guys will be subject to the same feeble restraints as their predecessors. Government, unlike private business, is not subject to the restraining effects of competition. The results that Tytler foresaw may be coming about with the threatened collapse since 2008 of the "European social model." A similar fate may await the U.S. economy.

Early democracies all originated among a small aristocracy—"citizens" in ancient Greece, barons in Britain, and male landowners in the U.S. Women, slaves and those without property were excluded. Restriction of voting to a small number of relatively wealthy citizens was the rule until relatively recently. Before 1832 and the Reform Act in Britain, a majority of members of parliament came from "rotten boroughs," each with a handful of voters and controlled by a local landowner. Even after the Reform Act, voting was still restricted to men who owned some property. Only one in seven adult males had the vote and constituencies varied greatly in size. It was a long way from one citizen, one vote.

Yet British democracy worked well even though, or perhaps because, voting was confined to people with skin in the game, to actual taxpayers. But everywhere pressure to extend the vote has been a steady force. Tom Paine in the *Rights of Man* (1791) argued for one-man, one vote (no women yet!) and his words had enormous influence in the U.S. Principles of natural justice self-evident to many seem to urge that no potential voter be left behind. After all, how can you justify the exclusion of the poor, of women, of once-enslaved blacks, of young people, from the franchise? So all adults and close-to-adults are now urged—or even compelled, as in Australia and Brazil—to vote. Voting ages have been declining in many countries. It used to be 21 almost everywhere, now it is 18 or even 16 in many countries. The U.S. voting age has been reduced from 21 to 18, lower than the legal drinking age—and there are pressures to reduce it still further.

Why does extending the franchise meet so little resistance while lowering the U.S. drinking age is well-nigh impossible? A cynic might respond that perhaps it is because the drinking age has a real effect on drunk-driving deaths, whereas the more people who vote, the less responsible their government need be. More likely is that it comes from blind adherence to a numerical view of democracy that has no basis in history and poses malign-hand perils.

In the UK, Margaret Thatcher's response to the Tytler problem was her hated "poll tax" (community charge) in 1990. The tax meant that the same fixed amount had to be paid every year by every adult.[10] The idea was that everyone, poor as well as rich, should have some investment in government. Thatcher's hope was that this rather modest but universal tax would encourage even net beneficiaries of government to feel some responsibility for government expenditures. But of course the same forces that drive inexorably towards a universal franchise will resist any attempt to limit it,[11] especially by a tax that seems aimed squarely at the poor. After several riots, Thatcher was ousted by her own party and the poll tax never went into effect. Many U.S. states had poll taxes, until all were abolished by the 24th Amendment to the Constitution in 1964. "No representation without taxation" has proved much less appealing than the converse. The forces against restricting, or even disciplining, the electorate in any way have been unstoppable.

Compulsory voting, which is the ultimate extension of the franchise, just compounds the problem, and can lead to one-party rule besides, as *The Economist* recently pointed out:

> One reason why liberals have been so muted since Brazil became a democracy again is that voting in elections is compulsory. This means that a large number of poor voters, who pay little tax but benefit from government welfare spending, help to push the parties in the direction of a bigger state. If the same system were to be applied to America, the Democrats might well enjoy a permanent majority.[12]

If you doubt that permanent one-party rule is a great idea (see "PRI in Mexico" for more than 70 years) maybe those "rock the vote!" campaigns aren't such a great idea after all!

There is a mechanism, universal in Europe, which does insure that every citizen makes some contribution to the national treasury: the value-added tax (VAT). The VAT is in effect a sales tax and it is substantial, 19 percent or more in the larger European countries. Tax competition within the EU is blocked by rules for so-called "tax harmonization" (nice euphemism!) that set a lower bound for VAT, so one country cannot gain advantage over others by lowering its rate below 15 percent. But VAT was not designed as a signal to the populace of their contribution to the government. *Au contraire*, it is a regressive stealth tax—regressive because the poor pay a larger fraction of their income in the VAT than the rich, and stealth because (unlike in the U.S.) the tax is concealed in the price of goods. Customers will look in vain for the line on their receipt saying "VAT £10" for a £50 item. Taxes are designed according to many rules—rewarding virtue, punishing vice, informing the public, etc. But VAT was designed according to the most important rule of all, which was described by Frenchman Jean Baptiste Colbert in the 18th century: "The art of taxation consists in so plucking the goose as to obtain the largest possible amount of feathers with the smallest possible amount of hissing." The VAT is useless as feedback to a responsible citizenry; it's great for raising money invisibly.

It's worth taking a little time to understand the root malign-hand problem for democracy. The problem is not one-man-one-vote or even progressive tax rates. The root problem is *income inequality* itself. Wide disparities in income are thought to be unfair, even unjust. Most people, even many rich conservatives, don't like the kind of wide income disparities that have taken hold in the U.S. in recent years. Libertarian former Fed Chairman Alan Greenspan, for example, commented in 2005: "This is not the type of thing which a democratic society—a capitalist democratic society—can really accept without addressing."[13] Super-rich investor Warren Buffett has quixotically complained that he pays a smaller percentage of income in Federal tax than his secretary, a claim that turns out to be misleading[14] but does show that many of the very rich share egalitarian social norms. On the other hand, conservatives, particularly, don't like the idea of confiscatory taxation of the rich, which seems to be the only way to remedy the situation. But is it? To know the answer we need first to know what has caused these disparities.

First, the facts, which are pretty staggering. The Gini coefficient[15] for the U.S. as recently as 1967, for example, was 34, but in 2005 it had reached 41—a huge increase in income inequality European countries and Canada have Ginis in the range of 30. A few other facts: in 1915, the time of the robber barons and the Gilded Age when, one would think, income disparities were at their height, the top one percent got about 15 percent of the nation's income. But in 2010, the richest one percent received 24 percent of the nation's income.[16] In terms of wealth, the disparity is even greater: the top one percent control 40 percent.[17]

There are two reasons to be concerned about this kind of disparity. One is moral: is it right that a small fraction of the population should be so much wealthier than the rest? Sure, no problem, say many libertarians and conservatives. They've earned their wealth—and indeed these days most of them have. As Chrystia Freeland has pointed out,[18] the new super-rich are usually not heirs of wealth and privilege as they used to be in centuries past. Many of them, like Steven Schwarzman, co-founder of Blackstone Private Equity, and Goldman Sachs' Lloyd Blankfein came from middle-class households. By and large they *have* earned their fortunes. And they know it and are not modest about it. Freeland has a few telling anecdotes: "When I asked one of Wall Street's most successful investment-bank CEOs if he felt guilty for his firm's role in creating the financial crisis, he told me with evident sincerity that he did not. The real culprit, he explained, was his feckless cousin, who owned three cars and a home he could not afford." No *noblesse oblige* here then! While this kind of arrogance is deplorable, it still seems reasonable to most Americans (not so many Europeans!) that so long as they pay their taxes and perhaps do a little charitable giving, people have a right to what they earn. The "politics of envy" have never gotten much traction in America, as (wealthy!) presidential candidates Al Gore and John Edwards found to their cost.

So the superwealthy are entitled to their billions. Well, maybe, but the second reason to be concerned is that almost everyone, even some of the wealthy themselves, is uncomfortable with income disparities and is more or less sympathetic to tax policies that do something to redress them. Some objections are raised to increases in tax progressivity, even though tax rates, and their progressivity, have been much higher in the relatively recent past. President Kennedy, for example, reduced marginal rates from the 20–90 percent range to 14–65 percent, a range still much higher than the current 10–35 percent. Nevertheless, there will always be some progressivity. What else are we to do?

The most popular objection to raising taxes has to do with the effect of tax rates on general prosperity. To update an old adage, maybe what's good for Lloyd Blankfein *is* good for America? In other words, perhaps too-high tax rates reduce economic growth? Perhaps they do, but it's hard to prove and in any case that is not the main reason to reject the idea that the income inequality problem can be solved through progressive taxation. The real problem is that highly progressive tax policies are bad in themselves, because they bring on the Tytler problem. Given the income inequality that prompted them in the first place, pretty soon, most people are either paying no tax at all or at least get back more than they put in. Redistributive policies may or may not be morally right. That's almost irrelevant. The real problem is that they create a majority who adapt to them (who behave rationally, if you prefer) in ways that undermine the financial stability of the whole democratic enterprise. The malign hand is free to act and the foundations of democracy are eroded. Soon we are trapped in a downward spiral. The economy allows a few individuals to amass huge wealth, which leads to tax and welfare policies to alleviate disparities, which provide a reinforcement schedule to which their beneficiaries adapt in ways that cut at the fiscal roots of democracy.

So we are in a bind. Huge income disparities are bad, but the tax and welfare policies that seem essential to ameliorate them are also bad. What *are* we to do? The answer is: try and understand the *causes* of these disparities. If we understand the causes, we can perhaps prevent severe disparities from occurring in the first place. As I will show later, this can be done without impairing—indeed while enhancing— general prosperity.

The pattern of changes in wealth distribution and total credit over the years provides a hint as to why inequality has grown in the modern U.S. As I pointed out earlier, the U.S. hasn't always suffered from massive income inequality. In the period from about 1942 to 1982, the "Great Compression" as it has been called, disparities were much less severe than now and prosperity by many measures was greater. The two graphs below are probably the most important in the book. The top graph shows how the share of GDP going to the top 10 percent of earners varied from 1917 to 2007. Disparities were bad from about 1929 to 1939 (the Great Depression): the top 10 percent got from 45 to 50 percent of GDP. After that, their share declined and did not reach the earlier level again until the late 1990s: the "Great Divergence."[19] What is going on?

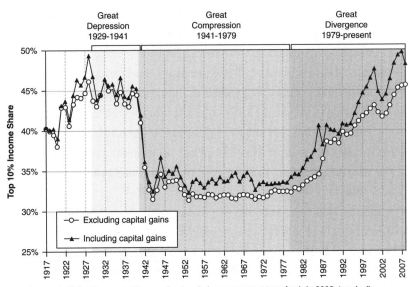

The Top Ten Percent Income Share, 1917-2008

Income is defined as market income (and excludes government transfers). In 2008, top decile includes all families with annual income above $109,000.

Source: Thomas Piketty and Emmanuel Saez.

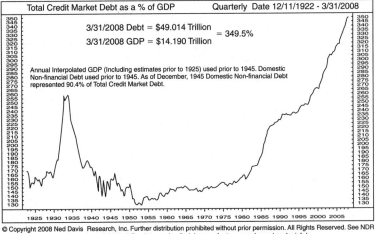

© Copyright 2008 Ned Davis Research, Inc. Further distribution prohibited without prior permission. All Rights Reserved. See NDR Disclaimer at www.ndr.com/copyright.html. For data vendor disclaimers refer to www.ndr.com/vendor info/.

Top: Share of national market income going to the top 10%, from 1917 to 2006. From Piketty & Saez, e.g., *The Quarterly Journal of Economics* (2003) 118 (1): 1–41, updated. Bottom: Total credit market debt as percent of GDP from 1917 to 2007. (Source: Kevin Phillips, *Bad Money: Reckless finance, bad politics and the global crisis of American capitalism.* Penguin, 2009, from Barrons, February 21, 2005, updated).

Figure 2-1

The lower graph provides a clue. It shows the proportion of the GDP that is owing to total *credit-market debt* at these different periods. The similarity between the two curves is striking. When income inequality is high, during the Great Depression and in recent years, so is total debt; when total debt declines, so does income inequality. Causation is something that is difficult or impossible to prove in macroeconomics.[20] But it looks as if a major, perhaps *the* major, cause of income inequality is massive debt-fueled growth in the financial sector. Since this huge debt is bad for many other reasons, as I will show in later chapters, this is surely the first place to look to solve the Tytler problem.

Timothy Noah, coming at the inequality problem from a very different angle in a *Slate* series on income inequality,[21] seems to agree. He lists a number of candidate causes for the growth in inequality. He concludes that race, gender, and single parenthood have no role; immigration, international trade and decline in labor unions have some share. But Noah puts a large chunk of the blame on the financial sector—"pampering of the Stinking Rich," as he tendentiously expresses it. I'm not sure the class-war rhetoric is helpful or that "pampering" is the right word. The problem is that malign-hand practices have been allowed to run rampant in financial markets. All involve the creation of huge amounts of debt. Gambling with created money has made many billionaires and impoverished, relatively and in some cases absolutely, everybody else. Now, like the cock crowing proudly as he produces the dawn, the mega-rich think that they are really responsible for their enormous wealth rather than almost incidental beneficiaries of a malign system. Not that they had no role in creating the malignancy—but that hardly qualifies as "earning" your wealth in the way that Bill Gates or Sam Walton earned theirs. The rest of this book is devoted to explaining how all this works and what might be done about it. But I must begin at the beginning, with some basic philosophy and economics.

Value and Reason

"[M]arkets have become too complex for effective human intervention, the most promising anticrisis policies are those that maintain maximum market flexibility.... Regulation, by its nature, inhibits freedom of market action, and that freedom to act expeditiously is what rebalances markets. Undermine this freedom and the whole market-balancing process is put at risk." So wrote Ayn Rand acolyte, free-market Chairman of the Federal Reserve—the "Fed"—Alan Greenspan just before the 2008 financial crisis.[1] In 2007 Greenspan had no doubt about the automatic, self-regulating properties of markets, which he likened to the control mechanisms of an autopilot: "We never, of course, know all the many millions of transactions that occur every day. Neither does a U.S. Air Force B-2 pilot know, *or need to know*, the millions of automatic split-second computer-based adjustments that keep his aircraft in the air." An interesting analogy, as it turns out, since it shows just how profound was Greenspan's misunderstanding of financial markets. Aircraft control systems depend on negative—error-reducing—feedback. But financial markets, as we will see, are riddled with destabilizing, bubble-inducing, *positive* feedbacks.

Greenspan also had no doubts about the markets' contribution to the general welfare: "The purpose of hedge funds and others is to make money, but their actions extirpate inefficiencies and imbalances, and thereby reduce the waste of *scarce savings*. These institutions thereby contribute to higher levels of productivity and overall standards of living." (my italics) He did not share John Maynard Keynes's occasional doubts about the social worth of financial markets: "Keynes, Fred Macaulay and most other 1930s intellectuals expressed the opinion that [financial markets] did not [have any socially redeeming value]."[2] More on Keynes in Chapter 9. Nor did he express any reservations about the concept of a free market. The idea that all regulation is bad implies that there is an ideal "free market," which modern financial markets more or less match. The very complexity of modern markets—"markets have become too complex for effective human intervention"—makes accurate regulation impossible, thinks Greenspan, so almost any attempt to regulate them is a mistake.

Is it unfair to single out Greenspan—who, we should remember, "has a legitimate claim to being the greatest central banker who ever lived" according to Princeton economists Alan Blinder and Ricardo Reis[3]—for being wrong about the perfection of the existing market system? He is certainly more responsible than most for what happened in 2008. On the other hand, many others, almost as influential, not just the "masters of the universe" on Wall Street, but the majority in government and Congress as well, believed that financial markets pumped out riches for the good of all. Opposition was muted and either ideological or technical. The first could be dismissed by partisans of the other side; the second was ignored by almost everybody. So the consensus was that no changes were needed. As the bubble grew and many prospered exceedingly, all seemed well with the world.

These quotes from Greenspan, "The Maestro," as Bob "Watergate" Woodward, Greenspan's biographer, called him—with no trace of irony—are worth a little dissection because they reflect so much of the thinking that led up to the 2008 crash. Here's a list of what I take to be Il Maestro's core beliefs about financial markets in Phase 1, i.e., before the crash of 2008:

1. Unregulated markets always give the right answer, they are "efficient" ("extirpate inefficiencies")
2. The money in markets is mostly *savings*.
3. Markets are irreducibly complex ("computer-based adjustments") so regulation is always bad.
4. Product innovation—hedge funds, securitization, swaps, etc.— makes markets more efficient ("freedom of market action")

5. Speed is always good ("freedom to act expeditiously")
6. Markets seek an equilibrium state ("market-balancing process")
7. Financial markets exist to allocate scarce resources.

In Phase 2, in shocked reaction to the 2007–8 credit crisis and sub-prime mortgage meltdown, Greenspan appeared to modify his views: "We are in the midst of a once-in-a century credit tsunami…"[4] Or did he? "…a once-in-a-century credit tsunami" sounds more like an Act of God than a design failure of the financial market system. I have no special insight into his mind but one suspects that Maestro Greenspan still thinks the 2008 crash was not a "market failure" in any real sense. He still believes the things I listed above.

In fact, all but the last of these seven claims are wrong: As I pointed out in the Introduction, even old Adam Smith knew that unregulated markets do not always promote the common good. More recent work shows more and more ways in which modern markets, especially financial markets, can fail.

Greenspan claimed that most of the money sloshing around financial markets is *savings*, which need to be allocated to efficient use, rather than opaquely packaged leveraged *debt*, money that never existed in the form of cash or tangible goods and could never be turned to productive use. Savings are but a small part of the total. Yes, markets are complex, but much market complexity is not intrinsic but created to confuse: complexity can be a weapon. Greenspan always believed in the absolute value of financial innovation: "part of the gains [in home ownership] have…come about because innovative lenders…have created a far broader spectrum of mortgage products and have increased the efficiency of loan originations and underwriting" he said in 1999[5]—as if the ingenuity of the mortgage industry did anything more than increase debt. The much-lauded "creativity" of market people—new inventions like securitization and credit default swaps—is as likely to destroy wealth (usually of people other than the creators, admittedly) as to create it. Speed, computerized trading and the like, can facilitate instability in ways I will discuss later. And, finally, markets tend to be *unstable*, especially in the long run. Whatever "rebalancing" there is, is often completely ineffective.

What *is* true is that the only real purpose of financial markets is to allocate scarce resources. On that point at least, all can agree.

Another point we can all agree on is that markets are complicated. But the solution when they fail is hardly just to leave them alone, as Mr. G proposed. Some pretty deep thinking will be necessary to understand them and come up with practical ways to regulate them. Just how keen the politicians are to go through this process can be gauged by the fact that the Dodd-Frank regulatory bill, which was advertised as a solution for the problems that precipitated the 2008 crisis, was signed into law on July 21, 2010, some six months *before* the report of the Financial Crisis Inquiry Commission,[6] which provided some insight into the causes of the crash. The politicians, at least at that time, had zero interest in understanding the causes of the crash or dealing with the systemic flaws that underlie it. They had every interest in defusing the political fallout from the pauperization of the middle class that the crash caused.

In the rest of this book I want to look at the factual and theoretical basis for the core beliefs that sustain financial markets in their current form. I begin in this chapter with *value* and *rationality*. The efficient-market idea needs a chapter to itself.

The idea of value is fundamental to all economics. If the idea of market efficiency means anything at all, it should mean that the price of something traded in a free market should be an accurate reflection of its value. In fact, *efficiency* of markets means something very different, as we'll see later. So what is *value*, other than price? The most popular suggestion for an independent measure of the value of (say) a stock is its *fundamentals*. The fundamentals include things like price/earnings ratio, cash flow and dividends, the competitive position of the company in its industry, the state of current and projected technology, efficiency of operation and so forth. Some of the problems with these measures are that a company may not do as well or as badly in the future as it has done in the past (P/E ratio, cash flow, etc. may change); predicting the impact of technology in the future often amounts to little more than a guess; competitors may arise and disappear unpredictably—and finally, very often, especially during boom and bust, the fundamental value computed using best practices nevertheless bears very little relation indeed to actual price. So fundamental analysis is not totally adequate either as science—to provide an explanation for stock price—or as practice—to tell us which stock to trade.

In the real world, price is unstable. For example, a simple name change can cause a substantial change in the price of a security. Burton Malkiel, in his modern classic *A Random Walk Down Wall Street*,[7] describes how, during the dot-com boom at the end of the last millennium, simply renaming a stock could cause it to blossom: "For example, American Music Guild, whose business consisted entirely of the door-to-door sale of phonograph records and players, changed its name to 'Space-Tone' before 'going public.' The shares were sold to the public at 2 and within a few weeks rose to 14." Stocks with "China" in the name have similarly boomed in recent years.[8]

Name—*brand*—is even more important in the retail world. Everyone knows that some "conspicuous consumers" will pay tens of thousands of dollars for a wind-up Breguet *Grande Complication* when they could get another watch as handsome, more accurate and requiring less attention, for a tenth, nay a hundredth, as much. But it is perhaps more surprising to see the same kind of bias in stock picking where (surely) the financials are all that matter.

Space-Tone returned to earth soon enough, as the bubble deflated. These returns to sanity are usually taken as evidence of market "efficiency." *But why should they weigh more in our analysis than the extremes?* Only because we share with the experts a completely ungrounded faith that there is a "real" value to every stock and we (sort of) know (always after-the-fact) what it is.

Economists are hardly unaware of the problem of value. Yet many of the most sophisticated, even as they acknowledge the problems, speak in Platonic tones as if there really is a "real" value for a stock or a house, or a work of art—although my 5-year-old grandson's masterwork, worth nothing on the open market, looks to my eyes indistinguishable from the casual scribbles of Wassily Kandinsky, with a market price of thousands. "Provenance" of course is everything in the art market: rubbish, unattributed, is worth nothing. The very same rubbish, convincingly linked to (say) Matisse, is worth a great deal. The history of an art object apparently often matters much more than what it actually is. Perhaps the oddest testament to the extraordinary valuations of *objets d'art* is the market in modern Britain for *car license-plate numbers*. If you thought four thousand florins for a tulip bulb is a primitive aberration of Holland in the 17th century (see "Tulipmania"—the first big free-market bubble[9]), try this: car registration "36KC" on offer for £24,000 or, if you prefer "6 BCL" a snip at £5,600.[10] Beauty may be in the eye of the beholder, but *value is in his mind*.

Sexual favors provide another bit of evidence that value is not an intrinsic property. Sex offered willingly, or even as the outcome of courtship or seduction, is usually valued more highly than sex simply purchased. The value of the end, as it were, is not always independent of the means used to attain it. Even the amount of money makes a difference. Recall the quote attributed variously to Winston Churchill and George Bernard Shaw after overhearing a discussion among some ladies of quality about a certain wealthy but unattractive man. When asked "Would you sleep with him for a fifty-thousand pounds?" one lady began to nod assent, at which point Shaw interjected "How about for a fiver?" To which she indignantly responded "Sir, what do you think I am!" To which he famously replied: "Madam, we have established what you are; we are only haggling over the price."

But of course, the lady was right and Shaw wrong. The price, and the form in which it is paid, does matter. Asked when her prejudice against wealthy but proud Mr. Darcy began to abate, Jane Austen's Miss Elizabeth Bennett, most intelligent and honorable of women, responded "I believe I must date it from my first seeing his beautiful grounds at *Pemberley*." It is, perhaps, easier to fall in love with a rich man than a poor one and the favors then given need not be tainted.

The philosophically inclined may notice that the attempt to define "value" in objective terms is an example of the *naturalistic fallacy*, so called by moral philosopher G. E. Moore in 1903. Moore argued that there is no objective, naturalistic, definition of "the good." The same is true for value. We are forced, I think, to the commonsense conclusion attributed to game-theory pioneer Oskar Morgenstern: "A thing is only worth what someone else will pay for it." But the idea of "pay" needs to be amplified a bit in light of new knowledge.

The link with payment does suggest an objective way to *measure* value, though it's not of direct help in understanding financial markets. Adam Smith, father of economics and a genius of common sense, called value "real price." In 1776 he wrote: "The real price of every thing, what every thing really costs to the man who wants to acquire it, is the toil and trouble of acquiring it."[11] This has become known as the *labor theory of value*. Smith's language allows it to be interpreted in two ways. One is simply to equate the value of a thing to the effort necessary to secure it. Thus, oxygen, which is freely available to everyone, would have no value, and gold, hard to get, would have much. This apparent contradiction—oxygen, essential to life, should surely be worth more than gold—led economists to make a distinction between "value in exchange" and "value in use" which papered over the immediate problem.

But there is another way to look at Smith's claim, a way that puts the emphasis not on the work but on the willingness. The behavioral psychologist can come to the economist's rescue here, because Adam Smith's definition of *value* is close to the psychologist's definition of *reinforcement*. A *reinforcer* is something an organism will work for, like money for a man or food for a hungry rat. It's the *willingness* to work, a property of the organism *and* the reinforcement schedule, not of the thing itself, that defines the value. So the difference between gold and oxygen in my example is not so much their real value as the usual *reinforcement schedule*—another term is reinforcement *contingency*—necessary to obtain them.[12] Oxygen is available ad lib., gold is not. A pigeon need not work for free food nor a man for free air. Thus, to compare values by looking at effort, the reinforcement contingencies must also be comparable. There is no doubt that if oxygen had to be worked for, we would all labor unceasingly. Indeed, even goldfish will work for oxygen,[13] as will a drowning man. When the schedules to get them are comparable, oxygen will have, as you might expect, a higher value than gold. This is all very reasonable but of little help in measuring the value of a financial instrument, stock or bond, say. Why? Because the schedule for a stock is always the same: you buy it. The work is gaining the money. The value is just the price, as Morgenstern proposed. But the reinforcement-schedule model does have useful implications for the economic concepts of rationality and marginal utility.

The labor theory of value is said to have been supplanted by the law of supply and demand and the concept of *marginal utility*. Marginal utility is simply the value of the next little bit of whatever it is you are interested in. Every economics textbook will have a diagram showing that the more you have of good A (pizza, say) the less value each additional bite will have. To maximize the value of a fixed money budget, the idea is to consume goods A and B until the marginal utility of the next bit of consumption is the same for both. Thus, with a choice between pizza and ice cream, you will not fill up with only one, no matter how cheap it may be. Instead you will sample each until the value of the next bite is the same for each. This is how static economics explains how consumers allocate their limited supply of money to different goods. The supply of labor is also supposed to follow the principle of marginal utility. The idea here is that there is a cost to work which increases disproportionately. When you are tired after working all day you are naturally reluctant to work a bit more: work cost shows *increasing* marginal (dis)utility. The marginal value of money wage, on the other hand, is assumed to be more or less constant, at least over the modest range of regular wages: each additional dollar has the same utility. The difference between these two curves, the more or less constant marginal value of wages and the exponentially increasing marginal cost of work, yields a bell-shaped *labor-supply curve*. It shows that people will work hard at first, but then peak at an intermediate amount of work.

This argument is for an individual worker, but of course much the same applies to an entire labor market: the better the wage the greater the number of people who will work and the more work they will do, up to a maximum beyond which further wage increases may actually cause total work to decrease. In the early 1980s, a few behavioral psychologists and economists noticed that people respond to the cost of a commodity rather as hungry pigeons respond to the amount of work necessary to obtain a bit of food.[14] The higher the cost, the more they will work for it, albeit suffering a slight drop in the amount obtained, until a certain maximum of work is attained. If the price (work) needed is further increased, labor output drops. So, in reinforcement-theory terms, *value* is measured by the amount of behavior (work) someone will perform, on a given schedule of reinforcement, to get the valued thing.

So how are reinforcement schedules actually used to measure value? Again, we must turn to simple experiments with animals. If you can bear with me for a mild technical digression, I hope that an example will show the principle and also shed light on the idea of adaptation to a schedule and why it is quite different from the flawed notion of rationality. "Operant conditioning" is learned behavior of the type that would normally be called "goal-oriented" or "voluntary." Most human behavior, certainly all the buying and selling behavior that make markets work, is "operant" in this sense.[15] Let's begin with a very simple operant conditioning experiment on choice. In a classic experiment, the subject (usually a hungry pigeon or rat, but humans work as well) is confronted with two choices. The payoff for choosing either alternative is an occasional reward (reinforcer, such as a piece of food). Choices must be made repeatedly because the schedule allocating reward is intermittent and usually random, so that a subject cannot know in advance when his response (choice) will be effective.

I begin with the simplest possible choice procedure, a Las Vegas-style 2-armed bandit: each choice pays off after a random number of responses. For example, the Left choice (a peck on an illuminated disk for the pigeon, a keystroke or lever-pull for a human) might pay off on average every 10 responses, whereas the Right choice pays off after every 20 responses; these are *random-ratio* schedules of 10 or 20 (RR10 or 20).

Even someone with meager quantitative skills can see that it's better to choose Left. A little further thought should reveal that it is in fact *never* a good idea to choose Right, because the payoff probabilities are unchanging—1/10 on the left and 1/20 on the right— so your chances are *always* better on the left than on the right. After a little experience with the outcomes from each choice both pigeons and people usually fixate on the higher-probability option—they maximize, an apparent win for "rational" micro-economic analysis.

Let's change the schedules a little bit. Still random ratio, but both choices are the same, say RR20. Now it doesn't matter what the subject does, the payoff will be the same: one in 20, on average. So rational-choice theory makes no prediction at all, since it doesn't matter which one the subject chooses. Well, under these conditions pigeons behave in an interesting way that provides clues to what they are really doing, which is not comparing outcomes in a rational way and picking the best. The clue is provided by the fact that when both options are the same, the animals' pattern of choice depends on the ratio value. If the ratio is small (say 20, i.e., relatively high probability of payoff) they tend to pick one choice and stick with it. But if the ratio is large (say 75, low payoff) they tend to alternate between the two. Why?

What seems to be happening is a rather simple incremental process of reward following and nonreward avoiding. After a reward for a Left response, say, the probability of a Left response increases; after a nonreward, it decreases—and similarly for a reward or nonreward for a Right response. The distinctive property of this process is just that, "At a given probability value, reward for a Right response increments it by the same amount that a reward on the Left decrements it—and similarly for a nonreward."[16] The details are not important, just the fact that each reward or nonreward bumps the probability of choosing a given option up or down in a rather simple way. What matters is that the apparently rational behavior we saw when the two options delivered reward with unequal probabilities does not reflect the kind of explicit comparison of the two choices implied by "rational" choice theory. What seems to be happening is a much simpler step-by-step process whereby the pigeon just adjusts the "strength" of the Left and Right response tendencies according to whether his last peck was rewarded or not. This process explains the odd behavior when the two choices are the same. When he gets a lot more nonrewards than rewards, switching wins over staying. But when his payoff rate is high, staying wins over switching.

It is important to point out that a rational-behavior analysis is not absolutely demolished by these results. The reason? It is *always* possible to come up with a rational (optimality) analysis (more about optimality in a moment) to explain *any* result. In this case, there are two ready to hand. One is *satisficing*, a term coined by polymath psychologist and Nobelist in Economics Herbert Simon (1916–2001).[17] Pigeons in the 2-armed-bandit situation behave as if they are settling for an acceptable alternative if it is "good enough" (RR20) but will not accept one that is not good enough (RR75). Satisficing is rational, from some points of view: if something is "good enough" why waste effort searching for better? But it is not of course optimal in the strict sense. It can be made optimal by changing assumptions, however. Suppose we assume that the animal has a pre-existing "default" expectation about the payoff to be had by leaving any given situation. Then if the situation delivers more than the default (e.g., RR20) he will stay, but if it delivers less (e.g., RR75) he will leave. "Ad hoc" you might say, and indeed it is. But it shows the flexibility of optimality analysis. There will always be a set of assumptions with respect to which *any* behavior is optimal.

At the same time that behavioral psychologists came to understand the limited rationality of animals, behavioral economists were beginning to show similar limitations in people. The limitations of animals are more profound than most of those that have been demonstrated in people. I say that for two reasons. First, it took people to discover the limitations of animals, not the other way round! And second, the limitations of animals hold up even if they are given repeated experience with the problem (indeed, since they cannot be instructed verbally, they usually must be given repeated exposure in order to learn the problem). Many of the tricks that behavioral economists have played on human subjects only work the first time or under highly controlled conditions where access to information is limited. Given repeated tries, or the ability to consult with others, people typically do much better.

The pioneer in unraveling human rationality was again H. A. Simon, who proposed the idea of *bounded rationality* and the companion notion of *satisficing* that I just discussed.[18] A subsequent economics Nobelist, psychologist Daniel Kahneman, and his longtime collaborator, the late Amos Tversky (1937–1996), had a huge impact on economics as well as psychology via a series of simple experiments that showed hitherto unsuspected deviations from rational behavior by human subjects.[19]

Three related and apparently irrational patterns that people show are *loss-aversion, framing* and the *endowment effect*. Loss aversion is the easiest to understand. Suppose we ask a group of people to choose between two options: Option 1: get $1,000 for sure; Option 2: get $2,500 with a probability of one half. Most people unhesitatingly choose Option 1, the sure thing, even though the *expected value* of Option 2, $2,500 \times .5 = \$1,250$, is greater than Option 1. To me, the most surprising thing about this result and others like it, is not the result itself, but that it was in fact surprising, even shocking, to most economists. People in these experiments are *irrational*! in violation of what was then—and still is to a large extent—a fundamental tenet of the economist's church, that humans faced with such stark and simple financial choices are invariably *rational*, in the simple, money-maximizing sense, and so should invariably pick the option with the higher expected payoff. Yet from a commonsense point of view, preference for a sure thing will as often be the norm as willingness to take a gamble.

Why do human subjects behave in this way? First, people exposed to repeated choices like this pretty soon get the idea and begin to optimize, choosing the option with the higher expected payoff. But the question still remains: why are they (apparently) so dumb the first time? A boring answer is that they simply don't trust the experimenter, so they want the sure thing, *now!* If that is ruled out, there are several possibilities (and that's part of the problem, deciding which is actually right). The endowment effect is Kahneman and Tversky's label for the fact that you will value more something you actually own than something you might own. People will not exchange a coffee mug they have been given even though, if they had been allowed to choose, they might have valued it less than another which is now offered in exchange. In a rather more dramatic experiment involving students at Duke University and basketball tickets, a good roughly equivalent in that culture to the Holy Grail or the elixir of eternal youth, Dan Ariely and Ziv Carmon found that students valued tickets they had "won" through a traditional and very effortful procedure at more than 10 times the price that other, presumably equivalent, students, who lost, would pay for the same tickets.[20] The endowment effect adds another example to Jane Austen's Mr. Darcy of the value of an object not being independent of the means of attaining it.

Kahneman and Tversky's result, the preference for $1,000 over a 50:50 bet for $2,500, might also be explained as an endowment effect. Since the $1,000 is certain, in a sense the subject already owns it. If he *frames* the situation as a potential *loss* of $1,000 (endowment) versus a gain of $2,500, the $1,000 might well be preferred — an example of *loss aversion*. But choosing the $1,000 versus the gamble is also an example of *risk aversion*, a very common factor in many choice situations. People usually prefer a sure thing to a gamble with a slightly better expected value. Risk aversion is readily explained by diminishing marginal utility: if each additional cookie is less valuable than the preceding one, then a cookie lost is worth more than a cookie gained. And a gamble between half a chance of two cookies is worth less than one cookie for sure. For example, if successive cookies are worth 10, 8, 5, 3, 1, according to some hedonistic scale of diminishing marginal utility, then a gamble between a 50 percent chance of both cookie 1 and cookie 2, expected value $(10+8)/2 = 9$, is obviously worth less than cookie 1 alone, the sure thing, which equals 10. It's hard to know without much extra work which of these accounts, risk aversion via diminishing marginal utility, or framing and the endowment effect, is operating in the loss-aversion experiment.

Loss aversion, framing, risk aversion and the endowment effect are just four of the heuristics, rules of thumb—or biases—call them what you will, that behavioral economists have come up with. Others are arousal (the effects of emotion), hyperbolic discounting, acquired value (placebo) effect, Pavlovian conditioning (associative learning), expectation, anchoring, reference-dependence, and social-norm effects—and I've probably left some out. These ideas are not all mutually exclusive, nor, with the exception of hyperbolic discounting,[21] are they easily quantifiable, which may account for economists' (a notoriously mathophilic group) initial reluctance to accept them. Economists might have accepted these concepts more easily had they realized that they are *not really in conflict with the idea of rationality* (however defined) once you realize what an organism must actually *do* to behave rationally.

Rational adaptation is *necessarily* a Darwinian process of variation and selection.[22] The subject must have available a set of different strategies (*variation*) and some means of comparing them (*selection*). If the set of strategies is rich and the selection rule appropriate, the result may be apparently "rational" behavior. If the set of strategies available is limited, or the selection rule imperfect, the subject will seem to be biased, to behave according to a heuristic, not to be "rational." *But the process that underlies irrational and rational decisions is in fact the same*: a repertoire of rules or strategies and a selection process that favors some or one over others.

If the selection is overt, via trial-and-error, with selection of the appropriate strategy by means of its immediate consequences, we have the standard operant-conditioning situation with its usually but not invariably optimal behavior. Conversely, if the selection is covert, "in the head," we have so-called "insight" when the correct behavior emerges spontaneously without any apparent trial and error. The result may be almost magical, as with human prodigies—like 13-year-old Jake Barnett who can recite the first 200 digits of the transcendental number Π—or the behavior of New Caledonian crows and even "bog-standard" English rooks that spontaneously learn to bend a wire into a tool to pull up a bucket of food.[23]

The point is that *there is no such thing as purely rational behavior.* There is only the set of strategies the agent has available to him and the ways that that one or more is selected to guide action. If the task is simple and (for animals) close to something in their natural environment, the subject will usually come up with a heuristic that works pretty well and is close to a commonsense optimum. If the situation is far from anything in the species' history—like the response-initiated timer in the animal experiments I will discuss in a moment, or (for humans) complex financial instruments on Wall Street—then subjects may not do so well. They may behave in apparently stupid ways, or behave "rationally" in the short run, with bad (hence "irrational") consequences in the long run, for example. The more complex the situation, the less obvious their "irrationality" will be. I'll explore these possibilities in later chapters.

Experimental psychologists and behavioral ecologists learned—an embarrassingly large number of years ago—that the very idea that behavior is "optimal" is flawed. Animals can make reward-maximizing decisions about simple situations with relatively immediate outcomes. When consequences are delayed, or the problem is complex, they often fail to behave in a way that maximizes benefit. It has taken economists much longer to learn the same lesson about human beings. The problem is not, however, that humans are "irrational." The problem is that human "rationality" is also limited to simple problems, with consequences not too-long delayed, especially if the delay is not explicit, like a mortgage or a bond, but implicit, like systemic risk. And of course the malign hand may itself be perfectly rational. It makes sense for people to act in ways that benefit them now but wreak collective havoc much later.

Behavioral ecologists and psychologists in the early 1980s came to the same conclusion about the way that animals, at least, adapt to reinforcement schedules, natural as well as artificial. Behavior can always be rendered rational/optimal once we understand the *currency* and the *constraints*, cognitive as well as environmental. By currency I just mean "that which is to be maximized/optimized"—money, in financial decision making, some proxy for Darwinian fitness in biology. The constraints are cognitive limitations, what the agent is able to figure out, and environmental limitations, what information and freedom of action is available to him. But rational or not, animals never, and people rarely, do it by what we might call explicit maximizing, directly comparing different strategies until they find the best one. What they typically do is come up with a simple rule of thumb or *heuristic* that works well enough most of the time. A well-known behavioral ecology textbook comments:

> A rule of thumb model...refers to the actual mechanisms used by the species...the fact that animals use rules of thumb...does not necessarily mean that they are suboptimal...what appears to be suboptimal within one set of constraints may be optimal when more are added....the rules of thu   mb used by a predator might be expected to work well in its normal foraging environment, but the rule may work badly in unnatural situations.[24]

So what are we to make of a statement like this[25] by an omnipresent contemporary economist: "After all, while there is only one way to be perfectly rational, there are an infinite number of ways to be irrational..."? The Paul Krugman quote represents the conventional wisdom throughout economics—and it could not be more wrong. As I have just argued, *there is no such thing as perfect rationality*. There is only rationality with respect to a given currency (which, in the real world, isn't always cash) and subject to a set of constraints—cognitive and environmental. This has been well known to ethologists and behavioral psychologists for very many years.[26] Apparently even some eminent economists have yet to discover it.

The belief of economists and policymakers that there is something called rationality that is independent of and goes beyond the necessarily fallible processes that we humans have for solving problems and doing what is best for us has led many of them, including free-market prophet Mr. Greenspan, to an extraordinary and almost religious faith in the power and self-regulatory properties of profit-seeking. There is confident talk about market stability, balance and re-balance, as well as a firm belief in the benign invisible hand. In succeeding chapters I will show that many of these beliefs are ill-founded. As they exist now, financial markets are not efficient.

Indeed, the concept of efficiency is meaningless in this context. Nor are they intrinsically stable. How may they be stabilized? We can't be sure of the answers, but perhaps by focusing on a different set of questions, we will come closer to finding them.

Now a final example to show how the automatic feature of some schedule adaptations—the fact that the organism is blindly applying a rule of thumb that works in most cases—can get the subject into trouble. The problem arises in a situation that differs in a significant way from the animal's "normal foraging environment." Let me introduce the procedure in two steps. The basic situation is even simpler than the 2-armed bandit. The organism has just a single choice. It gets a reward for the first response after a fixed period of time has passed since the preceding reward. This is called a *fixed-interval* schedule. At first, rats, pigeons and people will press their lever or peck their key all the time, getting intermittent rewards at fixed intervals of time. But, rather quickly, subjects learn that rewards are periodic, so they begin to pause after each reward. After a little experience, they respond only towards the end of the fixed interval. Perfectly sensible behavior, one might think. No point responding when you know the reward will not be delivered. But, people and animals cannot estimate time perfectly, so to avoid delaying the reward unnecessarily, best begin to respond a little early. Still, all perfectly "rational." The time between reward delivery and when the animal begins to respond again is called the *wait time*. Wait time is usually a fixed fraction, called the *wait-time ratio*, of the typical time-to-the-next-food reward.

The break with rationality comes in when we make a small modification to the procedure. Now, instead of starting after each *reward*, the fixed-interval timer starts only after the subject makes his first *response* (this is termed a *response-initiated* fixed-interval). What is the rational strategy now? Well, it's still very simple: respond immediately after reward to start the timer, then wait, as before. But animal subjects (and humans under some conditions) ignore the timer-starting requirement and behave just as they did before: waiting after the reward before starting to respond, thus delaying the reward unnecessarily by a time equal to the wait.[27] So our organism, which looked so sensible on a simple fixed-interval schedule, now looks pretty dumb when it fails to respond to start the clock on a response-initiated fixed–interval schedule. It is not optimizing at all, but following a simple timing rule: if rewards are approximately periodic, wait a fixed time, proportional to the inter-reward interval, after each reward before beginning to work for the next (this is called *linear waiting*).

And why do animals behave in this rather simple-minded way? Presumably because of a real limitation on their cognitive abilities[28]—a consequence of a "selection environment" (i.e., the environment in which the species evolved) in which the simple rule worked fine. Many contemporary species, including, especially, humans, live now in environments that have changed drastically in recent centuries—a short time in evolutionary terms. Hence many of their instincts may be poorly adapted to their current environment. After all, nowhere in nature will a pigeon encounter time delays triggered by a peck, nor have humans encountered credit-default swaps until recently.

The simple reward-initiated timing process works well under natural conditions, but it is easy to expose the animal to a situation that causes behavior to "blow up" in a way that resembles the boom and bust of financial markets. The key is *positive feedback*. I'll explain it in two steps. First, you need to know that linear waiting can work very quickly under some conditions. The pigeon will adjust his post-food wait time according to the previous interfood interval. It's easy to show this by presenting him with a sequence of changing intervals. If the interval duration changes relatively slowly from interval to interval, his wait time will track it, so that wait time in interval N+1 is set by the preceding interval N (wait time in interval N+1 is equal to the wait-time-ratio times the duration of interval N).[29] The second step is to introduce feedback by making the delay in interval N proportional to the wait in the previous interval. For example, the delay might be set to be, say, 2 times, so that if the animal waits, say, 10 seconds in interval N, the postpeck time until food will be set to 20 seconds in the next interval. If the animal has a constant wait-time ratio, it is easy to show that its behavior will be "rational" or "irrational" depending on the schedule multiplier.[30]

In this system, the feedback depends on the product of the multiplier (set by the experimenter) times the wait-time ratio (set by the animal). Thus, 1.5 multiplied by .5 is less than 1: the feedback is error-reducing (negative). But when the multiplier times wait ratio is $3 \times .5$, i.e., greater than one, the feedback becomes error-increasing (positive). The first result qualifies as rational—reward is obtained as soon as possible, the second as irrational—the reward is delayed indefinitely. Not only that, the cost of "irrational" behavior is much greater in the second case than in the first. But the truth is that the animals are *not* acting differently in the two situations. Both outcomes are the result of the very same adaptive process.

To anticipate future discussion of positive feedbacks in markets, notice that this maladaptive behavior is a consequence of two things: that behavior depends only on the recent past, and that the future depends on the actor's own behavior in multiplicative fashion (think "leverage"). Whenever these two things are true, the result can be unstable boom and bust.

The Platonic image of perfect markets has been shattered by recent global events. Despite several early warnings, not just the Great Depression, but recent crises in 1987 and 2000, the powers-that-be in government and the financial community were shocked, shocked! to see the financial universe come tumbling down in the absence of any external trauma. No 9/11, no Enron, not even Bernie Madoff can be blamed. A $65-billion fraud is small change compared to the value lost in bankruptcies and precipitous drops in security prices in 2007–8. Enron and Madoff are the swimmer rather than the tide in Warren Buffett's famous comment: "It's only when the tide goes out that you learn who's been swimming naked." (An odd comment, I have always thought, since it is the limpets not the swimmers that are exposed by the receding tide—but you get the idea.)

The faith of Maestro Greenspan and others at the pinnacle of finance in simple-minded ideas of rationality and value is based on several fallacies. From the point of view of economic theory, there is no such thing as the "real" value of anything; value is just price. There is no single rational strategy but many strategies, depending on what is to be maximized and the limitations of the maximizer. In practice, rational behavior depends on fallible and sometimes surprisingly simple rules of thumb. People adapt to financial contingencies in ways that resemble the much simpler adaptations of nonhuman animals. Yet another fallacy is the idea of the efficient market, to which I turn next.

4

Efficiency and Unpredictability

Efficiency is a good thing. Everyone would like to be efficient. It's a good brand characteristic. It is no accident, therefore, that the word *efficient* appears frequently in writing about economics and financial markets. The word is used in several senses. *Tax efficiency* is the simplest and most conceptually watertight: it's simply the idea that tax rates should be set to produce the maximum revenue at the lowest rate. Most important and most problematic is the idea of the *efficient market*. It's important to separate what is said about the efficient market from what can be done to test the idea. What is said is this: the efficient market theory[1] or hypothesis (EMT), like coffee, exists in three forms, weak, strong and semi-strong. All are said to involve *information*: "Weak EMH claims that prices on traded assets (e.g., stocks, bonds, or property) already reflect all past publicly available information. Semi-strong EMH claims both that prices reflect all publicly available information and that prices instantly change to reflect new public information. Strong EMH additionally claims that prices instantly reflect even hidden or 'insider' information."[2]

This is not how efficiency is defined anywhere else in science. Everywhere but economics, efficiency is a *ratio*: miles per gallon, lumens per watt, thermal energy is divided by mechanical energy out, etc. In economics there are a few sensible efficiency measures, like productivity and tax efficiency—man-hours or wage dollars per item produced, total tax revenue at a given tax rate—but the efficient market is not one of them. "Efficient market" *should* mean a market where price is an accurate measure of value. But as we have seen, there is no objective "value" other than price. So what on earth can an efficient market be? How is the efficiency of markets actually measured? What is this "information" of which they speak?

When in doubt, go back to the master—in this case Eugene Fama, father of the EMT, who writes with estimable frankness: "The definitional statement that in an efficient market prices 'fully reflect' available information is so general that it has no empirically testable implications."[3] But then Fama dives into a squid-ink sea of mathematical models: the "fair game" model, the submartingale and the random walk. But he was right the first time. All the talk about "information" is meaningless since the information in question cannot be measured. The efficient market theory amounts in practice to the idea that security prices vary more or less at random. Because if they didn't, the market would be a money pump. Unfortunately, such is the power of a good label, many people, including influential people like the head of the Fed, continue to believe that the efficient market is *really* efficient, in a meaningful human-welfare sense. Well, sometimes it is and sometimes it isn't, but the efficient market theory has nothing to do with the human-welfare effects of the market in either case.

In the rest of this chapter I look at the idea of market efficiency in more detail. There is general agreement among finance theorists that the prices of securities vary in a more or less random way. There are different kinds of randomness. The kind that seems to work best for financial markets is what is termed a *random walk*. But unconstrained random walks can be unstable; I give some examples and show later how they can be made more stable. The key to stability seems to be some restriction on the total amount of money and credit available to investors.

Despite its epistemological vacuity, market "efficiency" does refer to *something*, namely the obvious fact that there are no (or at least very few) free lunches. High returns generally go along with high risk; obvious discrepancies between "fundamentals" and stock price are usually soon eliminated, and so on. Nevertheless, there is no simple rule, no algorithm, for reliably making money in the market. Or, to express the same idea more simply: market prices are *unpredictable*, at least in the short term. A few studies have shown that "statistically speaking, stocks display short-term momentum and long-term reversion,"[4] meaning that if they increase (or decrease) in price from one time period to the next, they are likely to do the same over the next time period (momentum). and eventually they will return to their long-term mean (reversion). So prices are not perfectly random: close enough for random walk (explained in a moment) to be an OK approximation, far enough for a few shrewd investors to make money. In general, as Burton Malkiel (still a fan of the efficient market theory) put it: "No one can consistently predict either the direction of the stock market or the relative attractiveness of individual stocks..."[5]

The key word here is *consistently*. Once in a while someone does figure out how to predict the future price of a security, if only via inside information or by accident. There is continuing controversy about the meaning and prohibition of insider trading, which can be hard to define objectively. Milton Friedman thought insider trading a good idea because it contributes to accurate pricing; it was for a while quite legal in Germany. It was legal in the U.S. until 1934 and then became illegal only for people closely connected to the relevant company. It is still legal for members of Congress![6] But the definition has gradually broadened, and after the 2007–8 recession the regulatory hand grew heavier. By 2011 many prosecutions were ongoing in the U.S. Whether insider trading occurs or not makes no practical difference, however. Insider trading or not, markets are still mostly unpredictable. They are unpredictable for a pretty obvious reason. Just as soon as people begin to act on a prediction—buy a stock that is to rise or sell or short one that is to fall, the accuracy of the predictor is degraded: the stock falls or rises before many other players can act to make money from the prediction. This is the essence of the efficient market theory, although it has nothing whatever to do with efficiency. Many people have gotten rich predicting stock movements. Not all of them, probably, were simply lucky. But once a rule—like the famous Black-Scholes pricing model or the capital asset-pricing model (CAPM)—works, and is seen to work, the pattern it predicts is pretty soon obliterated by the trades it has inspired: "The practical triumph of the capital asset model had weakened its predictive power."[7] (This is not the only reason that financial models fail, of course. All models eventually fail, because financial engineering is not real engineering—not based on real scientific laws like the laws of physics. All the models are more or less imperfect and so all eventually miss.) Financial markets are information *sinks* because predictions are self-canceling. That is really all there is to the EMT.

That doesn't mean that stock prices are *really* random, however. Maybe they are, as the prevailing school believes, but no one can ever prove it—because proving something is random is proving a negative: randomness is the *absence* of any pattern. Proving randomness means proving that no pattern, no rule, no algorithm based on the previous day or previous 100 days of stock prices, has any bearing at all on today's price. Since the number of possible hypotheses is infinite, it is impossible to rule them all out. To see why this is true, imagine that stock prices convey a coded message. The job of the stock picker is to decode it. The aim of all encryption schemes is to produce coded output sequences that *look* random, even though they are not. To the extent that they succeed, they prove that looking random is not the same as being random.

Sometimes even a pattern that is completely determined can be missed. Suppose for example you were to ask a group of stock "quants" to study the following series of prices, representing successive trades of a rather volatile stock:

50,24,45,94,55,34,69,8,30,26,42,52,23,8,25,33,44,68, 50,35,26,19,31,18,81

Their task is to predict the next price. I doubt that any would be able to do it. But this series of numbers, with the "," added and leading zeroes deleted, is just taken from late in the infinite series for the transcendental number π, 3.14159 …, which is 100 percent determined. This is not, therefore, a random sequence at all. But the pattern is impossible to discover if you don't know the rule—and the rule may be extremely obscure. Or, as is very likely true of stock prices because of the multiplicity of more or less independent factors that can affect them, there may in fact be no rule at all.

So let's look a little more closely at the idea of randomness. In the modern era it all began with Charles Darwin's cousin Francis Galton (1822–1911). The multi-talented Galton, African explorer and amateur scientist, loved to measure things no one had thought to measure before. He was one of the first to study human reaction time, for example, and wrote the definitive textbook on fingerprinting. He was especially interested in human variation and was perhaps the first to notice that very many natural measures are distributed according to what we now know as the normal, Gaussian[8] or bell curve.

The picture (Figure 4-1) is taken from the 1892 edition of Galton's 1869 book *Hereditary Genius*, which ushered in a century and a half of controversy over the extent to which human talent—intelligence—runs in families, and if so whether this reflects nature or nurture. The picture shows the heights of an hypothetical island population, each dot being the height of one man marked against a post. As you can see, the average is about 5ft 6 in. (men were a bit shorter in those days) and the general bell shape is clear without adding the heights up and counting the totals in categories (5'-5'1", 5'1"-5'2", etc...).

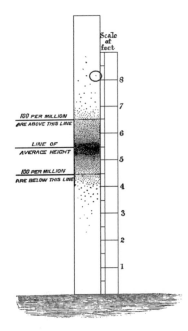

Figure 4-1

The normal distribution not only fits all sorts of natural data, it is also easy to handle mathematically, which makes it very attractive, possibly too attractive, to makers of mathematical models. It also follows from the central-limit theorem that the *average* of many *independent* processes, whether they vary normally or not, will vary normally—very convenient.

The normal distribution is the building block for countless statistical models, including models of security prices. The idea is that the price of a stock, say, which is certainly unpredictable, varies at random in a Gaussian fashion.[9] The simplest way to apply this idea is shown in the next picture (Figure 4-2), which is a very simple mathematical model of the price of a single stock (the black line) and the market average (the gray line) across trading periods. (This is a miniature market, with only 4 stocks, each starting out at a price of 8; just one is shown.

You can see three things right away: the market average varies less than the individual stock (no surprise there); the individual stock price varies a modest amount (between 7.5 and 8.5); and there is no

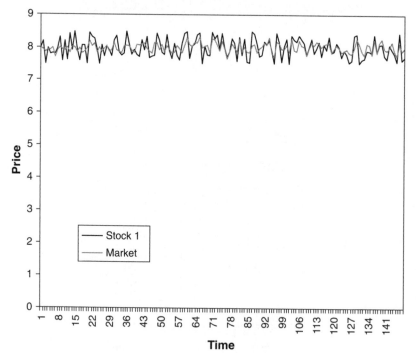

Figure 4-2

trend, because the random distribution, like the height distribution of Galton's soldiers, has a fixed mean (constant average).

There is a problem with the fixed mean in this model, though. One of Galton's themes was *regression to the mean* (what he called, after his Belgian predecessor Adolphe Quetelet, the "law of deviation"). He noticed it first in data rather than theory. The children of very tall parents tend to be shorter than them; and conversely, the kids of short parents tend to be taller than their parents. These facts may have nothing to do with genetics. They are just what you would expect if the height associated with a given genotype is normally distributed and individual phenotypes are selected at random. If you draw an exceptionally short or tall one, the next one is likely to be taller or shorter.

Regression to the mean, or rather the failure to recognize it, applies in some surprising places—the so-called "hot hand" in basketball for example:

> Despite the knowledge that coins have no memory, people believe that a sequence of heads is more likely to be followed by a tail than by another head. Many observers of basketball believe that the probability of hitting a shot is higher following a hit than following a miss, and this conviction is at the heart of the belief in the "hot hand" or "streak shooting." Our previous analyses showed that experienced observers and players share this belief although it is not supported by the facts.

So, rather depressingly (people like to believe in things like the "hot hand"), wrote Tversky and Gilovich in 1989.[10] The hot hand implies a violation of regression to the mean: that extreme is more likely to follow extreme—and it's not true. Missing a shot is apparently as likely after a run of hits as after a run of misses. The apparent discrepancy between the heights of parents and their children is perfectly consistent with the idea that heights are drawn more or less at random from a normal distribution. If you happen to pick an extreme, height (tall parent, say) from one tail of the distribution or the other, your next (random) pick (child) is likely to be closer to the average, just because most of the possible choices are to the left or the right of your last choice. Look at Galton's data again. If you just randomly picked the circled height, what are the odds the next random pick will be comparably extreme?

And that's what is wrong with the fixed-mean random model. If you know the mean of the distribution and its variability, then you know whether the current value is extreme, hence worth buying or selling. If the price is more than (say) one standard deviation below the mean then it should be a good buy, because pretty soon you can be sure it will increase, and conversely if it is significantly above the mean. In either case you can profit from a sale or a "short." Since nobody makes money that way in practice, the fixed-mean random distribution must be a poor model for the movement of real stock prices.

The solution to this problem is just to keep the randomness, but drop the fixed mean: let the mean shift with each data point. That's all a *random walk* is. At each stock value, the probability of an increase or a decrease is the same. In other words, the current value of the stock tells you nothing (the hypothesis says) about its next value. The next picture (Figure 4-3) shows our miniature market again, but this time the stocks (one is shown, plus the average of four), all starting at 8, move according to a random walk (sometimes also called *diffusion*,

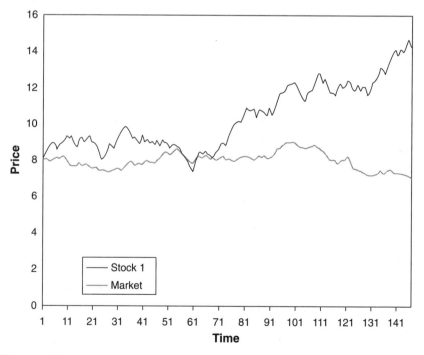

Figure 4-3

because it's like the diffusion of smoke in air or ink in water), with the same range of variability (−.5 to +.5) as before.

The general pattern does look much more like a real stock chart. Again, notice three things: As before, the market average varies less than the individual stock. The individual stock varies more, in absolute terms, than in the fixed-mean example, even though the range of random variation is just −.5 to +.5, as before. The individual stock varies from a low of 7 to a high of more than 14, compared with 7.5 to 8.5 in the fixed-mean example. Third, it looks as if there is a *trend*: the one stock shown seems to be on the rise.

The trend is an illusion. It's a stock-market equivalent of the basketball "hot hand." But it shows that apparent trends will be a reliable characteristic of any random walk. Because there is no fixed mean, there is nothing to restrain a random walk, which can stray indefinitely far from its starting point. But the direction in which it will deviate, north or south, is of course unpredictable.

There are still a couple of problems with this model, one empirical (to do with real stock data) and the other theoretical. The theoretical problem is that the model allows stock value to go below zero. Why is this unrealistic, you may ask; surely companies do go out of business from time to time? Well, yes, but less frequently than an otherwise-plausible random-walk model predicts.[11] And having stocks disappear at random from a sample makes analysis difficult. The empirical problem is that trade-to-trade stock-price variability—*volatility*—seems to be dependent on stock price. It's not constant as the simple random-walk model implies. The higher the price, the higher the volatility.[12]

One solution that I have seen in several secondary sources is deceptively simple: to solve both these problems at a stroke by assuming that the random walk affects not the stock price directly but its logarithm. Or, to put the same thing differently, just let random variation take place in successive price *ratios* not the price itself. Thus, a change in price from 8 to 9 represents not a unit change in price but a tenfold increase (if we are using base-10 logs). Similarly, a change from 8 to .8 also represents a unit decrease in log units. You can see at once that using a log scale means that stock price, like Zeno's Achilles racing the tortoise, can never reach zero, because each unit change just reduces the price by the same fixed fraction. Logarithmic random walk also produces realistic-looking stock charts.

But logarithmic random walk has the simple flaw as a model for stock movement that a unit increase is worth much more than a unit decrease. You can see it this way. Suppose you have a portfolio of stocks and you hold them for a while. For simplicity we'll assume they all begin at 10 (log 10 = 1). Half will increase in value and half decrease (of course, at the beginning you don't know which will increase and which decrease) and the average increase will equal the average decrease. Let's wait until the half that have decreased are at an average of 0 (antilog 0 = 1) and (since all are diffusing in log space) the half that have increased are at 2 (antilog 2 = 100), both showing an average log-unit change of 1. Now look at the actual value of our portfolio. Well, if half are at an average of 100 (gain = 90) and half are at an average of 1 (loss = 9), we've obviously made a profit—with no real movement in the market at all. So random walk in log-price space is a bad model for stock movements.

A better solution, which was adopted by the hugely influential Black-Scholes option-pricing model, is to retain linear random walk, i.e., walk in price space, not log-price space, but assume variability proportional to the value: "The stock price follows a random walk in continuous time with a variance proportional to the square of [equivalently, a standard deviation—SD—proportional to] the stock price."[13] This is the assumption of constant coefficient of variation (CoV: SD divided by mean) that psychologists have discovered in an amazing range of perceptual situations, where it's known as the Weber-Fechner law. The law, discovered by Ernst Weber (1795–1878) in the 19th century, applies to the perception of weight, distance, sound intensity, time and a host of other perceptual dimensions. It means that if you are just able to tell the difference between (say) a 100 g weight and a 105 g weight you will also be just able to tell the difference between 1,000 g and 1,050 g. Evidently the Weber-Fechner law applies to stock price as well. Weber-Fechner is probably only part of the reason; the fact that a higher number yields higher interest, which is a fixed proportion, probably also has something to do with it.[14]

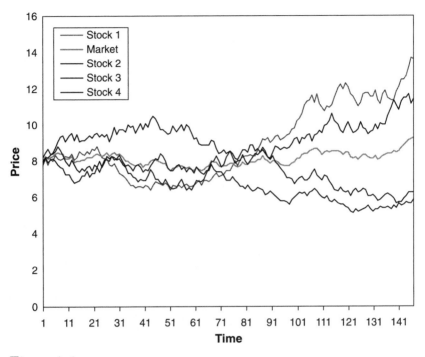

Figure 4-4

The next picture (Figure 4-4) shows an example of this *scalar random walk*, which looks much like the previous figure. The figure shows all four stocks and you can see the typical diffusion-like drift of the prices away from their initial value. The mean is stable, though. Because the walk takes place in linear (price) space not log space, a scalar random walk doesn't guarantee a profit just by waiting. Because variability declines with price, it doesn't seriously threaten to walk price down below zero.

In summary, the term "efficient market" expresses a wish not a reality. People working in finance like to think that the market is like some giant instrument whose keyboard they play with an invisible hand, in justly rewarded service to all—"doing God's work" as, Goldman Sachs CEO Lloyd Blankfein "impishly" put it in 2009.[15] But, absent an independent measure of a security's value other than its price, the concept of market efficiency is vacuous. When there *is* an independent measure of output—does the axe cut, does the pot hold water, does the food taste OK?—markets are indeed usually efficient, unbeatable as a way to diffuse supply and demand information and allocate resources efficiently, as Ludwig von Mises, his pupil Friedrich v. Hayek and the Austrian school of economics tirelessly point out.[16] No planned economy has worked as well as market economies and many have failed disastrously, as everyone now understands. When we do have independent measures—does everyone who needs socks, toilet paper, toothpaste, etc. have access to them? Or are the stores all out of essentials much of the time?—the idea of an "efficient market" makes intuitive sense. When we are dealing with independently produced discrete goods whose prices are largely uncorrelated, standard supply-and-demand theory works pretty well. But in financial markets, none of these things holds. When there is no measure of value other than price, when prices of different products are not independent, when the degree of non-independence can vary from day to day, when there are neither needs nor resources but only cash, promises and debt, "efficiency" is not so much a term of art as a term of hope. It is pretentious nonsense.

The words "efficiency" and "rationality" are barriers to clear thinking about markets because they suggest a level of objective knowledge that does not exist. Market "efficiency" is meaningless without an independent measure of value. "Efficiency" means in practice two things, neither really related to the word "efficient": that stock prices are unpredictable and that no rule for predicting stock prices works for very long. Markets are self-canceling information sinks. These two characteristics mean that the idea of a random walk is a tolerable mathematical model for stock movements. But random walk is not a stable process. Any individual stock price will tend to drift indefinitely far from its starting point. The market as a whole may show no change, but essentially no stock will remain close to the same value. And individual stocks may drift in a way that suggests a trend, even though none exists.

The Housing Bubble

E nough theory, for the moment at least. Let's turn to a real-world example, a preliminary look at the housing bubble that collapsed so painfully in 2008. The bubble had several components. Loose money and inadequate regulation permitted dangerous financial practices, such as securitization, "abusive swaps" (the phrase used in the toothless-but-dangerous Dodd-Frank regulatory bill of 2010) and the selling-on of mortgages, to proceed essentially unchecked. All introduced destabilizing positive feedback into the housing market.

A little history.[1] Bubbles all have similar ingredients: They usually follow a period of prosperity and cheap money (low interest rates); sometimes in the build-up an important regulation or two—strictures on banks or insurance companies, capital-gains tax on home sales, etc.— has been repealed or is cleverly evaded by an ingenious new arrangement; public enthusiasm is high for some new product (railroads, the internet, tulips) or for value rediscovered in an old one (like housing); sometimes a charismatic, often shady, individual, like John Law in the 18th century or Richard Whitney and Ivar Kreuger in 1929, galvanizes the mania; a majority of experts are willing to intone that "the fundamentals of the economy are sound" just when they are not (see the famous Yale economist Irving Fisher in 1929, Alan Greenspan in recent times), along with a minority of spoil-the-fun critics who know it ain't right but unfortunately cannot predict exactly when it will all go wrong (Nassim Taleb, James Grant in the recent crisis).[2] There is often rent-seeking, i.e., using the government for financial gain through its power to grant monopolies, impose restrictive tariffs or apply some other market restraint.

And some period of time since the last bubble must have passed—time for memories of, and the individuals involved in, the previous bubble to fade away—before a new boom and bust can have a chance to get off the ground. Twenty or thirty years are usually sufficient. Above all, there is always *debt* and plenty of it.

The recent housing bubble, in the UK as well as the U.S., is perhaps the easiest example to use to illustrate some general principles. The process here seems to be relatively easy to understand. I encountered the initial steps down the slippery slope myself when, after searching for a local bank in which I had confidence, I took out my own home mortgage nearly two decades ago. The mortgage was at a fixed rate, then common, and the scrutiny thorough. The deposit required was substantial, 20 percent of the house value, which was fine with me as I intended to pay if off soon. House prices at that time were pretty stable. Since this was to be my family residence, I had no thought of making a profit.

I was surprised and mildly shocked then, after a few months, to find that I was no longer paying my mortgage to the Hillsborough Savings Bank but to some remote entity I had never heard of. HSB had "sold it on."

That was my glancing introduction to the wonderful world of structured investment vehicles (SIVs): residential mortgage-backed securities (RMBS), collateralized mortgage obligations (CMO), "collateralized debt obligations" (CDOs), and a flock of other wonderful acronyms that put the U.S. military (the acronym king) to shame. Before I get to the further flowering of this market, let's ask the question I asked myself when I first discovered that my mortgage had been sold. What's in it for the bank, and what's in it for the purchaser of the mortgage?

The benefits to banks are clear. A retail bank makes money in two ways, via interest on its loans and through loan-origination fees, all those often opaquely named little add-ons that inflate your mortgage transaction cost so much above what you thought it would be when you started looking. The bank has relatively little control over the mortgage interest rate, which depends on the general interest rate and the actions of competitors (more on control of interest rates later). But the more loans it can originate, the more fees it receives. Anything that will enable it to get loans off its books is likely to be a plus. Banks must maintain a minimum ratio, the reserve ratio— currently 10 percent in the U.S.—of cash deposits relative to loans. When their loan total bumps up against this ratio, they can make no more loans until some are paid off—or sold off. Thus, banks will seize on any strategy that will enable them to evade the reserve ratio and let them make more loans. Selling their loans on does the job.

But why should anyone *buy* a mortgage loan originated by someone else? They don't know the borrower and must be at least somewhat uncertain about his creditworthiness. Well, we're from the government and we're here to help you. Started in 1934, in the depths of the Depression, the Federal Housing Administration (FHA) was the first in a series of steps by the Federal Government that allowed banks to essentially evade the (government-mandated) reserve requirement.

This is just the first of many features of financial markets that I encountered that might strike the average citizen as bizarre or verging on the criminal. The reserve ratio is set by the government, yet here is the government guaranteeing mortgages to allow them to be sold on so that banks can lend more, while still, ostensibly, satisfying the ratio. In other words, the government has created an entity that seems to exist simply to allow the banks to evade a government requirement. Why not just abolish the requirement? Or pass loan money to the banks in a more direct and easily accountable way? Nobody seems to question the practice of buying mortgages, yet it is, from one point of view, fundamentally dishonest. A bank must keep a certain fraction of its total obligations in cash. Once it has loaned nine times its cash reserves, a bank can loan no more. But if the Federal government, via FHA, Fannie Mae and the others, can buy up a few mortgages, the bank is once again free to lend. These agencies were in effect created, by the government, to allow banks to evade their reserve requirements—which were set up by government. How crazy is that!

Well, "jobs" was a mantra in 1934 just as it is now, and the FHA certainly created a lot of jobs for government workers—the paperwork involved in qualifying for a FHA guarantee is massive. Somebody has to be paid to read and approve all that stuff. The heads of the FHA and similar agencies created later also are exceedingly well paid, as we'll see.[3] And of course, selling mortgages makes lots of people lots of money. And people are in dire need of housing, aren't they? Not just housing, housing they *own*. The ostensible purpose for all these lethal gimmicks was, and is, to allow more people to buy houses. Why? How does the government know how many people *should* own houses, as opposed to renting them? It's not hard to go along with the idea that everyone, or at least as many people as possible, should have decent housing, though housing must be balanced against all the other government imperatives, like defense, border security, infrastructure maintenance—and servicing the national debt. It is not at all clear that everyone should *own* a house, especially as the apparatus created to ensure that this happens (not that it did) is dangerous as well as costly. But wait, there's more!

After the FHA was set up in 1934, and still in the midst of the Depression, FDR set up another agency. the Federal National Mortgage Association (FNMA: "Fannie Mae"), in 1938. Fannie Mae created a "liquid secondary mortgage market"—got that? What it actually did was buy up individual mortgages and package them, in ways that became increasingly obscure over the years, into *mortgage-backed securities* (MBSs) which could be created more or less at will. MBSs could be sold to all sorts of entities—municipalities, pension funds, businesses—wanting a secure (government-backed) source of interest income. The success of the secondary mortgage market thus pumped an indefinite amount of money into mortgage loans.

For 30 years Fannie Mae was essentially the only buyer of mortgages. At first, it bought only government-insured (FHA) mortgages, but this restriction was gradually lifted, and these other "mae's" and "mac's" eventually bought all sorts of mortgages.[4] The fact that for many years Fannie Mae was the only buyer, and that it bought individual mortgages, allowed for good oversight of primary lenders. The reinforcement contingencies were good in the sense that each party, pursuing its own self-interest, nevertheless promoted the common good—or at least did no great harm, other than creaming off a substantial chunk of money for fat salaries and bonuses. For many years, lenders, watched over by Fannie Mae, were reinforced for ensuring that mortgage holders were good credit risks and had substantial equity in their houses—10 or even 20 percent. In short, the loans were solid and purchasers of MBSs got a reliable return on their money.

This stable monopsony (single-buyer arrangement) began to erode in 1968 when Fannie Mae split into a private corporation and a publicly financed institution: "The private corporation was still called Fannie Mae and continued to support the purchase of mortgages from savings and loan associations and other depository institutions, but without an explicit insurance policy that guaranteed the value of the mortgages. The publicly financed institution was named the Government National Mortgage Association (Ginnie Mae) and it explicitly guaranteed the repayments of securities backed by mortgages made to government employees or veterans...To provide competition for the newly private Fannie Mae and to further increase the availability of funds to finance mortgages and home ownership, Congress then established the Federal Home Loan Mortgage Corporation (Freddie Mac) as a private corporation through the Emergency Home Finance Act of 1970. The charter of Freddie Mac was essentially the same as Fannie Mae's newly private charter: to expand the secondary market for mortgages and mortgage backed securities by buying mortgages made by savings and loan associations and other depository institutions."[5] Now we have not one but three potential buyers of mortgages: the Ginnie and Fannie Maes and the newly created Freddie Mac. The ostensible raison d'être for Freddie Mac was "to provide competition" for the private Fannie Mae. But on the selling side, Fannie Mae was already competing in the financial markets, which are completely indifferent as to the source of the securities on offer—whether mortgage-backed or based on other kinds of business—and care only for their risk and return. On the buying side, competition among the three entities, all government-backed more or less, was unlikely to be cut-throat.

Increasing the number of mortgage buyers from one to three had an unintended side-effect: the banks began to shed not just debt but *risk*. To the extent that there was real competition between the three, there was also pressure to weaken lending criteria. The reinforcement contingency went from good to not so good. A more honest way to achieve the same result—more mortgage lending—without distorting the banks' reinforcement schedule would have been for the government to lend them money directly, in proportion to their mortgage lending. Each bank would still be liable for its total debt, but because the reserve requirements had been directly eased. More honest, much less dangerous, but politically more difficult, perhaps.

The much-criticized Community Reinvestment Act (CRA: 1977), a Federal law intended to get more home loans to poor, especially minority poor, borrowers added a little more brushwood to a fire that was already well supplied with fuel. The 1977 law was intended to stop "redlining," the practice of denying home loans to some poor minority neighborhoods. The ostensible grounds for redlining are that neighborhood residents are bad credit risks, a claim denied by advocates for the CRA who blame racial discrimination. But economist Thomas Sowell has pointed out that if the discrimination charge were valid, loans made to blacks should be on average *more* profitable for banks than loans made to other groups, because only super-good, above average, black borrowers are being given loans. But loans to blacks are not in fact more profitable.[6] According to Peter Schweizer, Sowell's conclusion that loan practices are guided objectively, by credit risk, and not discriminatorily by race, is supported by recent data showing that "CRA-inspired loans [i.e., loans to people who would not previously have gotten them] were much more likely to fail than traditional mortgages were, in many cases three or four times as likely to foreclose."[7] Some influential scholars also dispute Schweizer's CRA claim: "default rates on the CRA lending were actually comparable to other areas—showing that such lending, if done well, does not pose greater risks."[8]

The CRA doesn't really matter for the real-estate bubble, I believe. Commercial real estate in the U.S., as well as house prices in the UK, also inflated without the benefit of CRA, Fannie Mae, Freddie Mac, and their various brothers and sisters, so the other factors I describe (credit insurance and cheap money—artificially low interest rates—especially) are probably more important.

The details are complex (naturally), but the bottom line is that there is now, and has been for some time, a substantial market for mortgage-backed securities—although non-government buyers are notably less enthusiastic since the events of 2007–8.

Increasing the number of mortgage buyers from one to three weakened lending criteria a bit, but the first of two knockout blows was delivered by the extraordinary process of *securitization*. As this process evolved, the links in the chain between debtor and the final holder of the debt multiplied and the connection between them became ever more tenuous. The term *securitization* is the all-time winner in the half-truth euphemism stakes, despite strong competition from many other entrants from the financial industry.[9] Even as securitization makes debt less secure, it promises just the opposite. The term and the concept were apparently coined by one Lewis ("Lewie") Ranieri, "godfather of the mortgage-backed securities business."[10] "Mortgages are math" declared Lewie—oh, really?

Here's how securitization works, according to two experts, Kenneth Scott and John Taylor:

> The bulk of toxic assets [paper of questionable worth] are based on residential mortgage-backed securities (RMBS), in which thousands of mortgages were gathered into mortgage pools. The returns on these pools were then sliced into a hierarchy of "tranches" that were sold to investors as separate classes of securities. The most senior tranches, rated AAA, received the lowest returns, and then they went down the line to lower ratings and finally to the unrated "equity" tranches at the bottom.
>
> But the process didn't stop there. Some of the tranches from one mortgage pool were combined with tranches from other mortgage

pools, resulting in Collateralized Mortgage Obligations (CMO). Other tranches were combined with tranches from completely different types of pools, based on commercial mortgages, auto loans, student loans, credit card receivables, small business loans, and even corporate loans that had been combined into Collateralized Loan Obligations (CLO). The result was a highly heterogeneous mixture of debt securities called Collateralized Debt Obligations (CDO). The tranches of the CDOs could then be combined with other CDOs, resulting in CDO^2 ["CDOs squared"].

Each time these tranches were mixed together with other tranches in a new pool, the securities became more complex. Assume a hypothetical CDO^2 held 100 CLOs, each holding 250 corporate loans—then we would need information on 25,000 underlying loans to determine the value of the security. But assume the CDO^2 held 100 CDOs each holding 100 RMBS comprising a mere 2,000 mortgages—the number now rises to 20 million![11]

Recall that in the first round of this process, the mortgage-backed securities were the outcome of the old practices, where the originator and creditor were one and the same. Since the banks paid the costs of defaults directly, their policies were relatively conservative and the loans were sound. So the process described by Scott and Taylor got off to a good start. The sold-on mortgages and bundles of mortgages were solid investments. But interest rates, forced down by dial-turner-in-chief Alan Greenspan,[12] remained low during this period, further lubricating loan origination—but limiting the income possibilities from the loans themselves. The reinforcement contingencies had turned malign and the "originate and sell" mortgage-business model was off and running.

Credit rating agencies—Standard & Poor's, Moody's Investor Service and Fitch Ratings and a few smaller others, played an important role in boosting securitization. But problems were triggered by a change in the reinforcement schedule of the agencies in the 1980s. In the early years, ratings agencies were paid by investors. Fair enough: investors benefit or lose according to the accuracy of ratings. It seems sensible that they should therefore pay for them.

But ratings can be shared, although it is far from clear why the buyer would *want* to share them, so perhaps *pirated* is a better word. In any event, this model began to fail (i.e., not be so profitable) and by the end of the 1980s, ratings agencies were selling their products to the *originators* of debt instruments. Bad reinforcement schedule because, obviously, originators are only interested in *good* ratings, not in *accurate* ratings: "The idea that the issuers of debt pay for their ratings is bizarre" in the words of Roubini and Mihm.[13] The shift in payoff schedule added to an earlier government mistake, an equally bizarre 1975 regulation by the SEC which "required that brokerage firms base their capital requirements on ratings"[14] by the likes of Moody's, Fitch and S&P rather than basing ratings on an independent assessment of risk. In other words, the government encouraged a shift in the responsibility for assessing risk away from those who would suffer losses, the brokerage firms, banks, etc., to those who would not, the ratings agencies. In any cosmic contest for governmental ineptitude, this must surely rank high. So, bizarre or not, the downward spiral began to turn.

How did the agencies rate these complex products? Ineptly? Irresponsibly? Worthlessly? Choose one...Michael Lewis's summary: "The ratings agencies didn't really have their own CDO model...The banks would send their own model over to Moody's and say 'How does this look?' Somehow 80 percent of what had been risky triple-B-rated bonds now looked like triple-A-rated bonds."[15] The structure of these instruments was so complex that the only way that rating agencies could understand it was through "quant" models supplied by—the CDO creators! "The banks [creators] were explicitly told by ratings agencies what their models required of the banks to obtain a triple-A rating," says Timothy Power, a London-based trader who worked with derivatives.[16] In other words, the CDO creators were invited to game the models to get good ratings. Why were the ratings agencies complicit? Because CDOs soon became very complicated; because the number of these things was potentially unlimited—just as there are more mutual funds than actual stocks, for example; and because they got fees for every rating—the more of this "crappy product"[17] the banks created, the more $$ the ratings agencies made— another ratio reinforcement schedule. But once again, the reinforcement is for the rating and not the rating quality.

> With these pieces in place—banks that wanted to shed assets and transfer risk, investors ready to put their money to work, securities firms poised to earn fees, rating agencies ready to expand, and information technology capable of handling the job—the securitization market exploded. (FINANCIAL CRISIS INQUIRY COMMISSION REPORT January, 2011)

The process of securitization was self-reinforcing in interesting ways. First, by distancing loan originator from final creditor, it encouraged a more relaxed attitude toward default risk. Deposits could be reduced, over-value[18] and interest-only loans and creative "balloon" products (easy-pay now, tough later) offered, poor credit ratings viewed in a more sympathetic light or even ignored entirely—because the originator would soon shed the loan. Second, injecting more money into the mortgage market inevitably caused a rise in house prices (because supply lags demand: new construction takes time), so that the risk of a loss caused by default was in any case reduced. Defaults could thus be faced bravely because collateral was increasing in value. All in all, a classic example of *positive feedback* (the bad, destabilizing kind): more money into mortgage market? increasing house prices? reduced loan risk? more money into mortgage market.

Fine! you might say: all shall have prizes—and why not! Why not? Because the value created is not a stable and persisting value, but the outcome of an inherently unstable dynamic process. Prices cannot rise forever because the very same process that causes the rise—increasingly dodgy loans many of which become more costly over time—also makes defaults more and more likely. As foreclosures begin to increase, because those creative repayment terms begin to bite and buyers become overextended, the same dynamic that produced the boom in short order produces a bust.

Most important of all, these changes in house prices and the changes in lending practices to which they led all took time to play out. It took several years for more and more complicated-and-indirectly-related-to-the-underlying-mortgages RMBSs, CLOs, CDOs and CDOs-squared (CDOs of CDOs) to begin to appear. It took time to develop the mathematical pricing models needed to justify the process and make it routine. And, that final financial security blanket, the credit default swap (CDS), could not come into existence until there was a plethora of risky instruments that could benefit from "insurance."

If you look at the housing market as a dynamical system, you can identify two simple feedback processes. The first is fast, and causes the rise in house prices caused by pumping mortgage money into a market where supply lags behind increasing demand. But the second is much slower and reflects the ever-weakening lending standards (NINJA[19] loans, "balloon" products, and all the rest) and the lagged increase in housing supply. The first process drives prices up, the second does the opposite.

The final knockout blow was delivered by credit default swaps (CDSs—what a wonderful name!). CDSs are an extraordinary creation, invented by people at JP Morgan during a banker bonding binge in Boca Raton in 1997: "They're called 'Off-Site Weekends'...One 1994 trip by a group of JPMorgan bankers to the tony Boca Raton Resort & Club in Florida has become the stuff of Wall Street legend... [they] were trying to get their heads around a question as old as banking itself: how do you mitigate your risk when you loan money to someone? By the mid-'90s, JPMorgan's books were loaded with tens of billions of dollars in loans to corporations and foreign governments, and by federal law it had to keep huge amounts of capital in reserve in case any of them went bad. But what if JPMorgan could create a device that would protect it if those loans defaulted, and free up that capital?"[20]

CDSs are a form of insurance. The buyer pays a periodic fee. In return, if a security defaults, the CDS will pay off its value. CDSs are not regulated like insurance even though that is what they are. They are sold by unregulated arms of insurance companies like AIG-Financial Products. Bank A could take out a CDS on its holdings with Bank B and get an exemption from lending restrictions from regulators, even without any proof that Bank B could pay up. What is more, Bank A did not even need to own the things it was betting on. This is called a *naked CDS*. It is like taking out insurance not on your own life or your wife's life but on the life of your wife's lover. Another really bad reinforcement contingency!

Although "naked CDSs" are a sort of gambling—worse, actually, because the bets are made with borrowed money—in 2000 federal law blocked states from regulating them:

The Bet That Blew Up Wall Street
Steve Kroft On Credit Default Swaps And Their Central Role In The Unfolding Economic Crisis

[T]hey are essentially side bets on the performance of the U.S. mortgage markets and some of the biggest financial institutions in the world—a form of legalized gambling that allows you to wager on financial outcomes without ever having to actually buy the stocks and bonds and mortgages.

It would have been illegal during most of the 20th century under the gaming laws, but in 2000, **Congress gave Wall Street an exemption** and it has turned out to be a very bad idea. (*60 Minutes,* Oct. 26, 2008, my emphasis)

Anyone who wants to absolve the federal government of responsibility for the crash of 2007–8 should be reminded of this extraordinary pre-emption of state restraints.

CDSs purport to insure the buyer against default or bankruptcy by the insured entity, something that was previously thought to be problematic if not impossible. Risk control in earlier days had been at the origination of a loan or a purchase. Care was taken then, by purchasers and ratings agencies, that the entity to be invested in was sound. But after purchase, you had to take your chances. After CDSs, risk could (it was thought) be mitigated even after you've taken the investment plunge. CDSs supercharged the "secondary mortgage market": "liquid" after securitization, it turned to vapor with the advent of CDSs.

There are, notoriously, two kinds of risk, made famous by Secretary of Defense Donald Rumsfeld[21] at the nadir of his popularity and subsequently in the title of his autobiography—although they were well known in the aircraft industry long before he made them generally known. Even earlier, American economist Frank Knight in 1921 wrote a whole book around the distinction between "risk" (where meaningful odds could be computed) and "uncertainty" (where they could not).[22] Maynard Keynes also emphasized the distinction in his many writings. It is unfortunate that "risk" and "uncertainty" mean much the same thing to most people, the distinction between them muddied.

The terms Rumsfeld used are "known unknowns" (Knight's "risk") and "unknown unknowns" (Knight's "uncertainty"). Known unknowns are risks to which a firm number may be attached. The clearest example is games of chance like roulette or poker, where the *sample space*, as statisticians call it, is precisely defined and the odds are exact (chance of getting your number is 1 in 37; chance it will go to the house anyway is 1 in 35, and so on). Probabilities in situations like roulette or dice are meaningful and precise.

When we go from roulette to the real world, things get a bit more slippery. But if two conditions are met—exact statistics are available *and* we can be sure that the future will be like the past—the same odds-making methods that work for games of chance can work in daily life. These two conditions hold for things like mortality, fire insurance and traffic accidents. Mortality and accident statistics are available, and absent a sudden epidemic or unsuspected design flaw which makes past history irrelevant, in mortality rates and insurance *we have every assurance that the future will look pretty much like the past.* In engineering the time to manufacture a standard product, a bolt or a stamped sheet, is well known: it takes x years to develop a new car model using familiar technology, for example. Problems will come up, but their outlines can be assessed in advance.

It is quite other with something like the Manhattan Project, development of a radically new airliner—or a war. Unknown unknowns, risks of a type that cannot be foreseen, will arise: an unanticipated need for a turbine-blade material of unprecedented strength or heat resistance, a computer problem that defies existing technology—or unexamined cascading treaties that turn a local conflict into a world conflagration. One of these problems may prove fatal; but the probability that some such a problem will crop up is simply *undefined*, hence unmeasureable.

Unfortunately, *market risk*, the chance that a company or financial instrument will fail, the risk insured against by a CDS, involves unknown unknowns that make assigning probabilities highly suspect if not impossible. The success of a company depends on many unpredictable factors that are out of its control. The future is like the past only if we restrict the past to a short period. Present and past will fail to match eventually—we just don't know when. There is no well-defined sample space of the sort that is essential to accurate statistical estimation. Making odds in such a situation is actually *worse* than gambling—in two ways. In roulette or dice, there are real, exact odds; and gamblers usually wager their own money.

There is a third factor that is also important. Fraud aside, present insurance should not change future risk. V. S. Naipaul, in his wonderful 1961 novel *A House for Mr. Biswas*, refers to a distressing Trinidadian practice he calls "insuranburn," which obviously makes insurance a dangerous business. The perpetrator takes out insurance for an inflated value on (say) a cheaply bought house with the intention of surreptitiously burning it down and collecting the difference. Insurance is not supposed to work that way. Insuring cars today does not (for example) render cars manufactured five years hence less safe, and life insurance rarely contributes to early death—indeed, suicide usually voids life insurance. So, if three things are true—the future is like the past, exact odds can be computed, and the existence of insurance does not affect future risk—insurance can be a good, stable business.

Unfortunately, market risk, unlike roulette odds or mortality statistics, *is* affected by the means used to limit it. To the extent that they are insured against default, holders of a security will be less interested in supporting the company that issued it. Buyers of CDSs on securities they do *not* own—a practice that, incredibly, is still perfectly legal—will be even less interested in the fate of the insured entity: "Credit default swaps have also faced criticism that they contributed to a breakdown in negotiations during the GM bankruptcy, because bondholders would benefit from the credit event of a GM bankruptcy due to their holding of CDSs. Critics speculate that these creditors were incentivized into pushing for the company to enter bankruptcy protection."[23] Insuring against market risk can therefore be very dangerous—not necessarily for the insured but for the system as a whole. It is a malign contingency. Yet such insurance is exactly what is promised by a CDS.

But the math, based on the idea that the future will be the same as the relatively recent past, was convincing and the need great. Once again, the viper in the ivy is an ineffectual and poorly conceived regulation-to-be-evaded. By taking out insurance in the form of CDSs, speculators can stretch legal credit limits. So CDSs provided a further boost to the process of securitization. Now—or so it seemed—the risk associated with CDOs, CMOs and the rest—"shadow banking beasts born of regulatory evasion" in the words of Roubini and Mihm[24]—need not be assessed directly, a difficult if not impossible process because of their complexity. Prudence, or at least its appearance, could be maintained, the law mollified, and risk eliminated. CDSs proved so attractive that the notional U. S. market for these malignant but oh-so-convenient instruments peaked at $464.7 *trillion* by June 30, 2008.[25]

The kind of risk-management thinking that led to CDSs is in fact routine in the financial industry. There is something called *reinsurance*, for example, which involves an insurance company insuring itself with another company, such as Swiss Re, hugely prosperous tenant of the famous "gherkin" tower in the City of London (Swiss Re was founded in 1863). Under some conditions, reinsurance looks like a reasonable strategy, although there seem to be simpler and less opaque ways to achieve the same end. For example, suppose an insurer runs into difficulties for extraneous reasons but still holds a number of life insurance policies—policies on which it might not be able to pay out. It can either sell the policies, or it can reinsure them and pass on some of the risk to another company. Selling the policies obviously poses less systemic risk, but if all are to be sold at the same time, the price may be seriously depressed. But reinsuring them may not startle the market or, to say the same thing slightly differently, it conceals the insurer's parlous financial condition from the market. In the language of the efficient market, reinsurance obscures relevant information and thus contributes to market inefficiency. But, in malign-hand fashion, it is good for the troubled company.

In addition to protecting the company by "shedding risk," reinsurance also allows it to take on additional risk without breaking regulatory reserve requirements. (What, then, is the point of these requirements, one might ask?) It will also, of course, make them more relaxed about writing policies in the first place. All good for the insurance company, and it obviously works for the reinsurers as well since these companies have grown prodigiously in the past few decades. But reinsurance often deals with a kind of risk that cannot be estimated as precisely as, say, mortality risk. And by spreading risk in opaque ways, reinsurance probably contributes to instability of the whole financial system.

The most recent efflorescences of this industry will strike many people as bizarre. Now there is a market for "catastrophe risk," even though catastrophes, by definition, are unpredictable—there's no way to compute accurate odds of one occurring—so it's "uncertainty" gambling on a massive scale. And, most recently there is an attempt to create a market in "longevity risk" which is betting not on life expectancy (that's life insurance) but on the probability that life insurers have guessed wrong.[26]

Even relatively conventional market practices can violate the "insuranburn" rule. "Shorting" is buying the right to sell a stock or other asset at a certain price before a certain date. Another way to look at it is that the "shorter" pays something to borrow a certain amount of stock for a certain time period. If the price of the stock falls, the shorter can buy what he needs to return the stock at a much lower price than he paid. For example, suppose the shorter borrows, for a cost of $500 for a month, 100 shares of AgriCo selling at $100. He sells the stock immediately, realizing $10,000 less his $500 premium for a net cost of $9,500. In two weeks, the stock falls to $50, he buys 100 shares for a cost of $5,000, returns them to the person from whom he borrowed them and pockets a net profit of $4,500 on an investment of just $100. Good deal, shorter! Of course, if the market goes the other way, if AgriCo goes from $100 to $200, for example, the shorter could be out a very large sum indeed, so the practice is risky. But it can also be very helpful in limiting market volatility. But the practice can obviously be abused because it violates the insuranburn rule in the sense that the shorter now has an interest in reducing the value of the asset he has borrowed. The risk is even greater with "naked" shorting, which is a simple bet that an asset—not owned by the bettor—will decline in value.

These risks are not academic. A couple of recent cases show them in action. For example, in 2011, "In a case simultaneously brought and settled [for a fine of $153.6M], the S.E.C. asserted that J.P. Morgan's investment bank had structured and marketed a security known as a synthetic collateralized debt obligation without informing buyers that a hedge fund that helped select the assets in the portfolio stood to gain, in most cases, if the investment lost value."[27] In other words, the product was actually created by people who had an interest in its destruction. By June 2011 a similar suit against Goldman Sachs was yet to be settled and investigations were proceeding against Deutsche Bank, Morgan Stanley and several other companies.

Like the process of natural selection, a change in the financial environment does not instantly produce the creatures best adapted to the new milieu. It takes time and, in this case, a degree of financial ingenuity, before mutation and recombination can take the financial phenotype from a simple loan, to a bundle of loans of type A to a bundle of types A, B and C, to, finally, a bundle of bundles. So we have progressed from insurance, to reinsurance, to something called "retrocession" which is insurance on reinsurance.

And of course as the new practices become common, they themselves act to produce still further changes in the environment, just as the environment in which human beings first evolved bears little relation to the human-dominated environment in which we now live. The grotesque CDO^2 could not come to life until CDOs had suitably multiplied, nor would there have been a market for such a thing early in the process, when the buyers were still under the influence of obsolescent beliefs, such as a suspicion of securities whose basis could not be readily assessed.

Delayed effects, some relatively short-term, others long, plus the essentially evolutionary nature of the whole process, make prediction, which is essential for conventional regulation, not just difficult but *impossible*. No one could have predicted 20 or so years ago the kinds of ingenious "financial weapons of mass destruction" (as Warren Buffett called them) that would spring to life in the ensuing years. Even after CDOs were first proposed, no one could have predicted their further evolution or the systemic hazards of which they are a part. The traditional concept of *regulation,* which assumes a more or less unchanging market with more or less independent goods like fruit, milk, or hog bellies, needs to be rethought in the face of the great and often destructive ingenuity of the financial world.

The rise in house prices caused by the transformation of the mortgage market had of course an effect in the real world. House builders competed to build new houses and the number of houses available for sale across the country, but especially in booming Sun Belt states like California, Nevada, Florida and Arizona, began to increase at an accelerating rate. This effect was both delayed and excessive. Delayed because it obviously takes time to plan, finance and finally build a "spec" house after you see that there may be a market for it. Excessive because builders compete for a growing market in considerable ignorance both of the size of the market and the number of competitors. Inevitably, in a climate of optimism, too many projects were initiated and, eventually, too many houses built. Competition, uncertainty about real demand and the unavoidable delay between the inception and completion of a project are the reasons that construction is a fundamentally cyclical business.

On the other hand, the housing bubble, like the railroad bubble and the Internet bubble before it, did leave us with lots of real stuff, in this case houses, even though in the aftermath of the crisis few could afford to buy them. Presumably most will eventually be occupied, however. This is the positive side of the boom–bust cycle. It is not certain, for example, that the railroads, here and in Britain, would have spread so far so fast without the bubbles that accompanied their construction. That will be a puzzle for policymakers in the future: can we still achieve what booms achieve without the collateral damage they cause?

The housing bubble that collapsed in 2007 shows the malign hand at work. At first, the mortgage lender, the local bank, was the mortgage holder. Good: he who took the risk bore the risk. Then, the Feds insured the risk (through the FHA): potentially not-so-good, except that the FHA did vet each loan. Next, Fannie Mae actually bought mortgages. Also not-so-good, except that with only one buyer, the lender could still be monitored for responsible lending practices. All the while more money went into the mortgage market forcing prices to rise—seeming to make even bad loans a no-lose proposition. The next step was the creation of Freddie Mac and friends to buy more loans and further inflate housing prices, so individual risk was further diluted and market risk increased. Two more steps finally brought the market down. Watergate bad boy G. Gordon Liddy in his radio show years ago used to give advice on how to shoot a mugger: "One to the body and one to the head, just like they taught you in the service" was his recommendation. The shot to the body in the sub-prime mortgage mess was securitization: the loan originator was finally severed from the holder of the loan as bits of hundreds of mortgages were bundled into an alphabet soup of "structured investment vehicles." The shot to the head was insurance in the form of credit default swaps. Now, with the necessary connivance of ratings agencies, risks could essentially be ignored by loan originators— "originate and sell" was born and the bubble was guaranteed to expand—and, finally, to burst with catastrophic results. The malign hand struck, big time.

The next chapter looks more closely at the idea of market stability and the dynamics of the housing market. I return to wondrous financial instruments in Chapter 10 and to the topic of risk in Chapter 11.

Market Instability and the Myth of Comparative Statics

L et's look first at the dynamics of the housing market. The lags and feedbacks in construction just about force real estate prices to be cyclic, although the cycle need not be simple. There are two ways to show this. One is by verbal argument, basically to hand wave. Such an argument can be compelling especially if it is wittily presented. J. K. Galbraith, an economist once invited to join the English faculty at U.C. Berkeley in an academic era when style was valued over obscurity, provides many brilliant examples. On the crash of 1929, for example, he writes "...now, as throughout history, financial capacity and political perspicacity are inversely correlated. Long-run salvation by men of business has never been highly regarded if it means disturbance of orderly life and convenience in the present. So inaction will be advocated in the present even though it means deep trouble in the future. Here, at least equally with communism, lies the threat to capitalism. It is what causes men who know things are going quite wrong to say that things are fundamentally sound."[1]

Galbraith is referring to short-term gain that leads to long-term peril, the malign hand. But he gives no clue to the means by which the peril comes about. This can only be shown by looking at the process, the mechanism, by which a market works. We don't understand the process; we do know it is very complex. But, and this is my second option, we can advance our understanding by making a miniature model of the sort of thing that seems to be going on. We can at least ask, what is the simplest possible process that seems to behave as a given market behaves? Can it tell us anything at all about the real market?

Suppose we boil down the housing market to the following simplifying assumptions:

1. An increase in average house price causes an increase in the number of mortgages available, reduced by a "drag" term related to the number of mortgage defaults. As defaults rise, the rise in house prices is slowed and, as we'll see, eventually reversed.
2. The number of defaults increases *disproportionately* as house prices increase.[2]

There are no explicit lags in this simple version, as there are in reality. But even without built-in lags, the feedbacks alone produce cycles, as I show in the Figure 6-1. The graph shows notional average housing price plotted against time. The black line shows a relatively stable situation when the "drag" default term is mildly disproportionate. The default term increases as the 1.9 power of housing price: in this example, it means that if the default term is 19 when average house price is 100K, it increases to 70 when the house price increases to 200, a more than 3 to 1 increase when housing price only doubles. What's critical is that defaults increase faster than prices. Under these conditions, there are a few initial ups and downs, but eventually housing price stabilizes. This amount of disproportion is not enough to destabilize the system, which eventually settles down at a stable price.

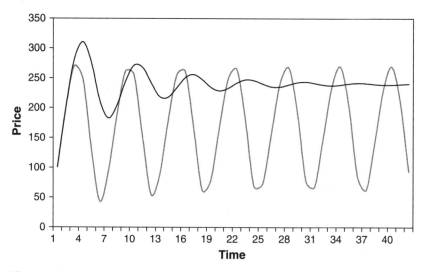

Figure 6-1

The gray line shows what happens if the default term is just a little bit more disproportionate (the exponent increases from 1.9 to 2), which takes the drag term from 30 to 120 (4 to 1 in response to a doubling of housing price). In other words, now defaults increase *much* faster than prices. This destabilizes the system, which begins to oscillate; there is no settled housing price. Instead we have a succession of bubbles. In other words, *a relatively small change in the proportion of defaults can transform this system from stable to oscillating.*

The current financial crisis, like so many in the past, seems not to be a response to some identifiable external shock, like 9/11 or the declaration of war. Instead, as shown in this example, it looks as if incremental changes in things like mortgage defaults at some rather unpredictable point caused the system to tip from stability into oscillation.

The way this happens is quite complex, even for this very simple system, as I show in the next Figure 6-2. The black line at the top shows the default parameter, the number which shows how sharp the increase in defaults will be as housing price increases. This number is one way to represent market sentiment—confidence, exuberance or their opposites. It starts at 1.5 (right-hand axis), and, as the other (gray) curve shows, house prices continue to increase over time. But then, as the default parameter creeps up over about 1.7, housing prices crash. When the parameter stabilizes at 2, prices begin to oscillate with increasing amplitude, finally settling down to the regime shown in the previous figure.

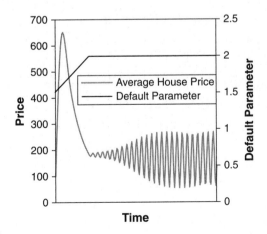

Figure 6-2

What this simple model says about the real housing market is that if willingness to write a mortgage increases as the level of house prices increases (true), and if the rate of mortgage default depends in a disproportionate way on the number of mortgages written (i.e., if the number of mortgages doubles, the number of defaults more than doubles—probably true), and *nothing else*, then house prices will oscillate in an unstable fashion. The real housing market is of course much more complicated than this. But what the model tells us is that these two simple processes alone are sufficient to produce instability. So this analysis by itself should ring a few alarm bells. Unless we can be sure that other, stabilizing, processes exist in the market, watch out!

In reality of course there are many complex dynamical systems running in parallel in the housing market, and the parameters of each are not likely to be fixed. As the national mood changes, banks may become more or less sensitive to the rate of default, builders more or less sensitive to buyers' enthusiasm. The resulting bubble cycle will not, therefore, be simply periodic. House prices are likely to fluctuate in a rather unpredictable fashion. But they *will* fluctuate. *So it is with most economic variables.* Fluctuation, sometimes cyclic but more usually unpredictable, is the norm in reality—but not in the discipline of neoclassical economics.

Comparative Statics. There is a core area of economics called *comparative statics*. It's a staple of Econ. 101 and economics textbooks, and provides the framework for many canonical works.[3] It sounds like *physics*, and that's no accident. Physics-envy is a well-known bane of the social sciences. Perhaps the simplest example of comparative-static analysis is supply and demand theory: as price increases, supply increases (the higher the price, the more widgets will be produced) but demand decreases (the higher the price, the fewer widgets will be purchased). The intersection of these two lines, demand descending and supply increasing as price increases, gives the equilibrium price, the price at which widgets will actually be sold. It seems obvious. This analysis is now so familiar that simple curves (often straight lines) of increasing supply and decreasing demand appear even in general interest books of the more thoughtful kind.[4] But more and more contrary voices, usually from noneconomists, are making themselves heard, saying that in all but the very simplest of situations the idea of economic equilibrium is a myth.[5] Let's look a bit more closely at supply and demand to see why.

First, those two lines in the supply–demand graph (Figure 6-3) are not real. They don't represent any actual *process* in the marketplace for widgets. Even if there is an equilibrium price, it doesn't come about because a little invisible price marker slides down the demand line until it hits the supply line where the two intersect. Not at all; what is really happening is much more complicated. First of all, there is a widget producer (or, more usually, a set of producers). He takes the initiative to produce widgets. How many should he produce? Well, it depends on his *estimate* of the possible market— how many people want widgets?—and the price he can expect to be paid: is it more than his cost of production? And on the other side is the consumer. When widgets are rare, a few consumers may be willing to pay a lot for each widget, but as more are produced, the price at which they can be sold will likely decrease.

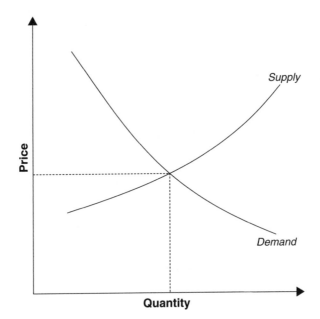

Figure 6-3

Let's see how a minimal model, a model much simpler than the reality but one that at least takes a stab at representing the actual processes of production and consumption—let's see how such a model might behave. I assume just two things: that widget supply increases so long as the selling price exceeds the cost of production; and selling price declines as supply increases.[6] The bigger the disparity between the price at which a widget can be sold and the cost of producing it, the more widgets will be produced. But the more widgets are produced, the cheaper they will have to be to corral more buyers. These two opposing processes capture the basics of production and consumption as simply as possible.

Under many conditions (i.e., parameter values), the model settles down in an orderly way that matches the static analysis (Figure 6-4): price decreases to the cost-of-production level, and supply increases to a stable maximum. But under other conditions—slightly different growth parameters but the same consumption–production model—price and supply fluctuate in a cyclic fashion (Figure 6-5). Under still other conditions, the changes are *chaotic* in the technical sense, meaning that although the process is completely deterministic, the data look random.[7] The process is unchanged, but changed sensitivity of supply to price or vice versa can move the system into a periodic or even chaotic regime.

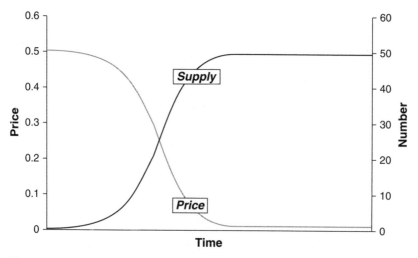

Figure 6-4

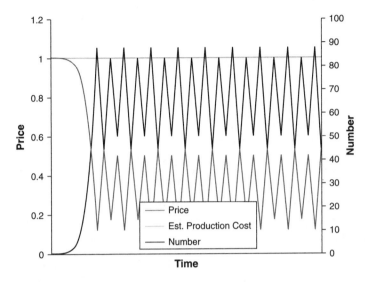

Figure 6-5

So yes, this simple supply–demand process often leads to an understandable, static, supply–demand equilibrium price. But with different parameter values, i.e., under different conditions of social context, "market sentiment," external competition—or what John Maynard Keynes more colorfully termed "animal spirits"—the same process can behave in a cyclic or chaotic fashion. As I pointed out earlier in connection with the "real" value of a stock, there is no reason at all to "privilege" the data that happen to conform to a favored model. The real world cannot be arbitrarily divided into "stable" and "unstable" (or real-value versus. depressed- or inflated-value) periods if there is no independent way to tell when we're going from one to the other. The stable/cyclic/chaotic-random nature of the system must be accepted as the only constant. Indeed, static models are *dangerous* because they give the illusion of comprehensibility. They do work some of the time, but we cannot tell in advance when they will fail. And they fail just when we need valid models most, during times of boom and bust.

Increasingly, critics, many from outside the economics community, are beginning to point this out. For example, Santa Fe Institute theorist Doyne Farmer and economist Duncan Foley recently argued in a major scientific publication that "the equilibrium models that were developed, such as those used by the US Federal Reserve, by necessity stripped away most of the structure of a real economy…When it comes to setting policy, the predictions of these models aren't even wrong, they are simply non-existent."[8] The frozen Platonic world of comparative statics doesn't exist. It would be good if macroeconomists ceased to believe in it.

We have all been rather misled by economists' talk of rationality and efficiency as market desiderata. "All will be well," they seem to say, "if people would just behave rationally and let the market be efficient." There are two problems with this. First, as I pointed out in earlier chapters, there is no single "rational" behavior. There are many, depending on the motives at work and the constraints, situational and cognitive, under which people must operate. And second, as many have now pointed out, the crisis of 2007–9 is not in fact the fruit of obviously *irrational* behavior. Omnicompetent jurist Richard Posner writes: "The key to understanding is that a capitalist economy, while immensely dynamic and productive, is not inherently stable." He goes on to conclude: "competition in an unregulated financial market drives up risk, which, given the centrality of banking to a capitalist economy, can produce an economic calamity. Rational businessmen will accept a risk of bankruptcy if profits are high because then the expected cost of reducing that risk also is high. Given limited liability, bankruptcy is not the end of the world for shareholders or managers."[9] The well-known stock analyst Henry Blodget, who has lost as well as won riding bubbles, says much the same thing: "most bubbles are the product of more than just bad faith, or incompetence, or rank stupidity; the interaction of human psychology with a market economy practically ensures that they will form. In this sense, bubbles are perfectly rational… a rational and unavoidable by-product of capitalism."[10] To say "unavoidable" seems to me a confession of failure; that most bubbles are the product of "rational" behavior, though, is indubitable.

If irrationality is not to blame, how about greed? A typical view of the current crisis is shown in the subtitle of a recent book: "How unrestrained greed corrupted a dream, shattered global markets and unleashed a catastrophe."[11] Rational short-term financial self-interest, otherwise known as *greed*, is ever-present in the financial world. These guys (they usually are *guys*) are not up at all hours out of a love of spreadsheets and real-time displays. They compete for *money*, the counter in a game whose stakes have recently grown stratospherically. Since greed is a constant, no particular bubble is to be explained by it.

An obvious cause of crises is unbalanced incentives—a malign reinforcement schedule. The schedule is bad in several ways. First, limited liability; these guys are playing with other people's money: "The men running Wall Street knew full well that any liability for their risk taking—once borne by their partners—now fell to nameless, faceless shareholders…The holy grail of investment banking became increasingly short-term profits and short-term bonuses at the expense of the long-term health of the firm…"[12] Upside gains were always much higher (for the players) than downside risks, but for the system as whole, the ratio was reversed. And, second, enormous leverage: the players controlled large sums while laying out very little cash up front. The result: a fragile dynamical system prone to periodic instability. It's the system that's the problem. If we can understand how it works, we may be able to improve it. As a first step, I end this chapter with a final example of instability on a grand scale.

It's time to return to the markets' random walk. As I pointed out earlier, there's nothing to restrain a random walk from drifting indefinitely from its starting point. On average, a random walk will depart from its starting point a distance proportional to the square root of the time elapsed: 1 point after 1 time unit, 4 after 16 units, 8 after 64 and so on. In other words, random walk is not very stable. Its only saving grace is that for every stock that drifts north another will drift south, so the average doesn't change.

But suppose it does change? Every stock tout hammers home the point that over a long time period, stock indexes show a consistent gain. The picture of the Dow Jones index from 1900 to 2008 (Figure 6-6) shows that the tout is basically correct: the graph is on a log scale, which much compresses the real gains. In reality, on a linear scale, it would curve steeply upwards through most of the era. The Dow Jones index is not exactly a pure measure, of course. The mix of stocks changes from time to time as some companies die (no more GM now, for example); stocks are weighted by price not capitalization; increases incorporate inflation effects, etc. But the rising curve does provide a psychological basis for the steady optimism, the persistent "buy" bias, in the stock market.

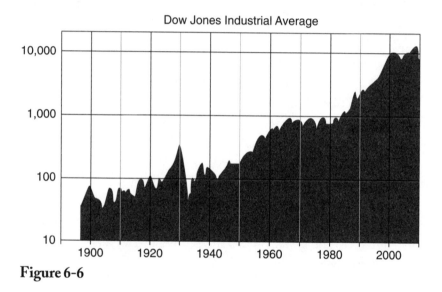

Figure 6-6

This bias, together with occasional apparent trends (see Figure 4-3 in Chapter 4), can easily cause runaway stock market boom or bust. The next figure shows what can happen when the drift in stock prices is even minimally sensitive to market trends. Recall that one property of the random walk is that a stock may quite by accident show a trend, that is, an apparently consistent bias up or down. Trends in the market average will obviously be smaller than trends in a given stock, but by chance the average will go up or down a few points from time period to time period. Now, suppose that the punters (as the Brits call them) are especially sensitive to market gains—they're optimistic. What will happen if they react to any positive change in the average more than they react to a negative change? Figure 6-7 shows what happens when any positive percentage change in the market average is added back to the value of every stock.[13] This is Keynes's "animal spirits"—the animals in this case being optimistic lemmings—induced here by a (random) increase in the market average. If the "zeitgeist" weighting is just unity, one stock begins to increase without limit; eventually all will. If the weighting is greater than one, the increase is very rapid. The market booms, based on ... *nothing* ... nothing but those animal spirits, amplified by the random-walk dynamic.

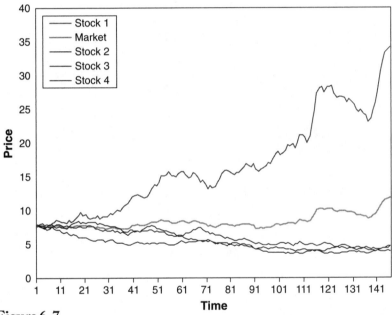

Figure 6-7

The time scale in these graphs is arbitrary. If those numbers refer to weeks, the drift to instability will be so slow as to be imperceptible. But if they refer to seconds, or hundredths of a second, instability can result almost instantly. In the last decade, automated computer trading has grown in practice enormously.[14] It should not be a surprise, therefore, to see that since trades can occur in microseconds, market instabilities now occur much more rapidly than in the past. The precipitous 1000-point drop in the Dow on May 6, 2010, the "flash crash," is only the most recent example.[15]

So, is the market really irrational? What else can we call the "animal spirits," or "irrational exuberance,"[16] or "market sentiment" that causes all stocks to go up because…all stocks are going up? But, as Keynes also pointed out many years ago, one "rational" investment strategy is to "anticipat(e) what average opinion expects average opinion to be."[17] If the average is going up, "average opinion" is telling us to "buy"… isn't it? The dynamic model shows in a formal way what is informally pretty obvious: that this "rational" behavior by individual players can easily lead to undesirable behavior by the market as a whole.

Real economics is not about equilibria but about *variation*. Even the simplest dynamic models of the housing market, supply and demand, or stock movement, very easily depart from the comforting equilibria of comparative statics. Static models are positively dangerous because they assume a stability that doesn't exist, and fail most dramatically when they are most needed, during boom and bust.

But several of the questions raised by any discussion of markets still remain. Of what real use are the financial markets? Should we share Maynard Keynes's misgivings about the social utility of the stock market? As the credit crunch peaked, many people wondered why government (i.e., the people's) credit was being used to bail out banks, rather than going back to the "real economy"—or letting the economy correct itself. Why not support the newly unemployed directly, rather than bail out the more-than-rich-enough? Or, since we don't understand it, leave the economy alone. How necessary is Wall Street to Main Street, really? I take up these questions, and the issue of regulation—what should, can, be done about stabilizing markets?—in the rest of the book.

Growth and the Conservation of Money

When Archimedes (*c.* 287 BC—212 BC) cried "Eureka!" and leapt from his bath, excited by his insight that measuring the amount of water displaced by an object would give him its volume, even an irregularly shaped object like the golden crown of his boss, King Hiero II of Syracuse, he was applying the first great conservation principle of science. Water is incompressible, so its volume remains the same no matter the shape of its container. Hence the volume of water displaced is the same as the volume of the displacing object.

After the principle of conservation of volume, and a few centuries, other conservation principles were discovered. French *gentilhomme* Antoine Lavoisier (1743–1794), a tax collector by profession, discovered oxygen and disproved the existing theory that "phlogiston" was a product of combustion. During the French Revolution at the time of the Terror he was guillotined, but during his short life he also discovered the principle of the conservation of mass. After mass, came laws for the conservation of energy, momentum, angular momentum, and charge. All were eventually linked by notions of space–time symmetry.[1] Conservation is obviously central to the stability—the very existence—of the physical world.

What is conserved in financial markets, and why should we care, or even think that the idea *should* apply to financial markets? Well, we should care, because conservation—a fixed total of something—does seem to be important to *stability* in many settings. The "green" movement, for all its quasi-religious overtones

("environmentalism is school prayer for liberals"[2]), is nevertheless correct in assuming that the earth's resources are finite. Hence,
human behavior which assumes the earth can absorb indefinitely
large amounts of pollution—or people—could eventually lead us to
disaster. (Just *when* that will happen is a matter of dispute, of course.)
Aspects of human behavior, like attention (our capacity to detect and
react to stimuli), for example, are also finite. I have argued that highway traffic-control practices in the U.S. that treat human attention as
essentially infinite may be partly responsible for America's distressing
record of traffic fatalities.[3] Conservation is an important principle.

The effects of limits are easy to ignore. They are often delayed
and the longer the delay, the harder it is to be sure that there really
is an effect that the putative cause has is in fact had the predicted
outcome. And in any case, delayed events affect us less than immi-
nent ones: "net present value" of $1,000 to be paid out a year hence is
considerably less than $1,000 delivered now—because accident may
intervene, and because a $1,000 in hand now would be worth more
because of interest or investment, in a year.[4] Skepticism about delayed
perils is therefore totally rational by any criterion. The costs of action
are certain and immediate; future benefits are unsure and remote.
As Keynes helpfully reminded us: "In the long run..."

The real-estate example in Chapter 5 illustrated how periodic
booms and busts in financial markets are delayed effects of positive
feedbacks. The fact that the systemic causes of market cycles act only
after long delays makes them especially hard to identify. Indeed, there
may not be "causes" in the conventional *stimulus* → *response* sense at
all. On October 19, 1987, for example, stock markets all over the
world crashed, declining 20 percent or more in a day.[5] No single
event has been identified that could have caused this great change.
Markets are to some extent like ocean waves, which rise and fall not
in response to any particular stimulus. They are simply the way that
a body of water, influenced by wind and gravity and governed by
the laws of physics, behaves with a complex periodicity. Once in a
while a "rogue wave," unrelated to any sudden change in wind or
weather, will occur — as one did near San Francisco on February 14,

2010, flooding spectators at a surfing competition. Rogue waves may have been responsible for some of the ships lost without a trace in the Bermuda Triangle. Like rogue waves, the surprising ups and downs of financial markets may often just reflect the action of the immensely complex psycho-dynamical systems that underlie them.

Unfortunately, the laws of the market are much more obscure than the laws of physics. Nevertheless, as I showed earlier, it is possible to get an idea of the process underlying the housing boom-bust with a pretty simple model which shows how a very small change in the mortgage-default rate may tip the system from stable to cyclic, to boom-and-bust. Imperceptible changes in key parameters may underlie many "market failures." Still others may be like the ocean waves: every now and then a really large wave will occur, even though general environmental conditions—wind, temperature, etc.—have not changed at all. Deep understanding of the very complex dynamic system that drives a market is necessary both to identify the critical factors in the system and predict the effects of small changes in them. We lack this under-standing now and for the foreseeable future. Yet without it, predicting the time of a market crash will be almost impossible.

That is why it is worth looking at the problem in a new way. Instead of looking for simple causes for boom-and-bust cycles, it might be better to ask: what kind of constraints, what kind of regulatory or tax environment, might work to *stabilize* random-walk markets?

Here conservation may be a key. For example, if all market participants have a fixed amount of money, and if a fixed propor-tion of that money were to be invested in stocks, the total value of the market would indeed be constant. And this might not be a bad thing, because it's pretty obvious that conservation of total wealth *would* tame markets. Look again at the simple random-walk stock-market model I discussed in the last chapter (Figure 6–7 in Chapter 6). Recall that if each stock price is bumped up just a little by increases in the stock-market average, by "market sentiment," the whole market can very quickly become unstable, with stock prices rising off the chart. (Indeed, even without a systematic boost, attending selectively just to stock increases can sometimes cause runaway instability.) This is because the most popular—and generally accepted—model for stock movement, the random-walk model, sets no limit to the total value of the market. With no bias, no "push" north or south, the average will indeed remain more or less constant (*more* if there are many stocks, *less* if just a few). But given just a little push, nothing restrains indefinite growth (or decline) if total wealth is *not* conserved. A random walk is inherently *un*stable.

But if a limit *is* set to total wealth, then the market behaves in a much more sedate fashion, even if random walk is boosted by animal spirits (Figure 7-1).[6] The reason, of course, is that because total wealth is conserved, an increase in the price of any stock must soon be balanced by a decrease in the price of one or more others. There cannot be a secular (i.e., long-term) increase or decrease in the market average in such a market—no boom, no bust. Moreover, if there is no overall trend, there is no possibility that a change in market average, through "market sentiment" can influence the price of individual stocks so as to produce the destructive positive feedback that underlies market boom and bust.

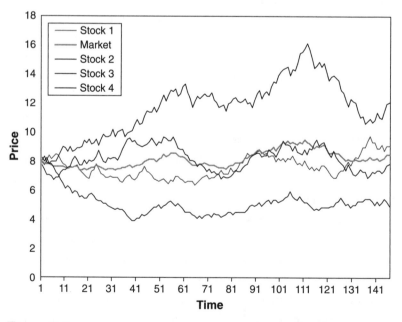

Figure 7-1

In the real world, total wealth (in the form of the total value of the stock market, for example) is not conserved. We have already seen the graph in Chapter 2 and here it is again: a graph of total credit, government debt and all other debt, over the past nine decades not only shows it increasing but *increasing massively in advance of the two great crashes of our time*: 1929, and 2007 (Figure 7-2). Correlation is not causation, as we all know—and equally often seem to forget—but it is hard not to see the explosive growth of credit in the run-up to all our big crashes as a necessary and perhaps sufficient causal factor.

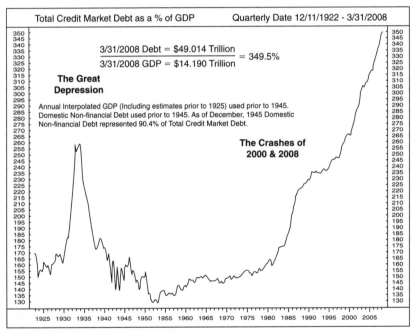

Total Credit Market Debt as a % of GDP   Quarterly Date 12/11/1922 - 3/31/2008

$$\frac{3/31/2008 \text{ Debt} = \$49.014 \text{ Trillion}}{3/31/2008 \text{ GDP} = \$14.190 \text{ Trillion}} = 349.5\%$$

The Great Depression

Annual Interpolated GDP (Including estimates prior to 1925) used prior to 1945. Domestic Non-financial Debt used prior to 1945. As of December, 1945 Domestic Non-financial Debt represented 90.4% of Total Credit Market Debt.

The Crashes of 2000 & 2008

1925 1930 1935 1940 1945 1950 1955 1960 1965 1970 1975 1980 1985 1990 1995 2000 2005

Figure 7-2

As goes debt so booms the stock market. So it is worth asking: why does collective wealth seem to increase, as indeed it appears to have done for most of the past 100 years (see also Figure 6 in Chapter 6)? Indeed, increase is both expected and desired: if the market systematically declines—recession or even depression—alarm bells go off. Since the absence of total-money-wealth conservation is clearly bad for stability, what *is* it good for? How essential is growth in money wealth, as indexed by secular increase in market indices, for example, to national well-being?

To ask the same question in a slightly different way: how about *economic growth*? Doesn't growth entail a rising stock market and a swelling store of national wealth? Doesn't growth necessarily violate a conservation principle? And if so, isn't placing a limit, by whatever means, on total wealth a bad idea? And in any case, how should/could it be done and by whom and with what safeguards?

So I ask first, what *is* economic growth: is it the same as an increase in GDP or the S&P index? If not, what is it? What is the role of *inflation*, i.e., increase in prices (and possibly wages) without increase in real wealth? Is some inflation necessary for growth and is *deflation* always bad? What is the role of the banking system in all this? And is economic growth, as conventionally understood, actually *good*, i.e., necessary for an improvement in collective well-being and the long-term success of society?

Economic Growth[7] Without thinking much about it, most people assume two significant things about national progress. First, that the nation's well-being can be reduced to a number—such as GNP, GDP, GDP per capita, or proxies such as the stock-market index. Second, that growth in those numbers always means that things are getting better, while a decrease means we are all in some way poorer, and thus worse off.

Not everyone agrees. A few years ago the tiny, Buddhist country of Bhutan had a go at finding an alternative to GNP in the form of "gross national happiness." Perhaps because the Himalayan mini-kingdom could not compete GNP-wise, King Jigme Singye Wangchuck suggested that it was more important to be happy than rich. More recently France's President Sarkozy, who is both rich and happy (or at least possessed of a beautiful wife) made a similar proposal, actually suggesting ways to measure "national happiness." Sarko also was criticized for moving the goalposts: "Critics have pointed out that measuring "happiness" will make France's struggling economy, famous for its short working week and generous social benefits, look better."[8] The editorial presumption was that Sarkozy's suggestion was a cop-out: real men, it assumed, seek real money.

One problem, of course, is that the happiness of a population cannot easily be measured with precision. And in social science (why does that so often sound like an oxymoron!), especially economic science, if you can't measure it, it doesn't really exist. Another difficulty is that happiness ain't all it's cracked up to be. Charles Darwin, a very smart fellow, once deplored too much happiness because it interfered with his ability to work. Others, of a more Aristotelian temper, have pointed out that some happinesses are clearly better, in some abstract, moral sense, than others.[9] Being happy by doing good is clearly more virtuous than being happy by taking drugs or molesting children, and so on. Finally, a happy culture is not necessarily a successful or long-lasting culture.

President Jimmy Carter, someone to whom the adjective "happy" is rarely applied, addressed the problem of quantifying "national happiness" through something called the "misery index." Created by economist Arthur Okun, MI is equal to the unemployment rate added to the inflation rate. The MI at least tries to quantify the common good in a more comprehensive way than GDP per capita, although it is open to many objections. A few other attempts to measure the state of the nation less simplistically than via GDP have been made, some serious such as the Barro amended "misery index," which adds a couple of statistics to the MI, and the Gini coefficient, that measures income inequality—and some less so, such as the "despondency index," which includes things like the annual rate of suicides from the Golden Gate bridge. The noted economist Joseph Stiglitz has tackled the problem of real national wealth and suggested several alternatives to GDP per capita, but again could not come up with a simple answer.[10] Happiness studies have even reached the Ivy League: see, for example, Harvard ex-President Derek Bok's new book: *The Politics of Happiness: What Government Can Learn from the New Research on Well-Being*.[11] Bok at one point reaches the alarming conclusion that most voters would like politicians to make them happy even against their wishes: "Most voters would probably prefer to be happy rather than have their representative mechanically accept their mistaken impressions of how to reach this goal." In other words, we know better than they what will make them happy, a statement that reveals much about Dr. Bok's respect for We the People. The multiplicity of suggested measures, and their failure to capture the attention of policy makers, just shows how impossible it is to really measure national well-being.[12]

But there is usually little dissent from the proposition that more money is better than less. So let's leave on one side for the moment whether money or happiness is the best measure of the common good, get back to simple economic growth, and ask a more concrete question: Is economic growth even possible if total wealth is limited? The answer seems to be an obvious "no," but wait…

To understand what economic growth actually means it's helpful to imagine how growth began at the birth of civilization. We can do little more than imagine, proto-history being mostly mystery. There are two main models. English philosopher Thomas Hobbes (1588–1679) thought of human origins as a war of all against all, with early man living a life that was "solitary, poor, nasty, brutish, and short." On the other side of the fence is the great Genevan narcissist Jean-Jacques Rousseau (1712–1778), who saw good *only* in proto-humans, uncorrupted by civilization. For Rousseau, private property was evil: "The first man who, having fenced in a piece of land, said 'This is mine,' and found people naive enough to believe him, that man was the true founder of civil society. From how many crimes, wars, and murders, from how many horrors and misfortunes might not any one have saved mankind, by pulling up the stakes, or filling up the ditch, and crying to his fellows: Beware of listening to this impostor; you are undone if you once forget that the fruits of the earth belong to us all, and the earth itself to nobody."[13] The tragedy of the commons was not a problem for Jean-Jacques, *évidemment*. This line of thought eventually led, via the French Revolution, Napoleon Bonaparte, and laws of inheritance designed to break up ancestral estates, to Pierre-Joseph Proudhon's (1809–1865) oxymoronic aphorism "property is theft," and thus to the rise of Marxism.

Neither Hobbes nor Rousseau even allows for a market much less advocates it. Hobbes's primitives fail because they were solitary, Rousseau's because they had no concept of private property. Both omit an essential feature of human nature most famously expressed by our old favorite Adam Smith: "The propensity to truck, barter and exchange one thing for another is common to all men, and to be found in no other race of animals."[14] So let's try a different model.

Imagine an early society in which every man is self-sufficient. Let's say each spends 50 percent of his time on just two essentials, growing food and constructing shelter. Then, following another of Adam Smith's suggestions, let's allow for the discovery of *division of labor*, a technological breakthrough in its day. Let half the population, group S, now spend all its time making shelter for everyone, and the other half, group F, spend all its time growing food. Because division of labor increases efficiency, we may guess that group S now spends only 70 percent of its time on house-building, even though it is making housing for the whole population (without division-of-labor efficiency gains, it should spend 100 percent of its time on construction) and likewise group F on food production. So now both groups have gained 30 percent of their time for leisure—or better housing, or something else.

Clearly, this mini-economy has "grown" in some sense, but how can we measure the growth? If money has not yet been invented, presumably the economy must function through some other arrangement, such as barter, the home-builders exchanging some of their housing for food, and vice versa. All that has increased, therefore, is the amount of time for leisure or some new activity. In this economy, time *is* money and total time of course remains constant. Yet "growth" has clearly happened, but growth in what?

This simple example should, by itself, make us suspicious of any measure of economic growth that rests on money, like gross national product or, if we are concerned with individual wealth, GNP per capita. Most important, this model shows unequivocally that an economy can "grow"—things can get better for all its citizens—without *any* growth in *any* global quantity, not total time, not the total of "money."

And is the word *growth* even the best one to describe what has changed, what has really improved, in this economy? What has in fact increased is *freedom*—people don't *have* to spend all their time on housing or foraging; and *resilience*—ability to adapt to change— neither of which can easily be reduced to a number. Because division of labor has freed up time, the citizens have more options than they had before. They can use the time for better housing, better food, or something quite new—weaving or warfare, for example. And this freedom makes their society more resilient, better able to cope with a new stress, like climate change or invasion by a hostile tribe.

The only downside is some loss of skills as individual citizens become more specialized. Eventually, perhaps division of labor might reduce us all to the human equivalent of ants, with individuals irreversibly specialized into workers, soldiers and drones—or perhaps politicians, bureaucrats, medical workers and IT professionals, plus a few other specialties—a *Brave New World* indeed. Which would be bad, wouldn't it? Except that ants *are* the most successful group on the planet: "On average, ants monopolize 15–20 percent of the terrestrial animal biomass, and in tropical regions where ants are especially abundant, they monopolize 25 percent or more."[15] For comparison, humans take up perhaps between 1/10th and 1/100th as much biomass.[16] Ants have also been on this earth roughly 30 times as long as humans, 60–80 million years vs. 2.4 million, max, for humans so far. If disaster should befall the planet, I'm betting on the ants. Specialization may not be so bad after all.

Resilience may be the most important common good, since it is so directly related to survival. It is no secret that the affluence and overwhelming superiority in numbers of the Inca and Aztec pre-Columbian empires could not protect them from the more energetic, more flexible, and technologically superior European invaders. Quite possibly, the GDP per capita of the Incas was superior to that of the Spaniards who invaded them. But in practice their wealth, far from protecting them, simply made them an inviting target. The indigenous peoples of the Americas lacked the flexibility, freedom and energy necessary to combat a threat that was essentially trivial in relation to the power that should have been available to them to crush it. Growth, economic and in population numbers, did not save them. Of course, the coup de grâce was delivered by diseases borne by the invaders, who were immunologically as well as technologically superior, and the whole process is complex. But it is certain that the affluence of the pre-Columbians did not protect them. It is interesting that despite strenuous efforts, Europeans were not so successful in Africa, where the indigenous people, though technologically inferior, were superior in their resistance to tropical diseases.

In modern economies, money is one way to achieve freedom and resilience. When the future is uncertain, people tend to save, to preserve their assets for emergencies that are expected but cannot be predicted. This is the so-called liquidity preference, something we will encounter again. But wealth measures for society as a whole are not quite the same as individual wealth, as we will see in a moment.

Incas and proto-humans, especially imaginary ones, may not convince skeptics that growth in collective "wealth," however measured, is not the same as growth in individual well-being or societal vigor. So let's look at a more modern example. Robert Reich, a professor at Harvard and Berkeley and Secretary of Labor in the Clinton administration, in his preface to a recent book on income inequality, writes, "Most Americans are worse off today than they were thirty years ago."[17] But by most conventional economic measures, Americans were much *better* off in the year 2004 than they were even 49 years earlier, in 1955. Average family income in 1955 was about $4,000 per year; in 2004 it was $34,000. That later is better is much less clear when inflation is taken into account, though. For example, the average price of gold in 1955 was $35.03 per oz., but in 2004 it was $409.72. If we divide the average wage by the average gold price to get a measure of average purchasing power, 1955 in fact comes out better, the ratio is 114 to 83. By this measure, people were actually worse off in 2004 than in 1955.

Of course, there are other measures of inflation, such as the consumer price index,[18] a tricky not to say arbitrary measure not totally free of political influence. The issue is complex because of tax effects, among other things—CPI does not take account of so-called "bracket creep" when marginal tax rates are not indexed to inflation—and because it depends on a "market basket" of products that reflects changes in consumer tastes and opportunities. But these tastes and opportunities are obviously themselves influenced by price changes. For example, in 1850 people lit their houses with oil lamps, so the price of oil, usually whale oil, would have been a critical part of the "market basket" on which a nineteenth century consumer price index might have been based. A hundred years later, the price of whale oil is irrelevant to the cost of living, but a new product, gasoline, is critical. So-called core inflation excludes the cost of food and energy. Yet food and energy are hardly luxuries. The stated reason for exclusion is that the prices of food and energy are subject to large fluctuations. But this is as close to nonsense as anything you can find in the rich lode of national statistics. I'm not sure why the concept of the moving average (not rocket science for economists) cannot be applied to these prices so that food and energy could be included in the inflation measure. And how volatile are food prices anyway? Try an average of quarter pounder hamburger prices at MacDonald's, Wendy's and a few other chains: just how volatile is that from week to week?

A critical problem is that prices are correlated both negatively and positively. If food and energy prices ramp up, people will have less money to spend on other things, and, as demand falls, their prices will probably go down. So real inflation in these essentials may actually produce apparent *deflation* in other measures. Leaving out the two most basic necessities of life from CPI makes the measure less credible, to say the least. Indeed, omitting any item that makes up a substantial part of the average budget renders any inflation measure worthless.

In any event, the CPI stood at 26.8 in 1955 and 188.9 in 2004. The comparable purchasing-power ratio here is 149 for 1955 vs. 179 for 2004. In these terms, people were a bit richer in 2004 than 1955—"a bit", not "much". Finally, the Bureau of Labor Statistics Web site tells us that $1.00 in 1955 was worth $7.05 in 2004, a ratio slightly less than the average-salary ratio of 8.5. It's hard to make the case that Americans were really *much* better off financially in 2004 than they were in 1955, though, especially as most families in 1955 had only one full-time worker (and food and energy were much cheaper).

How about income inequality, which is one component of the common good for most people? Well, as I pointed out in Chapter 2, the middle class now earns less in relation to the rich: the Gini coefficient in 1955 was around .38, in 2005 it was .47.[19] Recall, a Gini of 0 indicates that incomes are the same for everybody; a Gini of 1, everybody but one person with no income at all. European countries have Gini's in the range of .30.

Other statistics are less easily interpreted but no more favorable to "later is better." For example, in 1955 only 18.2 percent of women with children under 6 were in paid work compared to 62.2 percent in 2004.[20] What should we think of this? That more women were free to seek meaningful careers in 2004? Or that more women had to (or felt they had to) work in 2004? The answer is complex but involves at least the following ingredients: There were fewer work opportunities for women in 1955 than 2004; most families could attain an acceptable standard of living without the wife working in 1955 but not in 2004; being a housewife was probably more attractive in 1955, when most wives did it, than in 2004, when relatively few did— housewives in 1955 had a community of like women with whom to associate in a way they did not in 2004, when most women worked. It is lonely being a stay-at-home middle-class mom in 2004 in a way that it probably was not in 1955. And of course marriages were more common and longer-lasting, and a larger proportion of women were married in 1955 than in 2004. A report entitled: Married Couples Are a Minority in U.S. Households,[21] goes on to note that 51percent of women over the age of 15 were living without a spouse in 2005— either never married, divorced, separated or living apart from their husbands. In 2000, 49 percent of women over the age of 15 were living without a spouse. In 1950 the number was just 35 percent. So in 1955 there were fewer single women with a need to work.[22]

Even though more women stayed at home in 1955, paradoxically they needed to spend less time working for their children. For the most part, children got about on their own—walking, cycling or using public transport. What the Brits now call the "school run"—driving your kids hither and yon because they cannot go on their own—was unknown in the U.S. and UK in 1955. As a result, children were less dependent on their parents in 1955 than in 2004.

In 1955 *services* were cheap enough that even lower-middle-class people could afford laundry, dry-cleaning and seamstress help in a way they really cannot now. Of course, the people who provided those services were not well paid; and now almost everyone has a washing machine. Now it's almost cheaper to replace a shirt (made in a low-wage country) than have it dry cleaned (in this high-wage country). But overall, my guess is that middle-class parents now have *somewhat less* free time than they did in 1955, despite our apparent increase in national wealth.

On the other hand, we have many things today that we did not in 1955. The Internet makes incredible amounts of information available to anyone willing to type in a few search words. It supplies an almost equal amount of "noise," however: junk science and oddball rumor to support almost any wacko political agenda. Separating signal from noise is almost impossible when the question at issue is controversial or historical. like the causes and even existence of climate change, the "real cause" of the WTC collapse, or even, amazingly, the birthplace of President Obama.

Health and life expectancy are better now than 50 years ago (life expectancy at birth is 78.5 vs. 69.7 years[23]). But medical advances have made the end of life, though less painful than in the distant past, more protracted and more of a burden, financially as well as emotionally, on families than in those pitiless days when the sick tended either to recover or die without lingering. Longevity is not always a blessing—few die in relatively good health. A recent news program noted that in 2008 "Medicare paid $50 billion just for doctor and hospital bills during the last *two months* of patients' lives—that's more than the budget of the Department of Homeland Security or the Department of Education."[24] (my italics) This enormous expenditure went to elaborate treatments that slightly prolonged the lives of some very

sick people—kept them alive for a bit longer, but did not cure them—
a dubious but very expensive benefit. Historical statistics, of course,
are not readily available. But in Samuel Pepys's famous and still wonderfully readable diary (1660–69), he makes occasional observations
on ailing friends and relatives. I am still struck by the fact that these
unfortunates usually either recovered within a week or two—or died.
Modern medicine makes such decisive dispatch more and more
unlikely every year.[25]

On the positive side, we have many more cars and they are safer,
smaller, more durable and reliable, but (I suspect) less fun, now than
they were in 1955. And we have a continuously evolving plethora of
incredibly cheap new gadgets, from iPhones to video games, most
well beyond the imagining of 1950s science fiction. I can remember
as a young lad speculating that in 20 or 30 years things like radios and
even TVs (then a novelty) would be as cheap as a meal—and being
greeted with incredulity. I remember this prediction because it is one
of a select number of mine that have actually come to pass.

So. yes, we have gadgets aplenty. Underlying most of them is
the digital computer. What a boon computers are! Or are they?
Modern economies exist in a schizophrenic condition where governments strive mightily to keep everyone in work while employers, aided by computers, work even harder to reduce employment to
an absolute minimum. And employers have succeeded; firms in the
developed world become more efficient every year (the financial-
services industry is a huge exception, as I point out later). The result
is certainly an improved bottom line. But the improvement in quality
of life for everyone else is rather less obvious.

Some minor irritants: Many train stations in the UK have no staff,
most tickets are bought through machines or have been replaced by
swipe cards (next: use your mobile phone—you can already pay for a
parking space this way in the many places). Gotta question about the
trains? Tough— check your smartphone, if you have one and know
how to use it. Buses have no conductors and most places you pay for
your trip by card-swipe. In London, the hop-on, hop-off feature that
made buses so convenient in the 1950s has gone (reason: the vanished

bus conductor—plus health-and-safety-itis, I suppose[26]). Now you can only get on a bus at a proper stop—no hopping on at a stoplight. Airports and a few cities already have fully automatic trains; the next step will be automatic buses. In the U.S., of course, many buses and train lines have vanished over the past forty years so a car has gone from being a luxury to an essential.

The strong incentive to reduce the workforce, eased by automation at every level, is creating a one-man-band society where the consumer is pushed to do everything but actually make the product. Computers allow manufacturers and retailers to automate just about every aspect of customer service, from product information to purchase, as well as getting the consumer herself to actually control the flow of manufacturing and inventory via instantaneous point-of-sale feedback. But though it saves manufacturers money, this automation invariably costs the customer in time and attention—navigating phone trees and slow and erratic voice-recognition systems, learning new web sites, filling out automated-purchase forms and learning to use automatic checkout systems—plus all those passwords. And in the background is the constant buzz of "offers" and computerized "reward" programs that drain the attention of the distractible.

Computerized systems are *brittle*; despite constant efforts to build in stability and redundancy. When computer systems do break down, they tend to do so suddenly and catastrophically. When air-traffic control systems fail, thousands of people don't get to their destinations; millions can lose electricity when the power grid crashes.

Is the net result "progress" or not? Are all these new products and systems really worth the costs in terms of consumer time and attention, occasional massive failures, and the constant threat to full employment, not to mention waste-recycling problems of unprecedented scale? I'm not sure. But the point is that we should be very impressed by the fact that all this frenetic technological advance, steady money-inflation and push for economic growth, has in 50 years produced changes that in total are not *unequivocally* for the better. It should be shocking that after 50 years of relative peace and "progress" there could still be any argument at all about how much real progress has actually occurred.

This chapter has a short message about conservation (in the sense used in physics not ecology) and a slightly longer one about economic growth. The message about conservation is that without it, a random-walk process like a financial market is inherently unstable, prone to uncontrollable booms and busts. Unless there are limits on the total amount of credit, instability is guaranteed. Circumstantial evidence is provided by the massive growth in national credit in advance of the Great Depression and the crashes of 1987 and 2008. Credit is related to the money supply and the arcana of central banking, which I will discuss in Chapter 8.

Conservation principles seem to be essential to stability in the physical world. It is also easy to show that if the total amount of money invested in the stock market (say) is held constant—total wealth is conserved—major asset bubbles cannot occur. Yet economic growth, interpreted as an increase in total money wealth, is almost universally assumed to be essential to the well being of developed countries. But is it? Probably not. In the first place, growth in money wealth is not the same thing as growth in happiness, virtue, or resilience in the face of challenge, difficult as these things are to measure. For example, by comprehensive but inexact measures, it's by no means obvious that quality of life has improved that much for most Americans over the past 40 or 50 years—despite large increases in money wealth. That's an astonishing failure of public policy during decades of relative peace and technological progress. More concretely, the logic of the food-vs.-housing mini-economy shows that people's lives may improve without any growth in total wealth at all. As I will describe later, historical data from the U.S. also show periods of high prosperity and low or no inflation, hence no real growth in per capita income, although the dollar may have gained value relative to some other currencies and many prices will have fallen. In other words, low growth in total money wealth is perfectly compatible with prosperity.

Most important of all, actual growth in money wealth is largely illusory: $4,000 per year in 1955 is swollen to an equivalent-value $34,000 in 2004. "Growth" is mostly debt and simple inflation—growth in wages more than matched by growth in prices. In sum, real national wealth involves things like economic freedom and resilience (capacity to adapt to change) for which money is an imperfect proxy. Hence, an increase in total money wealth doesn't necessarily mean we are all better off in terms of style and stability of life. GNP is not easily related to what might be called *gross national fitness*. Nor is it clear, by vaguer but more comprehensive measures, that quality of life has actually gotten very much better for most people in the U.S. in the last 50 years.

CHAPTER

8

Debt, Inflation and the
Central Bank

Two things are missing from my proto-economic model: actual money and, what is inseparable from money—indeed it is what historically led to the creation of money—*debt* or *credit*, depending on whether you think it a good thing or not.[1] First, it's clear that it makes no difference whether ur-humans exchanged housing for food in a system of mutual obligation, or had a fixed amount of cash which Group S used to pay Group F and vice versa. In either case, the efficiencies of division of labor do the job of freeing up leisure/money for other uses. In neither case is it necessary for "growth" that the total quantity of money *increase*. The existence of money makes no difference to this argument.

The existence of money does complicate the situation, though. For one thing, unlike time, which is always spent, money can be saved. If some money is saved and thus not easily counted, the total money "value" of the market at any given time will not be constant and instability—price volatility—will increase. In good times, money will come out of savings and boost prices; when times are uncertain, the reverse.

So what *is* money? First, historically, came *commodity money*, something durable whose supply was limited and whose value was universally accepted. In much of the world, gold was the currency of choice, but other limited-supply objects, from cattle to cowry shells, have also served at other times and in less civilized places. In such a world, debts were few and largely between individuals who knew and trusted one another. But gold is heavy and too valuable for small

transactions. So it began to be replaced by cheaper, lighter alternatives: silver and copper coins. And then, in a decisive step, gold was
replaced by token *promises to pay*: gold certificates (paper notes), tally
sticks or something else in itself of no value but carrying a promise of
redemption in terms of gold or something else universally accepted
as having intrinsic value. The new-and-improved alternative to commodity money was in fact the creation of debt.

Governments soon stepped in to tie the value of banknotes, one
pound sterling, one U.S. dollar etc., to a specific quantity of gold.
This is the *gold standard*. Starting in 1837, for example, 20.67 dollars
was held equal to 1 troy oz (31.1 g) of gold, but this had slipped to
$35 per ounce by the end of World War II, and during the interven-
ing time dollar bills were by no means easily or even, for a while,
legally, convertible to gold by the common people. In 1933 specie-
gold ownership by U.S. citizens was declared illegal by executive
order 6102, an extraordinary, if not unprecedented, violation of a
citizen's rights by President Franklin Delano Roosevelt.

Precedents are many, however. For example, under the influence of
picaresque financial wizard John Law in 1720, the pre-revolutionary
government decreed that "the export of specie from France was prohibited and the hoarding of specie was gradually criminalized and
made subject to confiscation and fines…Other edicts prohibited the
wearing of diamonds and precious jewels, and the production, sale or
export of gold and silver objects. This was designed to prevent people
from converting the ever-growing emissions of paper banknotes into
these hard assets. In February, specie holdings were limited by law to
500 livres per person. In March, plans were announced to demonetize
gold and silver."[2]

FDR's crackdown on gold was an "emergency" measure, justified by the Great Depression—towards the ending of which it did
at best nothing. It did protect Federal gold reserves from claims by
the citizenry, however. Violation of FDR's order was punishable by
a fine up to $10,000 (about $170,000 in today's inflated money) or
up to 10 years in prison, or both. The Austrian economists think
this kind of coercion in fact goes hand-in-hand with fiat money: "At

no time in history has paper money been produced in a competitive market setting. Whenever and wherever it came into being, it existed only because the court and the police suppressed the natural alternatives."³ This is not all old history. In 2012 "an alternative currency was introduced in the Greek port city of Volos…Wherever you wander through the market area, one thing you won't need in your pocket is money.…From jewelry to food, electrical parts to clothes, everything here is on sale through a local alternative currency called TEM."⁴ When a group in Asheville, North Carolina recently tried to introduce a competing currency, their leader Bernard von NotHaus "was convicted [in April 2011]…of conspiracy and counterfeiting charges for making and selling Liberty Dollars."⁵ Governments guard their financial prerogatives jealously.⁶ So far the Greeks' TEM has escaped.

Gold ownership became legal again in the U.S. only in 1974,⁷ under President Ford. Any pretense at a gold standard (with the price set at $35 per ounce) was abandoned in the U.S. in 1971, whereupon the price of gold skyrocketed, fluctuating in succeeding years between extremes of $200 and $1,700 per ounce. In 2011 it again was up to around $1,700.

But freedom to own gold does not mean freedom to beat inflation: any dollar profit on investment in gold is subject to capital-gains tax, even though the gain may be due entirely to inflation, i.e., may represent no *real* profit at all. In March 2011, in response to this problem, and reflecting growing concern about the weakness of the U.S. dollar, the Utah State Legislature passed a law legalizing the use of U.S. gold and silver coins as payment in business transactions, and eliminated capital-gains tax on gold and silver sales. In order avoid Mr. von NotHaus's fate, however, the coins are deemed to be worth their face value, so that a dollar coin is deemed to be worth a dollar, not the $1,400 or so current market price. How, or whether, this move by Utah will amount to anything at all remains to be seen.⁸

Fiat Money We are now firmly in the era of *fiat money*, that is, a system whereby money is what the government says it is. British banknotes still include a promise to pay but the promise is empty. If you ask the Bank of England to redeem a £5 note, you'll just get another one in return—no gold, no cattle. U.S. currency is more honest: it simply affirms (in rather small letters) that dollar bills are *legal tender* and can be used to settle all debts.

Fiat money is abhorred by Austrian economists because its value depends upon the trustworthiness of governments. Since the value of a dollar, a pound or a euro is not tied to anything whose quantity is naturally limited, like gold, its stability depends entirely on the self-restraint of government in restricting the supply. When self-restraint is absent—during a financial or political crisis, for example, or when the government wishes to make large expenditures for which ready money is not available, such as paying for a war or bailing out AIG, the result is almost always *inflation*, an increase in the amount of paper currency required to buy a fixed amount of gold or goods.

In developed countries, the rate of inflation has been relatively modest for most of their history. But there are famous exceptions. The European numerical champ is Hungary at 4.19×10^{14} per month just after World War II, but the most famous example is Weimar Germany. From 1918 (the end of World War I) to 1923 the value of a single gold mark escalated from 1 to 1,000,000,000,000 paper marks. The inflation-impoverished populace was reduced to carrying wheelbarrow-loads of paper to pay for the most trivial items. The chaos caused by hyperinflation paved the way for Adolf Hitler and an authoritarian National Socialist regime that promised to restore order and stability, which it did, for a while. In the U.S. during the Revolutionary War the Continental Congress printed paper currency, the "continental," that was readily counterfeited and soon inflated. (Hence the expression "not worth a continental.") Indeed, it was this inflation that induced the framers of the constitution to insist on commodity (gold and silver) money for the states (Article 10, Section 1[9])—and they weren't even aware of fiat money. What they wanted to avoid were convertible certificates—convertible into gold! Federally issued paper money didn't arrive until the Civil War in 1861 when (lo and behold!) currencies on both sides inflated once again—most dramatically in the Confederacy, the losing side: "by the end of the war the Union's 'greenback' dollars were still worth

50 cents in gold [still pretty hefty inflation over four years!] but the Confederacy's 'greybacks' were worth just one cent..."[10]

Severe inflation is almost endemic among the wishfully named "developing" countries. A notorious recent example is the once-prosperous (when it was colonial Southern Rhodesia) central-African country of Zimbabwe. Under the thuggish regime of racist octogenarian Robert Mugabe, Zimbabwean hyperinflation hit 79,600,000,000 percent per month in November 2008.[11] Brazil, a country now edging towards first-world status, has attempted to cope with long-running inflation by converting its currency no less than four times between 1986 and 1994, each time valuing the new unit at 1,000 times the old: cruzeiro, cruzado, cruzado novo, then back to the real, the currency first introduced in 1690 or so. I can remember lecturing there in 1990 during a period when the inflation rate approached 100 percent per month. Merchants kept as little actual cash on hand as possible, so that finding change for a small purchase could be a problem. The banks, large opulent-looking structures for the most part, did a roaring trade as lines of customers queued up every day to move their money into and out of high-interest (hence partly inflation-proof) savings accounts as they earned money or needed cash for daily expenses.

Hyperinflation is incredibly destructive, and far more common than most people realize.[12] But what about mild inflation, 2–5 percent per year, say? Here, opinions differ. The downside is obvious: any inflation is in fact a *tax*, a flat tax, on both wealth and income, the only real flat tax our democracy is ever likely to see. But, unlike legislative flat tax proposals, which always have a threshold, excluding low incomes—so that the tax is always *progressive*, taking a larger fraction of higher incomes—inflation really *is* flat. It necessarily takes the same fraction of everyone's wealth, rich and poor alike. Such a tax is usually termed *regressive* rather than progressive.

What's good about *that*? you may ask. Well, Maynard Keynes for a while thought it was OK, because of something called the *money illusion*, the idea that a dollar is a dollar is a dollar. Workers think that a dollar has a fixed value but also expect salary increments every year.

Inflation is the solution: their salary goes up but their wealth does not—but they don't notice because of the money illusion. All this is more or less true. Gradual changes are always harder to see than abrupt ones. Obviously, people take a while to notice that inflation is eroding their wealth, whereas a salary increment is immediately apparent. Inflation statistics, the cost-of-living index, can be also "adjusted" to suit government policy, and so on. Whether it is morally right to deceive wage-earners in these ways is another matter.

But Keynes was also well aware of the dangers, and the immorality, of excessive inflation: "Lenin is said to have declared that the best way to destroy the capitalist system was to debauch the currency. By a continuing process of inflation, governments can confiscate, secretly and unobserved, an important part of the wealth of their citizens. By this method they not only confiscate, but they confiscate arbitrarily…"[13]

There is a sort of Puritan argument for modest inflation: it impoverishes misers. With inflation, misers are punished for hoarding their cash in a box, because it loses value every year. If they want to maintain their net worth, they must do something useful with their spare cash: spend it or invest it—so they or others can profit from it. This is an attractive idea to any country committed to economic growth. On the other hand, inflation also punishes thrift, so the consistent Puritan faces a bit of a dilemma.

For many years, the strongest argument in favor of mild inflation was something called the *Phillips Curve*,[14] named after A. W. H. Phillips, a modest and talented New Zealand economist (we will encounter him again in a moment) who made an interesting empirical finding. Phillips studied inflation and the unemployment rate in the United Kingdom from 1861 to 1957. Surprisingly for economic data, he found a simple relation, in this case an inverse relation, between them: when (wage) inflation was high, unemployment was low, and vice versa. This is the Phillips Curve. Even though Phillips himself quite sensibly saw these data as a reflection of supply and demand—labor shortage (low unemployment) causes employers to bid up wages—it turned out to be convenient for many policy makers to invert the causation and see high inflation as a cause of high employment. Soon, the powers-that-be came to believe that modest inflation was necessary to full employment. Indeed, part of the reason the Weimar government in inter-war Germany remained relaxed about its growing hyperinflation was its assumption that it promoted full employment.[15] Since governments are fans of inflation anyway, because it reduces the real value of public debt and thus softens the impact of overspending, faith in the benefits of mild inflation has proved hard to shift. But criticism by famous monetarist Milton Friedman and others in the 1970s, and accumulating contrary data from other periods and countries ("stagflation" in the UK in the 1970s, for example), led most economists to abandon the idea that inflation is necessary for full employment.[16] Inflation still has a few influential fans, however.[17]

But perhaps the most persuasive argument in favor of loose money and mild inflation comes from a much-cited comment in the *Journal of Money, Credit and Banking* (wake up at the back!) in 1977 on the Great Capitol Hill Baby-Sitting Co-op Crisis. (If you don't like ur-humans as a model for the U.S. economy, how about a bunch of baby-sitters?) "[It] changed my life" wrote famous Keynesian economist Paul Krugman in 1998.[18] The problem and its solution arose like this. A group of 150 or so young Washington, D.C., families with baby-sitting needs got together to form a baby-sitting co-op. "Scrip" —invented paper money— was issued to each family in the amount of (say) 10 hours of baby-sitting (this is the "money supply"). Then, rather than paying a teenager, a family can exchange scrip for baby-sitting time by another family. It looks pretty foolproof, especially as the scheme was drawn up with some care. Many of the people were lawyers; the charter ran to seven pages. Yet the scheme was prone to both inflation and recession. Sometimes too many people wanted baby-sitters (inflation: too much scrip chasing too few baby-sitters) and sometimes the opposite (recession: people hung on to their scrip for the times when they might really need baby-sitting).

Overall, recession seemed to be the major problem—and the solution was simple. Just issue more scrip, anxiety is relieved and the baby-sitting economy is unfrozen. It is this solution that so impressed

Krugman. The solution to recession is to print money. Some inflation may result, but that's a minor problem. The political convenience of a little inflation means that many governments, and even thoughtful commentators, readily accept it. Polymath Judge Posner blogs: "In a boom, inflation is a bad policy, because (among other things) it creates, as we know, asset-price bubbles. But in a bust, inflation is a good policy. This is partly because the biggest risk in a bust is a deflationary spiral, when as a result of falling prices the purchasing power of the dollar rises. Debts now become a crushing burden, because they are fixed in nominal terms and thus increase in real terms when they have to be repaid in dollars worth more than dollars were when the money was borrowed. And hoarding rises, because in a deflation the purchasing power of money increases even when it is just sitting in a safe-deposit box."

A small problem for policy makers, of course, is identifying just *when* we are in a boom or a bust. The list of "no boom" pronouncements by economic leaders during booms that are clearly apparent in retrospect is embarrassingly long. If we could identify booms with certainty many crashes could perhaps be avoided. But even if we can be sure when we are in a boom, monetary measures to control inflation take time to act, so the boom may persist only to be followed by a bust. You need to know much more about the dynamics of the financial system than we do now, or are ever likely to in the future, to apply the fiscal brakes in a way that guarantees a smooth landing, rather than ending in a crash or another boom.

No matter. For Posner and Krugman, deflation, not inflation, is the enemy, even in good times: "If the money supply did not expand with output, there would be deflation, which is more dangerous to an economy than inflation."[19] Steady expansion of the money supply is now the conventional wisdom, even for Keynes's critics like Friedman, although they are a bit more cautious: "Monetarists asserted, however, that a very limited, circumscribed form of government intervention— namely, instructing central banks to keep the nation's money supply, the sum of cash in circulation and bank deposits, growing on a steady path—is all that's required to prevent depressions."[20] The idea is that the growth of money should just match the growth of the economy, so as to prevent deflation. "[Central banks] decide this on the basis of how fast they believe the economy can grow, and they grow the stock of money proportionately. This is entirely sensible..."[21] The central bank, the Fed in the U.S., thus becomes a sort of thermostat for the economy, turning the interest-rate heater on (low interest) or off (high interest) to maintain the temperature (growth rate) at the desired level. Control of the economy about as simple as keeping your house warm—or so it was thought (and still is, by some).

But is the usefulness, and essential harmlessness, of government money infusions the real lesson of the baby-sitting example?[22] It is a fascinating and actually rather complex situation in which the major variables are surely psychological. What are the families' expectations about their future needs? How do they value the future versus the present—should they use their scrip now and not worry about the future, or not? What is the effect of the amount of scrip in circulation on the frequency of nights out? In a group of workaholic yuppies, after all, one might expect a rather limited night-out elasticity, so more scrip may mean rather few additional nights out. Surplus scrip might well be saved, not spent, and thus not be inflationary. And what about borrowing: why can't the organizers have a bank to lend scrip to the baby-sitting-deprived? What effect would that have? And what about price—the value of each piece of scrip was fixed at 30 minutes of baby-sitting time: how natural/sensible/market-like is that?

Given these complexities, I find the baby-sitters well short of life-changing. It seems rash to draw from this superficially simple example the happy conclusions that (1) the cure for recession is always to print more money; (2) the perils of inflation are exaggerated; and (3) deflation is more dangerous than inflation.

The so-called Paradox of Thrift is one other argument for loose money, made famous by Keynes with his usual gift for the memorable phrase. The idea has been around for some time.[23] It is supposedly another example of the malign hand: if everyone saves too much, consumption will fall, hence profits will fall, hence investment will fall—hence everyone will become poorer. The recession-prone baby-sitters are just a homey example. The point is that what is a virtue in the individual may be a vice for the community. I save because I'm uncertain about the future. If all save, the future gets worse for everyone. The solution: print money, to make everyone feel richer, spend more, and reverse the cycle.

But critics point out that other solutions are possible. If prices are flexible, increased saving should simply lead to a general drop in prices with total consumption left essentially unchanged. Or people may increase their consumption when prices fall—that is the standard supply-demand analysis, after all. In a modern economy, savings are rarely left under the mattress and totally withdrawn from circulation. They are invested or loaned to banks, which can then loan additional money in the ways I describe in a moment. So savings are not lost to the community. On the contrary, they stimulate spending and investment—perhaps at least as much as consumption. But the other problem, when there is a problem, is not so much *saving* as lack of *spending*, of course. Without some assurance that people will spend, entrepreneurs have no reason to make use of other people's savings to invest and produce. But *what* entrepreneurs—in Alabama, or South Korea? In what sense is the *U.S.* economy "stimulated" if people spend their free cash on Korean plasma TVs and Chinese refrigerators? It does make a difference. Doubtless there are situations, circumstances hard to specify with precision, when thrift is a bad thing. The devil, as usual, is in the details—exactly when and how much thrift is bad, and how much spending should be encouraged for how long? And is this problem in fact soluble?

In this context and in defense of government "stimulus" money, professional economists may raise the concept of the multiplier, the idea that an increment of \$x in government spending will lead to \$y of extra money in the economy, where $y > x$. The multiplier is the first step toward a real dynamic model of money flows in the economy. But only the first. Without much more detail, the sort of thing attempted in Phillips's MONIAC, discussed in a moment, it is an unreliable guide to policy.

The fundamental question is: are constant or falling prices really as hazardous as the conventional wisdom assumes? I think the answer is "no" and there is considerable historical precedent to back that up. In recent times, the real prices of clothes and electronic products have declined steadily because of advances in technology and the industrialization of low-wage nations in the developing world. Have the markets for these products stagnated? Well, obviously, no. They have thrived.

But what about the effect of low inflation on the economy as a whole: does low inflation always put a dent in prosperity? Well, no again. Take the period from about 1875 to the end of the 19th century. The price of gold remained constant at around $20 an ounce, inflation was essentially zero and "increases in purchasing power (*deflation*) [were] accompanied by the greatest period of economic growth in world history..."[24] Apparently even Alan Greenspan, once revered, but now under suspicion for years of loose-money policy, no longer believes that modest inflation is a good thing: "We had views about inflation in the 1960s...the desirability of a little inflation, which we longer hold anymore, at least the vast majority no longer hold as being desirable."[25]

But the idea that deflation is disastrous lingers, and modern Japan is usually cited as a compelling example. Here for example is that voice of the Establishment, *The Economist*, in December 2009: "Japan's economy has barely grown in nominal terms after two 'lost decades,' and is again suffering from deflation. Where Japan was once bearing down on America, it now feels the hot breath of China on its neck..."[26] But how badly off is Japan, really? Well, not too badly. In terms of standard of living and crime and employment levels, it is hard to see exactly what the problem with the "lost decades" actually was: "Have you any experience of Japan in the 1990s? Well I have. And it didn't seem too bad to me. Were there hordes of people begging on the subway? Not that I recall. Was it dangerous roaming the streets for fear of being mugged? No, it seemed safe enough when I was there. Was there high unemployment and general destitution? No." So writes Paul Wilmott, a well-known English financial quant.[27] In other words, in terms of the things that actually matter, it is not at all clear that Japan's financial state is an accurate measure of the real state of its people in the 1980s and '90s.

Deflation is bad *only for people and institutions that owe large amounts of money over long time periods*—mostly bankers, financiers and the government. It is bad for them because as time passes their debts grow, or at least fail to decline, in real terms, rather than shrinking as they would under inflation. But what about the little guy, people with mortgages—won't they suffer if house prices fall? No, probably not. Deflation is bad for mortgage borrowers only if house prices fall along with prices generally . But the reason for a big drop in house prices is a bursting bubble. If inflation is controlled, there should be no bubbles, hence no calamitous falls in house prices. But big borrowers, especially long-term borrowers in financial markets, will suffer from deflation. It is no surprise, therefore, that many loud voices are heard condemning it. Recently, for example, *The New York Times* opined that the Federal Reserve Bank should "make people believe that it is seriously committed to increasing the rate of inflation"!—and no, that is not a misprint.[28] But inflation hurts all those people who do not owe money, but save it. Inflation always erodes savings, and hyperinflation (there seems to be no such thing as hyper-deflation) can destroy civil society. On balance, I believe there is really no excuse for tolerating, much less encouraging, even mild inflation.

Without fiat money, inflation could not occur. The conquest of the New World, which added galleon-loads of gold and silver to the European stock, is an exception that proves the rule. The flood of new gold and silver caused a continent-wide inflation and contributed to the tulipmania bubble. So why is fiat money, inflation-prone as it is, now universal? Well, it is incredibly convenient for some people and, especially, for governments. A government-controlled central bank allows the state to in effect create money by issuing banknotes, which pay no interest, of course, and bonds, which do pay interest but at a rate that can be controlled by the bank (as I explain in a moment, interest rates now in the U.S. are maintained artificially low to limit government debt payments and "stimulate" the economy). The ease with which assets can be created through fiat money allows governments to react to emergencies such as war more easily than if they had to maintain a cash reserve. Fiat money frees governments from financial constraints and so allows them to...react promptly to emergencies? Or...to misbehave? Probably both.

Banking: Now we must turn to the subject of money and banking, a topic as unexciting as it is important. Fiat money begins to show its real muscle with *fractional-reserve banking*. It works like this. Imagine a bank that gets a deposit of $1,000. The bank legally need maintain a reserve of only 10 percent (say—the rate has varied over time) of its deposits, so it can lend out $900 to others. So long as they do not want immediate cash, these folk in turn create deposits in other banks to the tune of $900, which in turn allows those banks to lend out 90 percent, a further $810, and so on. So long as no one wants actual cash, this process can continue until a total of nearly 10,000 notional dollars has arisen from the initial $1,000 deposit. The original deposit is termed, in banking jargon, M0, the notional total of all accounts is M1. Obviously, M1 will fluctuate, depending on how a myriad of customers deposit and withdraw from their accounts. The classification goes on to include a number of other Ms[29] (money-supply measures) embracing different types of account. Once you have fractional-reserve banking, the total supply of money is a very elastic quantity indeed.

The stability of the fractional-reserve banking system depends, as does the stability of so much of finance, on *statistics*, the variation- and risk-reducing effects of large numbers. Banks have many customers and they usually behave more or less independently—they don't all want to withdraw their money at the same time, for example. When they do, when depositors don't behave independently, there is a bank "run" and, because it retains only a small amount of actual cash, the target bank will likely fail unless it can get a fast loan from someone else. But, exactly because banks loan to each other, when one bank fails, many are at risk. A run on one bank often presages runs on many. Bank runs were quite common in the 19th and early 20th centuries and many banks failed—though not as many as central-bank advocates like to claim.[30] A graph of bank failures from 1864 to 2000 shows that failures were relatively few until about 1920, peaked in 1933 when Glass-Steagall was passed, and remained low until the bout of deregulation that began in 1980.[31] All these early failures did not threaten the system, however. The banks were all small, nothing like the scale of the huge financial institutions that threatened to bring down the entire financial system in 2008.

The instability represented by bank runs is built into fractional-reserve banking. It was to avoid it that the U.S. Congress set up the Federal Deposit Insurance Corporation under the Glass-Steagall act of 1933. Guaranteeing deposits up to a generous limit (now $250,000) calmed depositors' fears that they could lose all their money even in a minor financial crisis and thus made bank runs unlikely. There has been no real bank run in the U.S. since 1933. But there was one recently in Britain, the first in the UK since the Great Depression. It was surely facilitated by Britain's lack of a robust deposit-insurance scheme. The devastating run on the building society (savings and loan) Northern Rock in September, 2007, finally induced the government to take it over in February 2008.

Perhaps the most intellectually honest attempt to understand money supply and its role in macroeconomics is an ingenious mechanism invented by the New Zealander of the eponymous curve, W. A. Phillips, while he was studying at the London School of Economics in 1949. The device, termed the MONIAC[32] (after ENIAC, an early digital computer), was a mechanical and hydraulic device, an analog computer, devised while digital computers were still running on relays and vacuum tubes, and intended to illustrate the flow of money around a modern economy. It is a much better metaphor for the real macroeconomy than any static model, if only because it makes plain how many things we either do not know or cannot measure with precision.

The MONIAC shows the circular flow of economic activity, defined as the sum of household expenditure, government expenditure, business investment and export sales, less purchases of imports. The water in the MONIAC represents the stock of money in the economy. As it is pumped to the top of the machine, this money becomes income. Some of this income is drawn off as taxes, which the government uses to fund its expenditure, which then comes back into the economy. The remaining disposable income can either be spent (consumption expenditure) or saved. The amount of saving depends on the interest rate and households' preferences. The money saved becomes loanable funds in the banking system, which firms use to finance their purchases of plant and machinery and buildings. This investment expenditure also re-enters the economy. This gives us domestic expenditure. As domestic expenditure reaches a certain level, domestic production cannot satisfy demand and goods and services are purchased from abroad. Money leaves the system as payments head offshore. Domestic products are also sold in foreign markets, generating export revenue that comes back into the economy. Imports and exports are affected by the prevailing exchange rate. Pen-writers trace out the level of GDP, the trade balance and interest rates.

Complicated as this sounds, it is still much too simple, of course. But the model at least attempts to understand the economy as a whole, and shows its dynamic (real-time) nature—water takes time to flow from one part to another—and the way that one part depends on many others. The water in the MONIAC is a good metaphor for money: it can't be reduced or increased in amount—like money, just as long as the central bank does not create any. Money like a fluid does indeed flow from one person and place to another and its amount (volume) is conserved, absent money-creation by the central bank.

"In 1913, the Federal Reserve Act was passed by Congress and signed by President Wilson. The panic of 1907, with its more than usual epidemic of bank failures, was the straw that broke the camel's back: the country was fed up once and for all with the anarchy of unstable private banking."[33] This is the conventional account of the origin of the current Federal Reserve System, most recent of two (or three, if a pre-Revolution attempt is included) previous attempts to create a central bank for the U.S. Recent events paint a darker picture, of course. Claudio Borio, of the Bank for International Settlements, in September 2011 began a highly critical article: "Central banking will never be quite the same again after the global financial crisis. The crisis will no doubt prove to be one of those rare defining moments in the history of this institution—an institution that, from its faltering first steps in the XVII century, has grown to become widely regarded as indispensable."[34] So, just how indispensable is the central bank?

The Federal Reserve is a quasi-government consortium of twelve banks that manages the supply of dollars available to all banks, the inflow to the MONIAC. Tired of the "anarchy" of private banking, the Fed was created to bring order and stability to the process. How well has it done? The short answer is: not well at all. It has presided over inflation well in excess of the rate that preceded its creation. Between 1910 and 1990 the dollar declined in value by a factor of about ten, compared to almost no change in its value in the preceding eight decades. And the Federal Reserve has failed to prevent financial crises more frequent in number and larger in extent than those that preceded it: the crash of 1921, the Great Depression from 1929 to the end of World War II, five or so recessions between 1953 and 1981, the stock-market crash of 1987 and the "dislocation" of 2008 and counting.

High finance is invariably conducted in high secrecy. The motives are, of course, honorable. Best not to scare the market, grave emergency, time of essence, need to maintain confidence, public good, stability, liquidity, etc., etc…By now the crisis-driven atmosphere surrounding the 1998 saving of Long-Term Capital Management, the first round of government bailouts, TARP 1, the saving of Bear Stearns and the abandonment of Lehman Brothers in 2008, is well known.[35] Not so at first, though. All those meetings were held in secret in an atmosphere of dire emergency. Is the crisis, this time and many earlier such times, real, in the sense that it affects the whole country? Or is it local, mostly affecting the financial industry? Are the measures recommended necessary for the common good, or just for the good of the people in those meetings and their friends and associates? These questions usually go unanswered.

Secrecy also surrounded the birth of the current Federal Reserve Bank. In 1910, in response to growing alarm in the financial community, Senate Republican leader Nelson Aldrich of Rhode Island and heavyweights representing the banks of Rockefeller,

J.P. Morgan, and Kuhn, Loeb & Co., met, not at Grand Central Station in New York City, where they would have been recognized, but in a suburban station in Hoboken, New Jersey, where they would not. According to one source, these gentlemen together commanded something like one quarter of the wealth of the entire planet at that time. Reportedly, though all were friends or acquaintances, they ignored one another until they actually got on the train where they addressed one another by first names only, so as not to give the game away to bystanders. The train took them, via Raleigh, North Carolina, to Brunswick, Georgia, from whence they finally arrived at privately owned Jekyll Island on the Georgia coast. They remained isolated on the island, at what is now the Jekyll Island Club Hotel, for ten days—still addressing one another only by first names. Paul Warburg ("Daddy Warbucks" of the Little Orphan Annie comic strip) of Kuhn, Loeb & Co. acted as master of ceremonies and laid out the main features of what would be called the Aldrich Plan, after Senator Aldrich. Thus was born the current Federal Reserve Bank, finally set up by Congress in 1913, a public entity with enormous powers to which the public will contributed precisely nothing.

The Federal Reserve is like the Holy Roman Empire, which was, famously, neither holy, nor Roman nor even an empire. The Fed is no more Federal than Federal Express, is not really a bank (it won't accept your deposits, for example) and—big problem—it has no real reserve. The System has a checkered history.[36] There have been three Feds. The current one is subject to the Administrative Procedure Act. It is not "owned" by anyone, is "not a private, profit-making institution." The Fed describes itself as "an independent entity within the government, having both public purposes and private aspects." Neither the Federal Reserve System nor its component banks are owned by the U.S. Federal Government.[37] The quasi-independence of the Fed is an acknowledgement of the dangers of unrestrained money creation by the central government. Unfortunately, the Fed's independence is more apparent than real. When it posted a profit at the end of 2009, for example, the money was returned to the Treasury. This is not standard practice for independent corporations! It's hard to know just how independent the Fed really is. The current Treasury head's "Team Geithner" seems to include Fed chairman Ben Bernanke as a key player, for example.

The Fed applies *monetary policy* through what are called *open-market operations*,[38] which "influence the availability and cost of money and credit to help promote national economic goals."[39] "When we read in the news that the Fed has 'lowered interest rates,' the writer is referring to something called the Federal funds rate, the interest rate at which banks lend to each other."[40] It is important to realize that the Fed *cannot control interest rates directly*. The idea that the Fed has a dial it can twiddle to set interest rates wherever it wants is an illusion. What it can do, create and destroy money, is something that therefore has effects that go well beyond interest rates.

The Fed lowers the interest rate by buying up short-term government securities (Treasuries or "T-bills") on the open market. The additional cash reserves give the banks more funds to lend, and because the banks are more anxious to lend, they are willing to accept a lower interest rate. Increasing the supply of credit lowers its price, the interest rate, in the usual supply-and-demand way. Control of interest rate by the Fed is better called *tuning* than setting. But it is tuning via the creation of money (reserves), money not earned by anyone and not tied in any way to the productive potential of the economy.

This account of interest rates is of course much simplified. Any loan has at least two dimensions in addition to the amount: the interest rate and the term. Open-market operations usually involve short-term debt, but they obviously affect long-term interest rates, sometimes in unpredictable ways. The Federal Open Market Committee adjusts interest rates so as to achieve "long-run goals of price stability and sustainable economic growth."[41] The argument of this chapter, however, is that these goals may not be good ones and that the process by which the Fed seeks to achieve them—control of interest rates—may impair the self-regulating properties of a properly designed market and thus contribute to boom-and-bust cycles.

Open-market operations are these days carried out largely electronically by simply increasing or decreasing (i.e., crediting or debiting) the amount of money a bank has on reserve at the central bank, i.e., at the Fed. The Fed can increase (say) Bank X's account in exchange for the bank selling a financial instrument such as government bonds, foreign currency, or gold. Or, newly created money can be used by the Fed to buy a financial asset in the open market. If the Fed sells this asset, the cash held by the purchasing bank decreases, reducing the total supply of money.

When interest rates are close to zero—in other words when the Fed's interest-rate lever has hit its limit—but the economy still shows signs of recession, the Keynesian solution is something with the emollient name of *quantitative easing*.[42] It's just like open-market operations, but now the government's purchases extend beyond government securities to other kinds of "paper"—corporate bonds, even mortgage-backed securities, etc. The money for these purchases comes not from government reserves, but out of nowhere. The central bank just creates it.

Money creation via easing or open-market operations is supposed to pull the economy out of recession without causing either inflation or another boom. But again, to avoid inflation the policy must presumably go into reverse at the right time. The government must stop buying securities and start selling them, so that interest rates begin to rise again. The theory gives no reliable guide to just when the brakes should be applied, however. So a frequent result of the attempt to control growth via these central-bank operations is simply to start another boom-bust cycle. If we are lucky, the boom period will be long and the bust short. But often, as in the Great Depression, the bust is protracted and the boom fails to arrive.

The best noninflationary version of the Keynesian approach I can come up with is as follows: The recession (almost any recession) is caused by people's unwillingness to spend (not sure how this works in the present case, given that U.S. savings rate was until late 2009 very low, so the population must have been spending flat-out—but press on). So, we put money into the economy, thus causing idle resources to come back on line. This doesn't cause inflation, because the now-active new resources produce additional goods to match the new cash (not sure how this works in the U.S. now, when most consumer goods come not from Chicago or Detroit but Seoul or Shenzhen, something to do with borrowing from China, I guess—but again, press on). And some of the new money is just held as reserves at the central bank,[43] allowing commercial banks to lend more (again, not sure how this is any different from delivering the cash directly, but no matter). As productivity improves, more cash can be released, but it will again be matched by more efficient production, so there will be no inflation. In other words, the fresh cash that is created by the central bank is benign because it is just a borrowing against anticipated future improvements in productivity (in Shenzhen?). As that productivity cuts in, we will need more cash if prices are not to fall (which is usually, but I think wrongly, assumed to be a bad thing). That's the presumption that sets a target of near-zero inflation combined with cash creation.

But even if the Keynesian view is more or less correct, there are serious problems—for both the lender and the borrower—with central-bank control of interest rates. Interest rate is in effect the price you pay for borrowing money. The borrower gains freedom now and the lender loses it for a certain time—*interest* is the borrower's cost for this privilege. If the lender thinks that the chance you will pay it back is less than 100 percent, or if the environment is uncertain so that he wants to retain full flexibility, he will charge a high interest rate—and conversely. What will be the overall effect of artificial interest rates on lenders' assessment of, and willingness to accept, risk and loss of liquidity? It is hard to say, except that their decision will be more weakly related to the real risks of lending than if interest rates were determined by market forces alone.

From the point of view of the borrower, the interest rate he must pay tells him something about the kinds of project he should contemplate. Absent an active Fed, low long-term rates mean that people are saving a lot—they don't need the inducement of high interest rates to save. Since they're saving, they will have cash in store to spend in the future. The low interest rates therefore signal two things: that the cost of a long-term project—a new airplane, a new production facility—will be relatively low, and that savings are available for people to spend later on the increased production from these new investments. Conversely, if rates are high, the entrepreneur will think more "short-term, high-profit." In other words, under Fed-free conditions, the prevailing pattern of interest rates helps entrepreneurs invest wisely.

But when rates are controlled by the Fed, borrowers get not valid information, but *noise*—misinformation about what they should do. For example, a conservative investor who would normally put his savings into government or corporate bonds will think again if these Fed-controlled assets earn negligible interest. He may instead put his funds into blue-chip stocks, which are bit riskier but earn much more. Which means that the prices of stocks in general are likely to go higher than they would when interest rates are free of government intervention and not artificially suppressed—a potential bubble. Something like this seems to have happened in the U.S. in 2009 and early 2010, producing general euphoria, and renewed hefty profits, in the financial sector. "Happy days are here again!" thanks to artificially low Fed-controlled interest rates. If interest rates are maintained by the Fed at a low level it likely means *not* that savings are available to spend in the future but in fact the opposite: that the Fed has incurred debt (by buying up T-bills to keep down interest rates) so that by the time long-term production plans come to maturity the country will be suffering under the new taxes necessary to pay back the debt. In other words, Fed-caused low interest rates signal that business will be bad in the future, rather than good. If this argument is correct, a Fed-induced boom just sets things up for a subsequent major bust.

And that's not the only argument against any attempt by the Fed to tune the economy. It is generally agreed among economists that governments do not "pick winners" wisely. A long list of failed government projects, from Concorde to the Japanese Fifth-Generation computer is testimony to this. Even if the government is no worse than the private sector in its judgments, its failed projects tend to be very expensive, they are propped up long after their failure has become obvious (Concorde again), and the money they lose is not voluntarily given, but extracted from taxpayers. Low interest rates favor capital-intensive, long-term projects over capital-light, short-term ones.

But the government cannot know whether this is the right emphasis—nor is interest-rate policy even motivated by entrepreneurial considerations. It is ostensibly designed simply to produce jobs, even if they amount in the long run to the equivalent of digging holes and filling them in again. This kind of argument leads to the conclusion that Japan's continuing recession will benefit greatly from the 2011 earthquake!

For the last several years, borrowers have used the cues from the Fed to invest in real estate, with the horrific results I have described. (What is even more alarming is that we seem to have learned nothing from this, and housing prices continue to be propped up.) The next capital-intensive bubble is likely to be in something "green" like wind farms, electric cars or solar-panel arrays, none of which is likely to get far without government sustenance. What is certain is that *by attempting to control interest rates, a central bank converts a more or less benign market into a potentially malign one that is distorted in unpredictable ways.*

A loose money supply means economic instability. "Countercyclical" (stabilizing) monetary and fiscal policies might be the solution, but in practice they eventually fail and a crisis ensures. They fail for three reasons. First, because it's hard to know where the economy is in the optimistically named "business cycle" so as to apply the necessary correction at the proper time—remember all those "there is no bubble" pronouncements by establishment figures? Second, because even if we were to know exactly where we are in the cycle, we don't know enough about how it all works to set the time and amount of monetary changes so as to precisely control the future course of the economy. Third and, perhaps most important, because the euphoric history of profits created by a boom makes all, policymakers included, reluctant to hit the "off" switch. Yet countercyclical policy, or at least expressed allegiance to such a policy, has been the norm for most of the time since the Great Depression.

The basic cause of financial instability is absence of any real restraint on the total supply of money. But there are other, subordinate, causes that contribute. One of these is *herding*, which works like this. The message of behavioral economics is that people are not infinitely smart (who knew?!). If the choice is between buying gas at a BP station for $X a gallon versus buying it at the Exxon for $Y, where X < Y, buyers have no trouble choosing BP. They are "rational." But if the choice is between buying or not buying a CDO^2 at a given price, or investing in a mortgage-backed security that supposedly yields a given interest rate with a given, computed (but how?) risk of default, punters really are not able to do the math. They literally don't know what they are buying.

Even if the object of desire is something concrete like a house, how do buyers assess the rightness of the price? Prices may scale sensibly—bigger, more luxurious, better-located houses are proportionately more expensive. But this kind of comparison has limited validity: how does the buyer know that *all* houses, or all mortgage-backed securities, aren't overpriced? Well, as we saw in Chapter 1, there are two main ways. One is the "method of fundamentals." Does X amount of money invested in a property yield rental comparable to what the same amount of money might yield in rent (if the property were to be rented) or in other investments? Are mortgage payments at "reasonable" levels in relation to wages? These are still comparison methods, but the comparison is wider, not limited just to houses or mortgage-backed securities. Does the MBS yield as much or more than other comparably risky (but again, how measured?) securities? By these criteria, real estate was considerably overpriced in the years leading up to the crash of 2008–9.

But there is another method, much more widely used; a method that gave steady "buy" signals on real estate for many years. The method says, never mind the fundamentals, *just look at what everybody else is doing.* The message of psychology is that if you can't figure it out yourself, you trust others. The more complex a security or an asset, or the more uncertainty about its real value, the more its price will be driven by the behavior of other people. Art investors rely on professional valuers. Even if most people, and even the buyer himself, think a piece is pretty hideous—if Bernard Berenson, John Canaday or Clement Greenberg think well of it, and if a few key people seem to agree, it will be expensive. For complex *derivatives* (financial instruments whose value depends on the value of other instruments), the calculations of credible quants (e.g., Black-Scholes experts), and the behavior of other players, will set the value.

The point is that the role of "herding"—watching the crowd as a guide to your own behavior—is inversely related to how well the buyer understands the issue himself. Confronted with a choice between cheap gas on one side of the street and more expensive gas on the other, most buyers would be unmoved in their choice of the cheaper by the sight of one customer going to the more expensive. Only a rumor that there's something wrong with the BP gas—or the sight of not one but a crowd of people thronging to Exxon—will change their choice. But if the choice involves a complex derivative or cash input to a quant's "money machine," then the buyer's behavior is likely to be almost entirely driven by others, ranging from "experts" to other buyers as ignorant as himself.

Herding is not necessarily irrational. But people's willingness to behave in this way is easily exploited by crooks, as Charles Ponzi understood many years ago. His early customers made money, as he paid profits to customer A from the new investment by customer B. Seeing the good earnings going to A and B, C, D and beyond joined his scheme. If money can be drawn into a market—either from savings or by "leverage" (i.e., debt)—and so long as the number of "takers" is limited (Bernie Madoff carefully vetted potential new customers, limiting their number while maximizing their gullibility), the law of supply and demand ensures that prices will rise. So, following the crowd is a simple, rational strategy that pays off much of the time. Only when the money supply runs out, or sentiment changes for some reason, will prices begin to crash and people begin to lose money—as they did in the housing and stock markets in 2007–9.

The causes of this instability are twofold: herding and a ready supply of new money. Since nothing much can be done about human nature (herding), and since following others is in any case an adaptive strategy in very many real-world situations, the place to look for a cure to bubbles like this is in the supply of money.

There is general agreement that financial bubbles require, and perhaps are in the end caused by, a loose supply of money. Charles Kindleberger, in his influential text *Manias, Panics, and Crashes: A History of Financial Crises*, concludes that "money supply should be fixed over the long run" but he goes on to add that it should be "elastic during the short-run crisis," presuming that we can know with precision when a crisis begins, and how much to open the money-supply spigot to fix it. I have argued in favor of the first proposition. But I'm skeptical about the second, because decision makers, either out of ignorance or a wish not to be party-poopers, rarely acknowledge a boom when it is occurring; nor would they know just when and how much to apply the brakes so as to ensure a soft landing.

Essentially every financial crisis during the modern era has been preceded by a period of low interest rates and high debt. The problem is that the resulting boom feels pretty good. People therefore expect and want it to be the norm, even though it is may be no more sustainable than high living funded by a home-equity loan. But if we want to avoid bubbles, then, somehow, the quantity of money must be held to a stable long-term level.

A *really* fixed money supply would call into question many things we now take for granted. As my ur-economy example in Chapter 7 illustrated, if total wealth is fixed, conventional measures of economic "growth" will not work. Purchasing power will increase and the currency may strengthen, but totals will not change. Stocks as a whole will not rise in price: the total value of the stock market, which, recession blips aside, everyone expects to increase steadily over the years, will not rise over the long term if the total supply of money is limited. If total wealth is fixed, why should it? Individual stocks may increase in price, but the average of all should stay roughly constant. Perhaps this thought should raise our suspicions about the real meaning of stock-market indices.

Even if average productivity increases, if the total supply of money is limited, improving efficiency just means that your dollar is worth more and more, you can buy more with it, over time. Prices should remain constant, or even fall year on year. You would not need more dollars to be richer. A corollary is that wages cannot be expected to rise routinely each year; indeed, some wages will fall, although workers need not on that account be poorer, because their dollars will be worth more. (The persistence of the money illusion means that there will be political problems with a truly fixed money supply, of course.)

Is this a utopian vision? Well, no; as I mentioned earlier, there were long periods of prosperity and price stability during the latter part of the 19th century in the U.S. What may be utopian is the notion that our political system, in its current dysfunctional state, can ever do what is necessary to achieve it. Can the public be educated out of the money illusion, the idea that a dollar is a dollar is a dollar? Maybe not; but it's worth asking, how might real stability be achieved?

There is a campaign, headed by Texas Congressman and 2012 presidential candidate Ron Paul, to "end the Fed," to simply abolish the central bank. Thus no new money could be created and interest rates would be free to find their own level. Even if such a step were politically possible, there are problems getting there from here. Every developed nation has the equivalent of the Fed, a central bank lender-of-last-resort (or counterfeiter-of-last-resort, if you prefer!) that tries to control interest rates and credit levels, and aid liquidity when financial markets "seize up" (if that is the right metaphor) for any reason. If we abolished the Fed, the international reaction would be shock and suspicion. Even if the political system had the will and power so to act, the resulting uncertainty and probable increase in the variability of interest rates and supply of money might have very bad economic effects. Uncertainty is always bad because people simply stop investing and spending money until the future appears more predictable.

We are probably stuck with the Fed. But are we stuck with the house-thermostat model that it uses to "control," the economy by interest-rate jiggling? Let us hope not. Remember Maynard Keynes's comment about the great depression: "We have involved ourselves in a colossal muddle, having blundered in the control of a delicate machine, the working of which we do not understand…"[44] The economy is indeed such a machine (*ecosystem* might be a better metaphor), composed of precisely interacting but delicate parts that if left alone may work together in harmony, but may also be blown about by animal spirits, intrinsic variability and the malign hand. *And we certainly do not understand it.* The idea that such a creature can be tamed just by fiddling with interest rates, widely believed for many years, is improbable, to say the least.

Abolishing the Fed is not really an option. But a first step would be to modify the Fed's existing "long-run goals of price stability and sustainable economic growth" by simply omitting the "sustainable economic growth" bit. The latter is an impossible target because no one in fact knows how to maintain economic growth. It's also verging on the ridiculous to set the Fed two targets that may sometimes be incompatible. *Let the Fed just worry about stability.* Real growth will take care of itself.

Finally, and more speculatively, we might ask just what it is that makes systems stable and see if what we learn might be applied to the Fed. In normal markets, competition is what holds prices steady against the power of monopolies to raise prices way beyond the costs of production. Competition is a stabilizing force. The Fed of course *is* a monopoly. It is the only source of legal tender. We shouldn't be surprised therefore if from time to time it creates too much money, with the resulting booms and ensuing busts. But there are twelve Fed banks. In principle they could be made to compete with one another. Each could issue its own currency, as banks in the nineteenth century used to do. And suppose that the staff of each bank had to be paid in its own currency. This would give them a further incentive to maintain its value. The result might be a better system, free of the wild swings and temptations to irresponsibility of the present one.[45]

When people must make difficult choices, between options they don't or cannot fully understand, they look to the behavior of others. "Herding" can often be a rational strategy, but it leads to market instability, the malign hand, only when the supply of money can expand without a clear limit. Since herding is both natural and under many conditions rational, if we wish for stability, we must look to limits on total debt, the total supply of money.

Money began as something valuable in itself and available only in limited quantities, like gold. Over centuries of societal evolution, human ingenuity, confronted with a need for capital to invest in productive projects, and human impatience—our unwillingness to wait until savings accumulate—broke free of the ties of gold and came up with fiat money. Most governments are now free to create money and, since the abandonment of the gold standard, are under no constraint as to its amount. The disease associated with fiat money is inflation. Many countries have suffered from hyperinflation over the past century, most dramatically pre-Hitler Germany and contemporary Zimbabwe. The U.S., we are assured, is immune from hyperinflation and, in any case, a little inflation is supposed to be a good thing. But is inflation necessary for prosperity? Historical data and logic say no. Several other arguments are offered for the benefits of inflation. The money illusion: workers can receive expected money raises even though their productivity or their bargaining power may not justify them. Full employment: for several years a little inflation was thought necessary to full employment, but the Phillips curve can be interpreted in other ways and the link between inflation and employment is no longer widely accepted. Government convenience: inflation is convenient for government and other big borrowers, but is this enough reason to encourage it? Demand management: following Keynes, recessions are often thought to reflect deficient demand, which can be enhanced by mild inflation, but are Krugman's baby-sitters a compelling argument? Critics have pointed out that many factors other than the quantity of scrip can affect this system— so increasing the amount of scrip ("quantitative easing") may not be the solution. The "paradox of thrift" sounds better, but it also has its critics. But Keynes's "demand management" idea remains influential. I look at Keynes and his influence in the next chapter.

J. M. Keynes and the Macroeconomy

The most influential advocate of a relaxed approach to government minting of money, and for downplaying if not denigrating the virtues of thrift, is the extraordinary figure of British economist John Maynard Keynes (1883–1946). Keynes looms over all current economic debates. He was an unusual person. Austrian economist Friedrich von Hayek (1899–1992), an intellectual opponent,[1] nevertheless wrote of Keynes after his death: "He was the one really great man I ever knew, and for whom I had unbounded admiration. The world will be a very much poorer place without him."[2] Brilliant by everyone's assessment, a talented mathematician (he wrote an important book on probability theory) as well as a gifted writer, he was the most influential economist of the twentieth century. He was vitally involved in designing the economic system that guided the West after World War II, culminating in the Bretton Woods Agreement (1944)—a strenuous wartime effort to save a bankrupt Britain that probably contributed to his relatively early death. In 1965, *Time* magazine famously announced on its cover "We are all Keynesians now," a comment later echoed by Republican President Richard Nixon. Keynes was a charming conversationalist, a member of London's "Bloomsbury[3] set" as well as a civil servant and for some years bursar (treasurer) of Cambridge's richest college, Kings. He did well by Kings and gave them some wonderful antiques and art by his friend Duncan Grant, the painter, and Eric Gill, sculptor and designer.

The "Bloomsburys," as they were known, were a small community of comfortably off, if not rich, esthetes and intellectuals who exerted enormous influence between the two world wars, especially in arts and letters but also in politics and morals. Some well-known members of the group were Virginia Woolf, darling of feminists for her essay *A Room of One's Own* and her novels, Lytton Strachey, an effete satirist who brilliantly if unfairly pilloried the Victorians, creating a stereotype that lives on still, the painter Duncan Grant, and E. M. Forster, author of *A Passage to India* and several other well-known novels. The philosopher and prolific popularizer Bertrand Russell (his *History of Western Philosophy* is essential reading) and the saloniste Lady Ottoline Morrell were on the periphery of the set.

The response of gay pacifist Strachey to a military tribunal examining his conscientious-objector status during World War I sets the Bloomsbury tone. Asked by an officer what he would do if a German soldier attempted to violate his sister, he responded:[4] "I should try to interpose my body" illustrating at once his pacifism, his wit and his affection for young men. In 1925 Keynes married the eccentric Russian ballerina Lydia Lopokova, but his sexual preferences in earlier days are said to have been flexible. Two excellent biographies of Keynes are by his friend Roy Harrod and the scholar and one-time Conservative Party minister Robert Skidelsky.[5]

Keynes, though not at all opposed to the free market, was also very comfortable with idea of government intervention in the economy. Politically the Bloomsburys were libertarian socialists; the libertarian bit applied to their views on personal morality, the Fabian socialism to their somewhat less well-formed ideas on such issues as government and social equality. There is no reason to think that Keynes differed greatly from the group. But none were as involved as he in government, politics and social science.

The following comment from late in his *magnum opus, The General Theory of Employment, Interest, and Money* (1936), shows Keynes's general attitude to government involvement in the economy, and summarizes his policy:

> In some other respects the foregoing theory is moderately conservative in its implications. For whilst it indicates the vital importance of establishing certain central controls in matters which are

now left in the main to individual initiative, *there are wide fields of activity which are unaffected.* The State will have to *exercise a guiding influence on the propensity to consume* partly through its scheme of taxation, partly by fixing the rate of interest, and partly, perhaps, in other ways. Furthermore, it seems unlikely that the influence of banking policy on the rate of interest will be sufficient by itself to determine an optimum rate of investment. I conceive, therefore, that *a somewhat comprehensive socialisation of investment* will prove the only means of securing an approximation to full employment; though this need not exclude all manner of compromises and of devices by which public authority will co-operate with private initiative. But beyond this no obvious case is made out for a system of State Socialism...[6] [my italics]

Keynes thought of his theory as not-socialist, not because it minimized government intervention, but because it permitted some freedom outside the government. His focus, during the depths of the Great Depression, was, appropriately, on unemployment—the great evil of his time and, increasingly, ours. His cure was what he called "socialization of investment." His premise: that the free market by itself cannot ensure "an optimum rate of investment"—assuming that there is such a thing, that it can be known and that government can achieve it. *Consumption* is his focus. Basically, he wants the State to be able to turn people's "propensity to consume" up or down on the assumption that this is all it takes to ensure full employment. *The General Theory* is a tract designed to convince his fellow economists on these points. It did so, in spades, right up through the Nixon years in the U.S. After that, Keynes was eclipsed by the Chicago school— the *monetarists* Milton Friedman, F. A. Hayek, et al.—for a few years under President Reagan and his successors, but Keynes returned with a bang under the impetus of the crisis of 2008–9.

This paragraph of Keynes's comes from the end of *The General Theory* when, as Paul Krugman (a huge fan) has commented, Keynes "kicks up his heels and has a little fun." Unfortunately (although it seems to have worked for Keynes!) the body of the book is tough going, with paragraph-long sentences, simple equations with obscure or hard-to-measure variables and arcane terms. His entire analysis is static (see Chapter 6), in the fashion of the time. Here is a relatively straightforward example:

> The post-war experiences of Great Britain and the United States are, indeed, actual examples of how an accumulation of wealth, so large that its marginal efficiency has fallen more rapidly than the rate of interest can fall in the face of the prevailing institutional and psychological factors, can interfere, in conditions mainly of laissez-faire, with a reasonable level of employment and with the standard of life which the technical conditions of production are capable of furnishing.[7]

Got that? Krugman, an excellent writer and perhaps the best known contemporary Keynesian, manages to summarize Keynes's position in four bullet points.[8]

- Economies can and often do suffer from an overall lack of demand, which leads to involuntary unemployment
- The economy's automatic tendency to correct shortfalls in demand, if it exists at all, operates slowly and painfully
- Government policies to increase demand, by contrast, can reduce unemployment quickly
- Sometimes increasing the money supply won't be enough to persuade the private sector to spend more, and government spending must step into the breach.

In attempting to analyze Keynes, the first thing to say is that he was *not* interested in market dynamics, in the boom that precedes bust, or in issues of stability. He was interested in fixing a serious problem, unemployment during the Depression, and had no inhibitions about interfering with markets to do so. He was not concerned that his fix might just postpone the crisis or even set the stage for a later, greater one ("In the long run, etc…").

Obviously questions can be raised about each of Krugman's bullet points. *Why* do economies "often…suffer from an overall lack of demand"? Is demand *sui generis* or does it depend on other things—like "animal spirits," for example? How tight is the assumed link between "demand" and full employment? Even if there is a link, where, in a global economy, will a consumption-induced increase in employment actually take place, in the U.S. or in some low-wage country? The Austrian economists might say, for example, that under free-market conditions (no intervention by the Fed), low demand may just mean high savings, hence, in a really free market, low interest rates and an incentive for businesses to invest in new production facilities—keeping employment up, not down. Of course, if interest rates are already low, because of action by the Fed, all bets are off. How (in)effective are the economy's natural righting processes? (If prices are allowed to fall, just how much will demand rise?) Hard to say, if they are not allowed to work without interference. What are the effects, bad as well as good, of "government policies to increase demand"? Is it really better for the government to pay people to dig holes and fill them in again, as Keynes at one point suggests, than leave them free to find something more productive to do? Even assuming that it is in fact necessary to induce the private sector to "spend more," is spending by government the best way to do it?

I have puzzled over Keynes for some time. I still have a copy of *The General Theory* I bought as a student. But I have yet to find a satisfactory answer to some of these questions. The one thing I feel pretty sure about is his emphasis on psychological factors. Here is the argument.

The continuing debate in economics between Keynesians and monetarists reminds me of a similar debate in psychology between Skinnerian behaviorists and cognitive behavioral economists. From one point of view, Skinner's approach to learning looks very much like the classical microeconomics favored by monetarists. Most behavior, he thought, is what he called operant behavior, that is, behavior guided by its consequences—like the behavior of the neo-classical economist's *rational man*. As I explained in the Introduction, much learned behavior of animals does seem to follow *reinforcement* (reward: money for humans, food for a hungry rat, brain-stimulation reinforcement, and so on). Animals and people on schedules of reinforcement often seem to adjust their behavior so as to maximize the amount of reinforcement they get—just as a neo-classical economist would expect.

But the resemblance is superficial, and Skinner's system, like the neo-classicals', is just half the story. It's pretty easy to find situations where animals and people behave in apparently irrational ways—tipping a taxi driver you will never see again is one example, I gave several others earlier. The newest incarnation of behavioral economics has focussed on examples of human irrationality and Keynes's "animal spirits" plays much the same tune. What can fallible human nature tell us about how people actually make decisions?

As I pointed out in earlier chapters, there are two kinds of failure to behave rationally. The easiest to understand involves cognitive limitations. If we ask a pigeon to solve a task that requires it to add or remember sequential information, or discriminate too-similar auditory or visual stimuli, it will fail. A human being asked to behave rationally in complex credit markets with securitized assets and complex insurance-like products such as credit-default swaps will defer to experts (rating agencies) and emulate the behavior of his peers. Because of positive feedback, herding often works, i.e., makes profits in the short run and so is "rational". But because it is based on flawed understanding—the experts often base their recommendations on faulty assumptions—if expert recommendations are followed the eventual result may be disaster. In the human as in the animal case, the problem is cognitive: financial whizzes are clever enough to invent complex financial instruments and even clever enough to make them sufficiently complex that buyers, and sometimes even sellers, are not smart enough to figure out their real value. None of our available heuristics—and humans have plenty, that's what *intelligence* is, a large bag of tricks—is adequate to solve this kind of problem. Indeed, in many cases, there may be *no* solution—the "unknown unknowns" I discussed in earlier chapters. Some problems will always be too tough. This is a familiar type of failure.

But there is a second "failure mode" that is more interesting and equally pervasive. To illustrate it, we need to go back to the some-times-behaving-optimally-and-sometimes-not animals. Rational (optimal)—reinforcement-maximizing—behavior is not achieved by animals, or even humans, through anything approaching the kind of decision-theory, compare-all-the-options analysis employed by economists.[9] As we saw in the Introduction, animals have a box of tricks, heuristics or rules-of-thumb, that works pretty well in most situations to which a given species has been exposed during its evolution. This set of tricks is the "variation" in the variation-and-selection process that *is* learning.

Let me explain. As I laid out in the Introduction, "learning"—adaptation that takes place from moment to moment and day to day—is a sort of evolutionary process. But it is one that operates ontogenetically (during the life of the organism) rather than phylogenetically (from one generation to the next). Darwin's great insight ("How extremely stupid not to have thought of that!" exclaimed Thomas Huxley, his young supporter) is that adaptiveness is the outcome of *two* processes, one environmental and the other endogenous. The endogenous process he called *variation*, the variability, phenotypic and genotypic, of individual organisms. The environmental process is *selection*, the differential reproductive success of different phenotypes—the antelope that is fleeter of foot, the chimp that is a bit smarter than his competitor in attracting females. If the traits that separate successful and unsuccessful phenotypes are *heritable*, then selection tautologically leads to a change in genotype and phenotype—generally in the direction of greater adaptiveness: the evolved antelope runs faster, the next-generation chimp is more intelligent.

So also in learning: the organism runs through its box of tricks, its trial-and-error heuristics, and each one is strengthened or weakened according to its consequences.[10] That's the "rational," Skinnerian, follow-the-reinforcement bit. In animals the selection process is pretty straightforward, the heuristic (rule-to-be-followed) that is closely followed by reward moves up the list, less effective heuristics are pushed down. Eventually, the most effective one is selected and we say that the animal has "learned" the task.

As I've tried to show, the process with humans is not all that different: the heuristic that leads to short-term success is favored. The trial-and-error list is longer in humans than animals, because we are more intelligent than they, but the basic process is the same. That's what people do when they behave "rationally" as well as "irrationally."

This process can fail, in pigeons and people, in several ways. The first is one we have already seen: the beast may have no heuristic adequate to the task. This is a pure cognitive failure. The second is a byproduct of the fact that the set of heuristics that comes into play *depends on the situation*. For example, a hungry animal in a situation where food is available is highly aroused, and this arousal, and the fact that the situation involves food, rather than water or danger or sex, say, limits the set of heuristics available.

Here is a simple illustration of the problem.[11] Imagine a hungry pigeon presented with two targets (stimuli) presented in alternation. Pecking one target yields a bit of food; pecking the other does not. Under normal circumstances pigeons have no difficulty learning this discrimination, pecking the positive target, not-pecking the negative one. But under special conditions when arousal is high (they are very hungry and food is delivered at short intervals of time) and the two stimuli share common elements, they fail. If the rewarded stimulus looks like this *** and the unrewarded one looks like this **Δ, for example, they will peck at the * in both stimuli and apparently fail to tell the difference between the two. Indeed, they will keep doing this even if errors (pecks on the **Δ stimulus) delay food for a while. This is called the "feature-negative effect"—they seem to ignore the negative feature, the Δ. In other experiments it's easy to show that they *can* tell the difference between the two displays: the pigeons' failure is not a perceptual problem.

Well, pretty dumb, you might say; but what do you expect of a pigeon! Well, dogs and people show the same sort of behavior: think "the madness of crowds," or the counterproductive enthusiasm of your dog (well, mine anyway), who jumps up and prevents you from putting on your shoes she is so excited at the prospect of walk

What is going on here, and how is this relevant to human decision-making errors? The feature-negative experiment is an instance of a venerable psychological principle called the Yerkes-Dodson law.[12] In 1908, Yerkes and Dodson pointed out that people learn a difficult task best when they are aroused, but not too aroused.

If the task is too stressful, or if they're not interested at all, they don't do as well, but if, Goldilocks-fashion, they have an intermediate level of arousal, they do best. So it is with the hungry pigeons, if they are less hungry or food is delivered in a more leisurely fashion, they can solve the problem. But if they are really aroused, pecking, the pre-eminent food-related response, comes to the fore and they cannot inhibit it.

The general point is that the *repertoire* of heuristics/behaviors/tricks that people bring to a situation is not fixed. It depends on the type of situation, the person, and his history. This is the Keynesian bit: market sentiment, confidence, animal spirits, call it what you will.

The take-home message for understanding economic crises is that neither the pattern of incentives, the *reinforcement contingencies,* in Skinnerian jargon, or "rationality" in economic language, nor Keynesian animal spirits (market sentiment, confidence), is sufficient by itself to explain economic behavior. We need to understand both what people are willing to try and where this willingness comes from, the source of "confidence" or lack of confidence—as well as the consequences of their actions—to comprehend any market situation.

The hungry pigeons in the feature-negative experiment showed behavior that was both stereotyped—rigid—and excessive: they had too much "confidence." In a boom, this is investors' bias. In a slump, it is the opposite. Confidence describes the options that the investor is willing to entertain. An investor is confident when his liquidity preference is low, he seeks anxiously for something to put his money into, and doesn't look too carefully at the details. If confidence is low, he may not look at any options other than simply hanging on to his cash. His liquidity preference is high. If he is very confident, his animal spirits are high, he's "irrationally exuberant," and game for anything from solid investment to mega-fraud Enron. But if his confidence is in the in-between range, he is willing to invest, but likely to look at more options and analyze them more thoroughly.

The supply–demand model that I described in Chapter 6 can be used to illustrate the devastating effect on an economy of a change in market confidence. This is the model that, with suitable parameter values, shows a stable, orderly supply-and-demand relation (see Figure 6-4). Now suppose that producers begin to notice that profits are

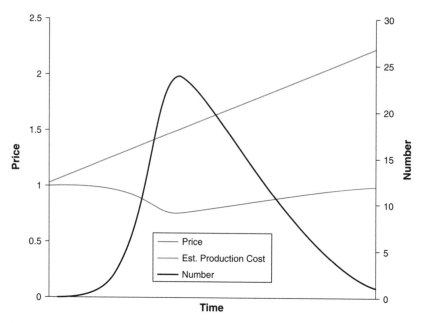

Figure 9-1

declining. In this very simple model, that is equivalent to a slow increase in the cost of production. The next picture (Figure 9-1) shows the effect. The rising straight line is the increasing (estimated) cost of production. The flattish light gray line with a little dip is price. The heavy black up-and-down line shows that although cost of production is increasing steadily, the amount produced (starting from zero) first shows a rapid rise and then a fall: it eventually crashes, even though price has not changed much: a mini-slump caused by loss of producer confidence.

This is not a realistic model, except in one respect: it shows that given highly simplified but plausible dynamics, a gradual change in a variable like producers' beliefs about future profits may cause a rather sudden crash in the amount actually produced. The real dynamics are much more complicated, but similarly sensitive, sometimes showing rapid changes in output in response to small psychological changes.

Compare this account with Maynard Keynes's famous analysis of the Great Depression. Let me paraphrase Keynes, whose prose is not always easy to follow.[13]

We are living this year [1930] (he wrote) *in the shadow of one of the greatest economic catastrophes of modern history. But now that people see what's happening they are full of fear, too much now as it was too little previously. But people should relax; this crisis too will pass. We are as smart and technologically sophisticated as we ever were. All these resources will again soon be brought into play* (sound familiar?).

The slump is nevertheless a violent one. Soon, the output of primary producers (e.g., agriculture, fishing, forestry, mining and quarrying industries) will be restricted almost as much as that of manufacturers. And this will have an adverse reaction on manufacturers, since the primary producers will have no purchasing power to buy manufactured goods—and so on, in a vicious circle. This can lead to behavior which is beneficial to the individual but injurious to the system. Keynes here sets up the original version of the recession-prone-baby-sitter model.

For example, restricting the output of a particular primary commodity raises its price, so long as consumers continue to consume. But if consumers reduce their consumption, then reduction of output is matched by reduction in demand, and no one is better off. Notice that Keynes does not say *why* the consumers reduce their consumption, nor why reduction in price does not reverse this trend—why the "law" of supply and demand fails to work. The effects of differential time lags—dynamics—are also ignored here. It matters a great deal how quickly demand responds to price changes. *Same thing for wages: if a particular producer or a particular country cuts wages, then, so long as others do not follow suit, that producer or that country is able to get more of what trade is going. But if wages are cut all round, the purchasing power of the community as a whole is reduced by the same amount as the reduction of costs; and, again, no one is further forward.* Similar problems: If country A cuts its costs and it gets more business, it will also be able to purchase more and thus increase trade with other countries. Why will this not help to lift all out of the spiral of decline?

Thus, Keynes argues, neither the restriction of output nor the reduction of wages may serve in itself to restore equilibrium. Moreover, re-establishing output at the lower level of money-wages appropriate to (say) the pre-war level of prices will entail another problem. Since the end of World War I, European countries were all stuck with massive amounts of currency-denominated debt. This is also true of the U.S. now, of course, not because of a world war, but because we have financed entitlement overspending, and two small but expensive wars, by borrowing billions of dollars, much of it from other countries, notably China and Japan. *If currencies increase in value, if the price level goes down, the debt burden increases.* (Here, is the argument for inflation again.) *And it's all unnecessary.* Keynes reminds us again: "all the time, the resources of nature and men's devices would be just as fertile and productive as they were. The machine would merely have been jammed as the result of a muddle." Knowing this is presumably the reason (though not the only one) why, early in a crash, public figures continue to insist that all is, and will be, well.

Keynes goes on to give examples of debt that would weigh heavily on economic recovery: for example, *if we were to settle down to the pre-[WWI] war level of prices, the British National Debt would be nearly 40 percent greater than it was in 1924 and double what it was in 1920; agriculturists and householders throughout the world, who have borrowed on mortgage* (sound familiar?), *would find themselves the victims of their creditors.* In such a situation, he argues, it is doubtful whether the necessary adjustments could be made in time to prevent a series of systemically destructive bankruptcies, defaults, and repudiations. Alleviation of this huge debt load is the real argument for inflation, which duly occurred.

Keynes then gives a highly simplified, verbal account of the sequence of events that drives the world to depression. The core of his account is this. He begins with what he calls the total costs of production, which he divides into two parts: the cost of capital-goods and the cost of consumption-goods. Capital-goods include factories, machinery, tools, equipment, and structures which are used to produce products for consumption. Consumption-goods are goods that directly satisfy human wants or desires, such as food, clothes, movies, etc. (What about other kinds of goods, I hear you ask? Can the whole economy really be dichotomized like this? Never mind; bear with me. All that's necessary for Keynes's argument is that there be a dichotomy into consumption–goods and everything else.) These two parts define the whole economy. But, Keynes notes, the economy, considered as the total income of the people, can also be divided in another way that partly overlaps with the first: into expenditure on the purchase of consumption-goods and *savings*. Common to the two dichotomies is the cost of consumption-goods. The rest is either made up of the cost of production-goods or, looked at in the other way, the amount of savings. So the issue for Keynes is whether the proportion of total wealth devoted to savings is greater or less than the amount devoted to capital-goods. He writes:

> Now if the first proportion [savings] is larger than the second [capital goods], producers of consumption-goods will lose money; for their sale proceeds, which are equal to the expenditure of the public on consumption-goods, will be less (as a little thought will show) than what these goods have cost them to produce. If, on the other hand, the second proportion is larger than the first, then the producers of consumption-goods will make exceptional gains. It follows that the profits of the producers of consumption goods can only be restored, either by the public spending a larger proportion of their incomes on such goods (which means saving less), or by a larger proportion of production taking the form of capital-goods (since this means a smaller proportionate output of consumption-goods).

So, he argues, production of capital-goods will not be ramped up unless the producers think they will make a profit, and they will not so believe if capital-good purchasers continue to save rather than spend, which they will do so long as consumers do not increase their consumption—the malign hand, tragedy-of-the commons version. The situation reduces to what is called *liquidity preference*: "[capital-goods producers' profits] depend on whether the public prefer to keep their savings liquid in the shape of money or its equivalent or to use them to buy capital-goods or the equivalent." That's why putting cash into the hands of consumers so as to keep the merry-go-round turning has been the Keynesian government solution to financial crises.

By Keynes own admission the problem is not lack of those real resources that are "just as fertile and productive as they were." It is lack of "belief" by producers that they will make a profit and of consumers that they will have the resources to consume. But the details are expressed in a verbal argument that, despite its occasional profundity, or at least opacity, cannot deal adequately with the multiplicity of little-understood time-dependent processes that drives the real economy. For all its complexity, Keynes masterwork is in fact much too simple as a description of a real economy.

So what is the real message? It is, I think, not blanket approval for the dumping of created money, but attention to the sources of peoples' *beliefs* about their own futures. How rich will I be in a year? How likely is it that people will buy my product? Since the real strengths of the economy were not injured by the slump, then or now, the real problem is just *confidence*. Producers need to feel that if they produce they can sell; consumers need to feel that they can afford to buy and invest and not store their nuts for a rainy day.

The problem for the political system is how best to restore confidence while harming as little as possible innocent victims of the slump, and not rewarding, but perhaps even punishing, those responsible for causing it—and avoiding moral hazard in the future. The question for our time is whether delivering large dollops of cash, not distributed throughout the system, perhaps via the famous deflation-fighting "helicopter drop" favored, tongue-in-cheek, by Milton Friedman, but delivered right at the very top, to the major Wall Street banks, meets these requirements or not. It certainly makes many people outside Wall Street pretty unhappy.

This is obviously a complicated issue both economically and in terms of the politics involved. Economically it makes a difference whether the money delivered by the government to prop up the system is in the form of loans, which have a chance of repayment, or something like unemployment benefits, which do not need to be repaid. But if unemployment benefits simply limit the suffering of the people and allow the government to stay its hand, to not interfere and let the self-organizing restorative efforts of a market economy work—then the costs of unemployment benefits may be recouped via economic growth and increased tax receipts in the future.

In terms of politics, money, whether delivered via helicopter or in a less flamboyant way, is in any case an indirect way to help those who need and deserve help the most, namely people who lost their jobs not because they or their companies were inefficient or their government[14] offices unnecessary, but because of the collapse of the financial system. Money for Wall Street is indirect even as a way to restore confidence, loss of which, Keynes and many others[15] have argued is at the core of crises like the present one.

The core is always psychological, but the psychology may or may not be based on real changes in fundamentals. In the crash of 2008, people belatedly began to see that prices of stocks and real estate were in fact too high when defaults increased and the sub-prime (oh wondrous euphemism!) mortgage market collapsed. This was rational in the sense that these prices were pushed up by unsustainable debt and temporary limits on supply. Given a small change in public sentiment, asset prices proved unstable and crashed and, for most part, are crashed still.

At other times, as economists point out, confidence may be lost for no good reason. But if the system is unstable the resulting depression may still persist for years. For example, the depression of the 1890s followed a boom, but then the collapse came "as a total surprise, with no logical cause."[16] Some prices begin to fall; employers put pressure on wages; workers object and the whole thing spirals down. In 1893 there were bank runs; with no deposit insurance and embarrassingly small reserve requirements (only 6 percent), a financial crisis ensued. The reasons for the bank runs are still pretty obscure—something to do with historically based suspicion of banking institutions, the introduction of bimetallism (should silver rather than gold be the standard??!) and gradual expansion of legal tender: "as government gold reserves fell some people got a feeling that something did not look right, and their confidence likewise fell."[17] But the very low bank-reserve requirement, and great buildup of debt in the rest of the economy, doubtless had something to do with the persistence of the 1893 depression.

I have already mentioned another example, the events of October 19, 1987, when stock markets all over the world crashed, declining 20 percent or more in a day. It seems not to have been associated with anything in particular and the economic system of the day seems not to have contained too many destabilizing elements. Accordingly, markets recovered relatively soon. The most recent precipitous drop occurred on Thursday, May 6, 2010, when the Dow plunged almost 1,000 points in less than 30 minutes. The causes are still being debated.

My conclusion is that Keynes's understanding of the economy, in 1936 and now, is not adequate. For Keynes the problem is lack of demand. His analogy was to pump-priming, where "demand" is the water in the pump and level of employment is the water out. If we add enough water to get above some imaginary threshold, the pump will be primed, a stream of water will emerge and the economy will recover. But, staying with hydraulics, suppose the economy is not like a pump but like a leaky bucket, with a steady inflow of water. Water level is employment level. So, with a steady inflow, it will settle down at a point determined by the size of the hole: the bigger the hole the lower the settling level. Adding a cup of water—an infusion of government-created cash—to the bucket will indeed lift the water level. Employment will increase—for a while. But only for a while. When the infusion ceases, the initial level will be restored to a lower equilibrium level where outflow again matches inflow. If the economy is like the leaky bucket, the solution to the problem (raising the water level) is to reduce the leak (make structural changes in the economy) or permanently increase the inflow (inflate?). The odd added cup won't do the trick.

Systems theory provides a more neutral metaphor. For Keynes, the economy is a system with multiple equilibria. Some equilibrium points sustain full employment, but others do not. His claim is that an infusion of government-created cash can move the system from a low-employment equilibrium to a high-employment equilibrium. But the details are obscure, to Keynes and, still, to us.

Pump or leaky bucket, which metaphor is correct? I'm not sure, but I am sure that a bucket-and-pump level of understanding is not adequate. On the other hand, Keynes's emphasis on animal spirits, on people's level of optimism or pessimism, and their beliefs about the future, is an essential part of the story. Rationality, even the limited short-term rationality that seems to hold most of the time, is the other half. Either alone is inadequate. People's actual behavior is the adaptive interaction between these two: the animal spirits that generate a repertoire of potential actions, and the prospects of short-term profit they believe to be associated with each. Rational and irrational behavior both are the product of these two processes.

Maynard Keynes was a brilliant and humane man, but his persuasive analysis of depression economics is open to so many objections that it seems unwise, if not foolish, to defy common sense and apply a policy that in effect amounts to pouring the gasoline of created money on to the fire of the excessive debt that led to the crisis in the first place. On other hand, since all adaptive behavior, both rational and irrational, depends on the interplay between variation and selection—people's repertoire of rules and strategies and the good and bad consequences of them—Keynes's emphasis on confidence, animal spirits—*behavioral variation*, in my language, still stands. What is much less certain is that confidence can best be restored by Keynesian methods—least of all, I will argue in the next chapter, by bailing out the icons of Wall Street with borrowed cash that must eventually be paid back by taxpayers, either directly or via the slow theft of inflation.[18]

The political system confronts not one problem but two: First, what to do about the current crisis. But second, and more important, what to do to prevent this kind of crisis from happening again. These are the topics of the next three chapters.

PART

II

Financial Markets are Different, I: Problems and Some Solutions

Financial markets are unstable by nature. If the random-walk model is even approximately correct, small but measurable events, like a change in mortgage-default rate (Chapter 5), or large unmeasureable ones, like a change in animal spirits, can cause substantial swings in asset prices. So the occasional crisis is to be expected. Unfortunately, the time scale of this instability is long, years and decades rather than days or weeks. Our short lifespan, our instinct for short-term profits and indifference to long-term costs, especially if they are shared by others—and our human ingenuity—has favored policies that don't just ignore long-term fluctuations but invite them. Technological advance combined with the ingenuity of the modern financial industry and collusion by government and the central bank has exacerbated the intrinsic instability of markets. "Financial business is creating credit without limit until a crisis occurs" in the words of Chinese economist, and chief adviser to China's Banking Regulatory Commission, Andrew Sheng.[1] In 2008, these forces led to a shocking economic crisis whose aftershocks will linger for years. The system needs serious reinvention. What can be done to mitigate the present crisis? What should be done to stabilize the system in the long run? The next chapters outline a new design.

CAUSES AND CULPRITS

Delaying the next crisis means understanding what caused the most recent one. These last three chapters draw together the various threads started earlier. I first review the institutions, practices and beliefs that seem to have midwifed the crisis. The next chapter looks at flawed, but generally accepted, assumptions about risk and competition that have derailed regulatory policy. The final chapter discusses possible preventive measures and ways to mitigate the present crisis.

Nine possible causes of the 2008 disaster have been identified in this and many other books. As I go over them one by one, remedies will become clear. The culprits:

1. The Fed: by holding interest rates too low for too long, the money supply was increased excessively, allowing debt of every kind to balloon.
2. The political system, for encouraging home ownership over many decades without asking itself (a) Why is this a good thing? (b) Are the means employed the best way to attain the objective? Are they even necessary? And (c) What are the implications for the rest of the financial system?
3. The same, for repealing the Glass-Steagall act and allowing FDIC-insured banks to play with excessive risk.
4. The same, for easing up on market regulation in general.
5. "Financial engineers," who created complex derivatives and then convinced themselves and others (including regulators, the federal government, rating agencies and the Nobel Prize committee) that they understood the risks.
6. "Shadow" bankers who figured out ways to leverage (borrow) 40 or more times their cash base.
7. The same, for finding ways to diffuse risk from those who chose to take it in the first place.
8. The same, for devising incentive schemes that allowed them to earn (is that the right word?) stratospheric bonuses by behaving badly if not illegally.

9. "Too big to fail" financial institutions that took excessive risks, secure in the belief that if they tripped, the government would pick them up.

Let's take a look at each of these.

The Federal Reserve Bank A central bank, like any monopoly, is the malign hand incarnate. There are only two ways to stop it: either some unbreakable limit on the money supply such as a gold standard—or competition, let the best currency win. Perhaps individual banks should issue their own currencies, as was done for many years early in the Republic, so that the public can pick the most reliable. Without one of these two blocks to money creation, every time the Fed prints money, a small number of people—bankers, speculators, investors—benefit at once. Perhaps, as the Keynesians believe, the "stimulus" produces economic growth so that everybody eventually benefits to some extent. But whether there is general benefit or not, a relatively small group of financial players always benefits first. If the stimulus fails, as increasingly they seem to,[2] the result will be an increase in the national debt which must be repaid through inflation or future taxes. Any costs, in other words, are delayed and shared, but the benefits are immediate and focused: the malign hand.

It's clear to essentially everybody—on the political left as well as the right—that the Fed's policy of holding down interest rates for a long period contributed to the housing bubble: "In virtually every interpretation of the crisis, the Fed was at the center of the creation of this and the previous bubble."[3] Which means, of course, that there is every reason to expect another bubble so long as rates remain low. What is less clear is just how effective the Fed can be in reversing a crash. If confidence is low, interest-rate manipulations lose their power, because interest rates cannot go below zero. On the other hand, if confidence is high, low interest rates just add fuel to the fire and the pressure to keep them low is strong. As I argued earlier, the Fed should do no more than seek to stabilize the supply of money and avoid artificially constraining interest rates, and it should leave regulation to the market—assuming that the rules under which the market operates limit the malign hand. As for employment, the

Keynesian theory that links employment to inflation and interest rates is much too uncertain a basis for policy (see Chapters 7 and 9). The Fed should leave employment alone.

The Fed controls interest rates by buying up Treasury bonds which it has sold previously. The money it uses for this purpose can come from reserves or, more usually, is simply created. In order to keep the interest rate at a low level, the money supply must therefore be much increased. If, as many have argued, an uncontrolled money supply is a major cause of market instability, it's clear that messing with the interest rate is very dangerous. It follows that it should not be possible for the Fed to incur more than a strictly limited amount of debt. Yet, as things stand now, the creation of such debt is regarded as the main function of the Fed and the main "fix" for recessions. America, we have a problem!

Debt is thought to be bad because it is, well, debt! A loose money supply is bad because it can lead to inflation. I argued in Chapter 2 that increases in national debt are associated with growth in income inequality, which undermines democracy. All true, but perhaps the most potent reason to fear a massive national debt is that *it is a root cause of instability in the financial markets*—compare Figure 6-7 and 7-1. Some means of limiting the total amount of debt is essential if future crises are to be avoided. Traditionally, making paper money convertible into something like gold that is more or less fixed in total amount—the *gold standard*—is the way to do this. But the U.S. has systematically retreated from the gold standard, even to the point of forbidding private citizens to own specie[4] gold for more than forty years—probably because of the very limits a gold standard imposes on the creation of government debt. But events since 1933 should surely tell us that these limits are not just a free-market shibboleth. Gold is not a "barbaric relic" as Keynes called it. Limits on money creation are essential if we really want economic stability.

Unfortunately, there is reason to doubt that everyone wants stability, because two influential classes of people are in favor of money creation. Governments and politicians like money creation for reasons I discussed earlier: it gives them freedom to do things the country could not otherwise afford, like wage war and create vote-buying pork, subsidies and welfare schemes. Financial markets like instability, because a small number of financial players make large amounts of money when a bubble inflates. And, generally speaking, they don't lose it when the bubble pops—compare the post-1929 period in the top and bottom graphs in Chapter 2. The graphs show sharply rising debt (bottom) and sharply increased share of national income going to the top 20 percent (top) up until 1929. The bottom graph shows credit collapsing right after 1929, but the top graph shows the share of national income going to the top 10 percent staying high until the onset of World War II in 1941. A few shrewd speculators even make money when a bubble pops, as I will describe in a moment. There is no reason to believe, therefore, that the financial sector has any real wish to smooth out boom and bust. They just want to be bailed out during the "bust" part—and for the most part, they have been. Returns to the super-rich will be more modest, and the financial sector will be much smaller, if markets become stable. This would not be a bad thing.

Leverage The Fed's loose money policy allows the instability that eventually results in boom and bust. It is, if you like, the final cause. But the efficient or proximal cause is leverage, the assumption of huge amounts of risky debt by financial institutions. This is crystal clear in the present crisis. John Cassidy,[5] for example, has shown that in the 50 years since 1956 during which national debt has more than doubled, the lions share of debt has been due to leverage (debt) created by financial institutions.

Politics and Home Ownership How important is it that most people own their own homes? This is a philosophical question not to be settled here, but it is worth noticing that many European countries where most people rent seem perfectly happy.[6] Owning a home in a declining market makes it hard to sell your house. If you lose your job, it makes it hard to move to where there is work. In a rising market, however, it may be quicker to sell a house than run out a rental lease, so this is an argument for a booming housing market—or for short leases. And of course "ownership" even in the U.S. rarely means real ownership, since most homeowners have mortgages. The bank is the real owner.

But, assuming home ownership is an absolute good, are the FHA, Fannie Mae, Freddie Mac and all the other government-created inducements to home ownership even necessary? "Are [Fannie and Freddie] really so indispensable?" Roger Lowenstein asked in the *New York Times*.[7] Well, no, because they have made little difference to home ownership. Lowenstein continues: "If homeownership was the goal, securitization barely made a dent. In 1980, 64 percent of Americans owned their homes; three decades later, the rate is 67 percent. What the twins accomplished during the bubble was to help some people who could not afford mortgages temporarily pose as owners."

The UK provides another comparison. Home ownership in the UK peaked at 75 percent in 1981[8] (numbers continued to increase, but the percentage has dropped slightly since then). Home ownership in the U.S. has been relatively stable since 1960, at a somewhat lower level, less than 70 percent.[9] Apart from the one-time boost to UK private-home ownership provided by Prime Minister Margaret Thatcher's privatization of council (public) housing in 1980, the UK has no government intervention comparable to Fannie and Freddie. Indeed, mortgage interest is not even tax-deductible as it has been in the U.S. since 1944. In a world-wide comparison of home ownership, the U.S. ranks only 17th, behind Chile, Italy and Israel.[10] "Economists don't agree on much, but they do agree on this: the interest deduction doesn't do a thing for homeownership rates."[11] In other words, Fannie-and-Freddie, the Community Reinvestment Act and all the rest may have added little or nothing to U.S. home ownership rates, which might well have risen without them.

We are therefore forced to the conclusion that political support for these agencies gains its strength from something other than the questionable boost they provide to private home ownership in the U.S. What might that be? One suggestion is that they provided a sort of "cover" for the Federal government; their original purpose was "to camouflage, hide, or understate the extent to which [the U.S. government] actually intervened in the economy."[12] Maybe, but once they were established, other functions took over. F & F executives got huge bonuses even after their organizations cratered. In April, 2009. "Fannie Mae and Freddie Mac expect to pay about $210 million in retention bonuses to 7,600 employees over 18 months..." said the *Wall Street Journal*.[13] "Retention bonus" is of course a term not of art but of artfulness. If an organization, like Fannie or Freddie, has tanked, why would you want to retain those who were at the helm as the propeller rose above the waves? The mind boggles. In any case, these jobs, managing and packaging a portfolio of mortgage loans, are hardly at the cutting edge of creative capitalism. No bonuses should be required. Evidently, other forces are at work.

I'm afraid it's all too clear what really kept the F & F behemoths upright all these years.[14] Fannie and Freddie, and the policies they implement, were profitable for a great many people, many with political influence. This is not a novel insight. In 1979, for example, the *Wall Street Journal* commented: "The Federal Trade Commission has looked into the government's housing policies and discovered that they are driven by something other than pure altruism...the main thrust seems to come from the people who make money building housing [there's a shock!]—contractors, bankers, labor unions, material suppliers, etc..."[15] The source of all this money is the edge given to Fannie and Freddie by their implicit federal guarantee—worth around $7Bn a year as early as 1995, according to a 1996 CBO report.[16] Of this huge unearned amount, Fannie and Freddie passed on only about two-thirds to mortgage holders. The rest went into political activities and those whacking bonuses. The situation was worse by 2003 when, by one estimate, the benefits to F & F were on the order of $150 billion, of which the shareholders retained around $100 billion: "two–thirds for us, one-third for you, the homeowner."

By 2007, the number of Federal teats had grown to feed not only the housing industry and its financiers and suppliers but numerous well-connected figures inside and close to the government. On December 18, 2006, U.S. regulators filed 101 civil charges against Fannie Mae chief executive Franklin Raines, chief financial officer J. Timothy Howard, and the former controller Leanne G. Spencer.[17]

The three are accused of manipulating Fannie Mae earnings to maximize their bonuses. The lawsuit sought to recoup more than $115 million in bonus payments, collectively accrued by the trio from 1998–2004, and about $100 million in penalties for their involvement in the accounting scandal. In June 2008 the *Wall Street Journal* reported that Franklin Raines was one of several public officials and congressmen—"friends of Angelo" (Chief Executive Angelo Mozilo)—who received below-market-rate loans from mega-mortgage-loaner Countrywide Financial (now, after financial difficulties, taken over by Bank of America). He received loans for over $3 million while CEO of Fannie Mae. It is the care and feeding of these people, rather than the needs of the poor, that has sustained these grotesque programs for so long. The long-delayed end-result of this unsavory process, the sub-prime-initiated crisis described in earlier chapters, eventually brought down the whole financial system.

Another problem with housing is what might be called the *target price*: how expensive *should* people's homes be? The assumption for most consumer goods—cars, appliances, clothes, etc.—is: the cheaper the better. Yet houses are regarded quite differently. For housing, serious price drops are regarded as disasters. Why should this be? If we want people to own their own houses, then the cheaper the housing, the more achievable that should be. Low housing prices should be a *good* thing. What on earth is going on?

Two things: People buy houses with mortgages, and people treat their homes as investments. Both of these are a source of problems.

A house represents debt, and mortgage debt is often, depending on the jurisdiction, *non-recourse*, meaning that if the debtor defaults, all the lender gets is the house; the borrower is free of further obligation. This means that both the lender and the borrower have an interest in the price of the house: they don't want it to decrease, and the borrower would like to see it increase.

The borrower, especially, is happy because of *leverage*: if his deposit was 10 percent of the purchase price, and his house goes up by 10 percent, he has made a paper profit of 100 percent on his money. If the price does decrease so that the mortgage is "underwater" (the borrower owes more than the house is worth), and if the mortgage is non-recourse, the temptation for the borrower to "walk away" and leave the lender facing a loss on the sale of the property is strong. But to a buy-to-rent house buyer whose exposure can be as low as zero, if no deposit is required and closing costs are also amortized, buying a house might well look like free money.

If house prices increase mightily, the lender is freed from risk and the homeowner feels rich, as unrealistic as that feeling may be. He may even refinance the house at the new higher value and pocket the difference or, equivalently, take out a "home-equity" loan and live high on the proceeds. Most people don't know that only the Federal Government can get away with that! Because many homeowners treat their residences as investments, falling house prices are politically disastrous.

But of course, treating your *home* as an investment[18] is (technical term) *nuts*. It's treating ransom money as disposable income. Sure, you can spend it, but then the kidnapper shoots you. Sure, you can spend the home-equity loan, but then where will you live when you can't pay the new, higher mortgage? And if you sell your house, unless you have been lucky enough to buy in an area where house prices have risen more than the average, it will cost you just as much to move to a comparable house somewhere else. If everyone is richer, you can't expect to do any better. But people think they can; it is the house-price equivalent of the money illusion. You need a home like you need your liver: but neither is an investment.

What can be done? First, the Fannie-Freddie practice of buying mortgages from the first-lender now looks like a dangerous idea. Selling a mortgage—converting it into a tradable security— commits what should be a cardinal financial sin: the separation of the risk-taker, the bank that chose to make the original loan, from the risk-bearer, the new holder of the sold-on mortgage. People like me (and probably you), who are not in the financial industry, who look at all this "naively," usually see this first step in breaking the link between the loan and the institution that knows the customer, makes the initial loan, and is in the best position to assess the risk, as slightly crazy, not to say dishonest. I think that events have proved us right.

But at first it was OK, because Fannie Mae was the only buyer and could therefore discipline irresponsible loan originators. This discipline was diluted somewhat when other government-sponsored buyers, the other Maes and Macs, came on the scene. But the big break, when the danger changed from potential to actual, came with the practice of securitization. As I pointed out in Chapter 5, securitization compounds this problem by making it almost impossible for the holder of the security to track back to each one of what might be a very large bundle of individual borrowers. Control over the loan originator, possible when loans are traded one at a time with one or a few buyers, is completely lost. Unfortunately, financial sophisticates regard tricks like securitization as high art. No doubt Salomon's Mr. Ranieri was proud[19] of his ingenuity and, as we've seen, the world of finance boasts a zoo of similarly innovative "products" it has evolved over the past two or three decades. But "innovation" (like "change") is not always good. "I wish someone would give me one shred of neutral evidence that financial innovation has led to economic growth—one shred of evidence." So spake not Ralph Nader or Noam Chomsky, but Paul Volcker, onetime head of the Federal Reserve.[20] There are more bad new ideas than good ones. Innovations that reap a quick benefit for the financial institution all too often turn out to be disastrous for the common good. Innovation can be dangerous, especially in finance. More on this later.

If all mortgages were recourse loans, so that the borrower remained liable no matter what the value of the house, the lender would have much less interest in the value of the house and correspondingly greater interest in the creditworthiness of the borrower. Lenders might find themselves once again requiring some equity interest from the borrower, perhaps as much as 20 or even 40 percent, before they make loans. The problem with this idea, of course, is that it would impede the growth of housing bubbles and the mega-profits that go with them. This would not be a bad thing. Real-estate buyers should be liable for the amount they borrow, not for the fluctuating value of the property only. Changing mortgage law is one obvious step towards stabilizing the system.

But what about helping poor people to own their houses? There are ways to do this that don't violate elementary principles of prudence—not that any special steps are necessary, as the UK's success in advancing home ownership without any governmental intervention shows. There are solutions that can increase resources in the mortgage market without breaking the responsibility link between lender and borrower. Instead of the bizarre practice of buying up mortgages, and thus severing risk-taker (the bank or mortgage originator) from risk-bearer (F& F, alias you'n me; and the securitization market—our pension funds), why not just extend favorable government loans to banks in amounts equal to the number of low-income mortgages we think they should offer? The bank could make more loans, but it would still be liable for its own debt. Excessive profits could be easily limited by the government-loan interest rate, so the bankers are unlikely to embrace this idea.

But surely a better solution here should be the same as the solution to poverty generally. People have become better clothed, shod and transported over the years via lower costs for shoes, clothes and cars. Why on earth should the same thing not be true for housing? If you want more people to own their houses, make housing cheaper. Pumping more money into the system, the current practice, has three effects: it aids buyers to some extent in the very short run and by increasing housing demand it stimulates building, the supply of new housing, which aids them in the long run. But before either of these effects, the practice acts as a positive feedback that simply elevates house prices. It is the latter effect that has dominated in recent years. It's like giving everyone in New York City the same cost-of-living bonus. Pretty soon, no one is better off and all prices are higher. It is very likely that the same process is partly responsible for the chronic above-inflation rise in health-care costs. More and more money goes into the system, mostly from government programs, while little or nothing has been done to remove all sorts of existing limits on the competitive supply of medical services. (But that's another book!)

Making houses cheaper will not be easy. Builders in Las Vegas, with 10,000 empty, foreclosed homes in mid–2010, have started to build yet more homes, with mortgage down-payments as low as 3.5 percent. Why? Because they can sell them. How can they sell them in these tough times? Because mortgage interest rates are artificially low. Why are they so low? Because they are kept that way by the Fed. Since the Federal takeover of Fannie and Freddie in 2008, more than 90 percent of mortgages are now government-owned or backed. The momentum behind the present price-inflation system is tremendous. Despite the financial crisis, house prices have fallen relatively little (as of late 2011) and seem to be stabilizing at a still-high level.[21] To compound the madness, the politicians seem to think this is a good thing: "That's why we're working to lift the value of a family's single largest investment—their home. The steps we took last year to shore up the housing market have allowed millions of Americans to take out new loans and save an average of $1,500 on mortgage payments. This year, we will step up re-financing so that homeowners can move into more affordable mortgages."[22] If even the President thinks that a home is an investment; if he thinks that house prices should be *higher* not lower; if he thinks that pumping more money into a bulimic real-estate market is a cure rather than a disease, then we must all despair. But of course propping up house prices does benefit financial institutions and the favored few who run Fannie and Freddie, even as it makes things tougher for first-time home buyers.

Glass-Steagall The 1933 Glass-Steagall act was one of a number of legislative attempts during and after the Great Depression to mitigate its effects. G-S did two important things: it established the Federal Deposit Insurance Corporation (FDIC) which, as we've seen, insured bank deposits up to a fairly substantial level (now $250,000). FDIC insurance successfully prevented bank runs. This insurance is paid for by a fee paid by the banks that depends on the size of deposits and degree of FDIC-assessed risk. Nevertheless, the fee doesn't come anywhere near covering the real costs of a systemic crash. No matter: FDIC insurance is also backed by "the full faith and credit" of the U.S. government.

The second thing Glass-Steagall did was separate investment banks from regular commercial banks. Only the commercial banks benefited from FDIC insurance, and only the investment banks were allowed to trade securities of all sorts, organize mergers and acquisitions, etc.

Bankers saw that G–S prevented them from making profits from financial operations, and pressure to change this mounted until, in 1999, Glass-Steagall was repealed in a flush of anti-regulatory zeal. Thereafter, commercial banks began to engage fully in the much more risky activities of investment banks, even though they were still covered by a Federal insurance at a price based on the commercial-banking (least-risky) part of their business. Plain-vanilla "boring banking" began to be a thing of the past. Large banks, much increased in size since the repeal in the 1980s of old laws restricting banks to in-state operations, grew even larger after the repeal of G–S.

In retrospect, relaxation of G–S and the intra-state limit on banks has proven to be a disaster. The only defense for these moves is the increased profit possibilities for banks. These did indeed materialize. But it is now obvious that the short-term benefit to bankers is more than counterweighted by the malign-hand long-term boom-bust risk to the economy as a whole. Abolishing size limitations (the restriction on interstate banks) has contributed to "too big to fail," which has caused huge problems (more on this in a moment). And in the early days of the credit crunch, it seemed that "community banking"—lending by local banks to small businesses that create the most jobs, the kind of lending favored by the interstate banking restrictions that were abolished in the 1980s—was exactly what had failed. Absent drastic changes in the whole banking system (abolition of the Fed and fractional-reserve banking, etc.) new rules, comparable to Glass-Steagall, need to be devised. More on regulation in a moment.

Market "Efficiency" and Complex Financial Instruments
Alan Greenspan was singing the investment bankers' song when he said: "The purpose of hedge funds and others is to make money, but their actions extirpate inefficiencies and imbalances, and thereby reduce the waste of scarce savings. All these complex financial products are thus justified by their efficiency in allocating scarce resources." Yeah, right! one might say. And several notable people

have, albeit less sarcastically: "It is hard is to distinguish between valuable financial innovation and nonvaluable." (I'll argue in a moment that it's not in fact that difficult.) "Clearly, not all innovation should be treated in the same category as the innovation of either a new pharmaceutical drug or a new retail format. I think that some of it is *socially useless activity*" (my italics). Thus spake Adair Turner, head of the UK Financial Services Authority (equivalent to the U.S. Securities and Exchange Commission), in the summer of 2009.[23] Maynard Keynes many years earlier had similar reservations: "When the capital development of a country becomes a by-product of the activities of a casino, the job is likely to be ill-done. The measure of success attained by Wall Street, regarded as an institution of which the proper social purpose is to direct new investment into the most profitable channels in terms of future yield, cannot be claimed as one of the outstanding triumphs of *laissez-faire* capitalism..."[24]

Adair Turner's cautious reservations nevertheless elicited a storm of protest. The financial markets are supersensitive about any suggestion that they are—not failing the public good, which is not thought possible—but perhaps contributing less than the huge sums they take out? Turner was rebuked for "talking down the city" and "going beyond his remit" and told that he should "foster the health of the sector, irrespective of its size."[25]

The financial community believes that innovation is always good. Any new financial product that makes a profit for the vendor and is not actually fraudulent is assumed to be socially beneficial—remember Lloyd Blankfein of Goldman Sachs and his "impish" comment about "doing God's work." Tim Geithner, current Chair of the Fed, has no doubts about new types of credit instruments. In 2007, when head of the Federal Reserve Bank of New York, he said things like[26]: "The rapid growth in these new types of credit instruments is, of course, a sign of their value to market participants [would you expect people to use them more if they were *losing* money? Is profit its own justification? Apparently yes.]... By spreading risk more broadly, providing opportunities to manage and hedge risk, and making it possible to trade and price credit risk, credit market innovation should help make markets both more efficient and more resilient. They should help make markets better able to allocate capital to its highest return and better able to absorb stress.... We cannot turn back the clock on innovation or reverse the increase in complexity around risk management.... The stronger these shock absorbers, the more resilient markets will be in the face of future shocks." Nice metaphors: "efficient," "resilient," "able to absorb stress," "shock absorbers" (as on a Maserati, perhaps?). Let's all happily "trade and price credit risk"—a pretty dangerous, not to say nonsensical, idea as I will show in a moment. Does anyone really know what half this stuff means? Is anyone supposed to know? The fact that so much rhetoric about these heavyweight financial issues reads like advertising for shampoo ("Damage Therapy Volume Boost"—Dove) should raise everyone's suspicions about what is going on.

But 2007 was the height of the boom. Perhaps young Tim lost some of his enthusiasm for the wonders of financial innovation after 2008? Well, no. In 2010, unlike his elderly predecessor Paul Volcker who seems to be coming to his senses, he was still wittering on about "the benefits of financial innovation."[27]

As I pointed out in the Introduction, financial "products" are very different from traditional products like cars, cookies and cameras. They are not "end use;" that is, they are of no use in and of themselves. They are reinforcement schedules useful to those that work under them only for the money they can make. They are useful to the rest of us only for their "efficiency in allocating scarce resources." Because financial products can be created at will, and because their raison d'être is trade, they may have effects that go well beyond their source. So it is necessary to ask: what is the real use of some of the financial products that have appeared over the past couple of decades? Do they really "allocate scarce resources" in the most efficient way? Do they do it in a way that justifies the enormous profits they have yielded to their originators in recent years? No.

The efficient market theory (EMT) seems to provide support for belief that for financial innovation, profitability is its own justification. I argued earlier (Chapter 1) that the concept of the "efficient" stock market is, from a logical point of view, absolute nonsense. There is no independent, objective measure of the value of a stock; *ergo,* there is nothing with which to compare its price; *ergo* it is not possible to assess the "efficiency" of the pricing process (the market). I can't tell you how efficient your car is if you won't tell me anything but the number miles you have driven.

It is truly incredible that the remaining advocates of the EMT seem to be unmoved by, or perhaps even unaware of, the defects in their position. Recall, the basic idea is just that stock prices, say, accurately reflect all of the available information. The theory sounds hardnosed, yet what can it possibly mean? How is this information to be measured? Not in terms of Shannon-Weaver bits and bytes, presumably, which is the technical concept of information. And information by itself does not lead to action. Even if I tell you that you are standing in the path of a careering truck, without the motive of self-preservation you will not move. All those antipodean animals that evolved without predators just sat still and got eaten when the foxes arrived; they had the information but not the instinct. On the stock front, suppose your spies tell you that the Saudis are injecting CO_2 into some of their oil fields. What will you do with this "information"? You need to know that this procedure is usually used only when the oilfield is approaching depletion, that this suggests oil shortages in the future, and that this in turn suggests that buying certain kinds of security (in this case, oil futures) is likely to be profitable—unless a lot of other people also have this information, in which case oil prices probably reflect it already, so no action is necessary (this is the self-contradictory aspect of EMT). Or perhaps the Saudis are just being socially responsible by sequestering CO_2, an action which would have no market implications at all.

In short, information has to be converted into action. In effect, saying that stock prices reflect all possible information is to say that the stock market is both omniscient and endowed with all the appropriate motives. It is a position that is not rational but religious. And this should have been obvious when the term "efficient" was first proposed.

If this conclusion seems a little harsh, listen to the comments of Eugene Fama, the chief exponent of the efficient-market theory. Asked by interviewer John Cassidy, the *New Yorker* economics writer[28]: "So you still think that the market is highly efficient at the overall level too?" Fama responded: "Yes. And if it isn't, it's going to be *impossible to tell*" (my italics). So, a vital part of the EMT is apparently *untestable*. Fama goes on to say that "bubbles" don't exist, apparently because they are not predictable. A commentator then reminded him that earthquakes are also unpredictable.

Fama also seems to think a recession is a cause rather than an effect of economic processes. As for what causes recessions, he admits: "That's where economics has always broken down. We don't know what causes recessions." It is good to admit ignorance. But why does Fama not go on to ask: of what use is economics, if it only works in "normal" times—but can't tell the difference between "normal" and "bubble"!?

Eugene Fama is an academic; he can perhaps be excused for holding some rather unrealistic, not to say outlandish, views. How about Alan Greenspan, "The Maestro" of the Fed, onetime EMT-fundamentalist but a realist par excellence, one might think? Well, no. From August 26, 1996 to June 1, 1999, Brooksley Born was Head of the Commodity Futures Trading Commission (CFTC), the Federal agency which oversees the futures and commodity options markets. When she tried not to regulate but just to look at the possible problems with derivatives she was explicitly blocked. At the prompting of Greenspan, Robert Rubin, Lawrence Summers and other Clinton administration figures, Congress explicitly curbed the CFTC's ability to regulate derivatives via the Commodity Futures Modernization Act of 2000 (Congress must have a Euphemism Office that comes up with these names...). So great was Greenspan's faith in the magic of free markets that he assured Born that Federal policing even of fraud is unnecessary, because the market will always detect it.[29] But everyone knows—Greenspan must have known—that when booms collapse, frauds are revealed by the dozens. (Recall Warren Buffett's naked swimmers.) Bernie Madoff is only the largest and most notorious boom-aided fraudster, but there have been many, many others. How efficient was the market in detecting *them*?

So we can't assume that money-making financial devices are ipso facto contributors to the common good. But Adair Turner's criticism and Keynes's reservations do suggest where we should look for a real measure of market efficiency. Not at navel-gazing market measures, but at the effect of market practices on society at large. Here is the *real* market efficiency. So how efficient *is* the financial sector?

It's not an easy question to answer because there is no well-defined measure of the common good, as I pointed out earlier. The glow of untold riches illuminating a "hot" financial marketplace also makes dispassionate analysis very difficult. Nevertheless, I think the answer is pretty clear when we look first at particular practices and then at the sector as a whole. It turns out that most financial innovations are subject to the malign hand, and growth in the financial sector goes along with the growth not of the economy but of social ills like third-world levels of income inequality.

Securitization I'll look again at two particular practices we've already encountered: securitization and credit-default swaps. Let's start with securitization: how dangerous is it, and what general benefits does it confer? Securitization is the selling on of real-estate mortgages or other interest-bearing instruments to an investment bank or a Federal agency that then combines them into bunches, layered according to risk. By a sort of magic,[30] many rather risky instruments, when bundled together, supposedly become "safe" or at least "safer." These bundles which, as we have seen, can be extremely complex in their structure, are then sold on to financial institutions, such as banks and pension funds, around the world that are looking for a reliable source of income.

The dangers of securitization, which have been known to some economists (but neglected by many others) for many years, are:

1. Severing the link between the entity that takes a risk from the entity that ultimately bears it. This is rather misleadingly called "information asymmetry" by economists but, as I've argued, more than just the comfortingly abstract notion of "information" is involved. Thus, the original mortgage writer, typically a local

bank or savings-and-loan, sells the mortgage to an investment bank, which then "securitizes" it. The buyer does not really know, and the seller does not really care, about the real risk associated with the mortgage. As I explained in Chapter 5, this worked well enough at first, because the local bank was still operating under the old rules. The bundled mortgages were based on solid evaluations of the borrowers' creditworthiness. But eventually, the new reinforcement contingencies began to kick in, house prices began to rise, apparently without end, the borrowers became less and less creditworthy and the sold-on securities became dodgier and dodgier. The process violates what should be a cardinal rule in financial markets: in general, *he who assumes (voluntary) risk should bear the risk.* (More on risk in a moment.)

2. The supposed safety of these bundles of mortgages rests on a key assumption: that the chances of default by each borrower are *uncorrelated*. If each risk is independent of the others, the average risk will obviously be much reduced. In other words, if John Smith defaults, that should have no effect on the default probability of another mortgage holder, Carol Carrera. And the chance that both John and Carol will be both subject to one of those unpredictable recessions that Eugene Fama talked about is also negligible. So, if A defaults that has no effect on B; and the chance that A and B are both affected by C (recession) is negligible. Notice that if the assumption of independence fails, if individual risks become correlated, the model not only fails, but the overall risk is much increased. The recent financial unpleasantness shows the assumption that individual mortgage risks are more or less independent of one another to be plausible only in the short run.

3. Size: the securitization process allowed hundreds, even thousands of debt instruments in the thousands of dollars to be combined in MBSs, CDOs and so on, each of which could be valued in the hundreds of millions. In the buildup to the recession, the process thus reached across continents, as financial institutions all over the world bought these things.

4. Securitization merely compounds the risk problems created by Point 1, above. A security that is just a bundle of other securities obviously suffers from the risk-severing I just mentioned. But it adds a malignancy all its own: *complexity*. People are not infinitely smart (remember?). They must buy CDOs largely on trust because they are not in a position to disentangle them. Distinguished economist Joseph Stiglitz comments: "The financial markets had created products so complex that even if all the details of them were known, no one could fully understand the risk implications."[31] I can add "although they thought they could." Stiglitz continues "The financial markets deliberately created complex products as a way to reduce effective transparency within the rules." Or, in plain English: they made things complicated to fool the customer.

Complexity is a Weapon It's worth noting that complexity is an important tool of the financial industry.[32] Not because it is necessary to market efficiency or anything of that sort. On the contrary, it probably impairs efficiency, properly measured. But it is mighty useful as a way to limit *competition*. Financial products are just numbers. You can't really brand them (a rating by a reputable agency, if such there be, is the closest to a brand) or offer them in different colors. They should be easy to compare—but they're not. Almost any financial instrument, from a home loan to a credit card, will be offered by different vendors in different forms. This complexity serves the interests of the vendor in two ways: it makes it hard for the buyer to even know how much he is actually paying. And, perhaps even more important, it makes it very difficult for the buyer to compare essentially equivalent products. If you're looking for a mortgage loan, for example, and the only ones on offer are fixed-interest rate for the same term, your choice is easy: you pick the one with the lowest rate. If collusion among vendors is prohibited, in such a competitive market loan-interest rates will be driven down to the lowest possible level. This is real "market efficiency"—but it is not pleasing to lenders. The incentive for them to come up with a range of more complex products, variable rates for different periods with various goodies tacked on (closing costs or even a sort of "cash back" included, for example), is high. This is often called giving the buyer "choice." The luxuriant efflorescence of this process in the credit card industry has even led to (somewhat feeble) attempts to restrain it through regulation, the most recent one being the Credit Card Act of 2009 that came into force in February 2010.

Vendors can offer a stronger defense for the noncomparability of many consumer goods (although even there it is hard to see sometimes: how real are the differences among washing machines or TV sets, for example?) But *caveat emptor* works well enough in this market because buying a washing machine or a TV has few knock-on effects. On the other hand, the complexity of financial products is much less defensible because the sums involved can grow almost without limit, so the effects of bad practices can affect the economy as a whole. The malign-hand potential is large. Unless a complex product—reinforcement schedule— can be shown to be, if not beneficial, at least not harmful, to the system as a whole, some thought should be given to controlling or even abolishing it.

Legislating simplicity has many pitfalls. Would you want to trust a government bureaucrat to know simple from complex? Check out the consequences of the so-called Paperwork Reduction Act of 1980: notice how much simpler Federal government forms and regulations have become since then (not!). Notice also the many new Federal jobs that have been created to enforce this act (see also the Economic Growth and Regulatory Paperwork Reduction Act of 1996). What should/can be done without exacerbating the problem or limiting people's freedom in an unconstitutional way?

The pharmaceutical industry is required to do clinical trials to establish the safety and efficacy of its potentially toxic products. There are problems with the slowness and cost of this system, of course: some government-required trials take years to complete and cost in the hundreds of millions of dollars, effectively blocking potentially beneficial drugs from the market. But the bad effects on the financial markets of similar inefficiencies are likely to be very much less—no one will fail to be cured of a fatal illness as a consequence of laggard regulators, for example. The world may survive quite well without another tricky financial product—although bankers may complain. On the other hand, we have certainly experienced recently the toxicity of many financial innovations. The rules I will propose in Chapter 12 will go a long way to eliminating many of these bad effects. Nevertheless, something like clinical trials is necessary for some aspects of the financial industry.

At the very least, the obscurity and complexity of financial products and agreements should be subject to some kind of check. Perhaps something as straightforward as giving citizens the right to petition for a simple empirical post facto comprehensibility test of financial agreements (credit card, mortgage, etc.) might work. If average-IQ citizens cannot understand the contract within a limited study-time related[33] to the amount of money at risk, then the agreement could be declared null and void. Psychometricians would be delighted to devise valid comprehension tests for this purpose. The requirement that products be easily and provably comprehensible would be a strong incentive for vendors to simplify and pre-test their agreements so that customers could not use a contract's demonstrable opacity to wriggle out of it.

So the potential costs associated with securitization are substantial; what about the benefits? The benefit to investment banks is clear: they derive fees from the bundles of securitized loans, the bigger the bundle, the larger the fee. (In fact, it's not really clear why the size of the fee should be proportional to the value of the deal. It takes much the same time to type six zeros as five, and the computer doesn't care how big the number is.) The benefit to buyers is less clear. MBSs were sold as relatively risk-free investments yielding a rate of return not much less than the average mortgage (the difference being the fees the bundling banks collect), but with much less risk. The law of averages, that great savior of financial markets, was supposed to make the overall return from a bunch of mortgages, each of which might be somewhat risky, a great deal less risky. And so it should if each risk is independent of the others. But if it is not, and if a substantial number of the bundled securities begin to go into default, the MBS holders have few options. It will be difficult or impossible to track back to the original borrowers to try to recoup some of their money.

So long as default rates remained low, MBSs provided an attractive risk/return combination—but they did so by violating a golden rule: under normal circumstances, once again, he who takes the risk should bear the risk. *This rule should be a bar to securitization in all its forms.* "What a blow to market efficiency!" cry the financiers. To which the proper response is a hollow laugh at the hollow concept of "market efficiency." Less dismissively, we can repeat Joseph Stiglitz's challenge: "It is not even clear that these new instruments were necessary.... no one has ever shown that the increased efficiency in risk-bearing that resulted [from derivatives] would ever come close to compensating the economy, and the taxpayer, for the damage that resulted." Absent such a proof, it's not clear that securitization should be permitted at all, especially as there are many other much less systemically risky means for diversification, such as mutual funds. If they don't yield quite as much as securitized instruments, so what? Stability has a (small) price, but the systemic savings may be much larger. Stiglitz concludes his devastating critique on a fatalistic note, saying "Securitization will not go away. It is part of the reality of a modern economy."[34] But I cannot for the life of me see why it should be, given the dangers it poses to the community as a whole.

The first step in the malign chain that ended with securitization was of course the practice of buying mortgages in bulk by Fannie and Freddie and others. This practice violates the golden rule—he who takes a (voluntary) risk should bear it. The ostensible aim, creating more mortgages for poor people, could have been achieved in many less risky ways. Doing nothing at all works pretty well, as the British experience attests. But if something must be done, the government could loan matching money, at low interest, equal to an agreed total of mortgage loans, to local banks. The banks would retain the mortgages and bear the losses of default. If a bank lent too generously, it would go bankrupt and be wound up by the FDIC in the usual way. Its shareholders, not the public, would take the major hit.

Credit Default Swaps Credit default swaps (CDSs) are another derivative that has come in for considerable criticism. The buyer of a CDS makes a series of payments to the seller for which he gets a payoff if a credit instrument (typically a bond or loan) defaults in some way. "Default" includes actual default but may also refer to some loss of creditworthiness by the bond issuer. Sounds like insurance, but CDSs have a couple of wrinkles that move them out of the regulatory corral of "real" insurance. First, you don't have to own the bond in order to buy a swap on it. These are called "naked" credit default swaps. This is quite different from regular insurance. I can't buy insurance on the life of a third party to whom I am not related, for example. I have to be at risk of a real loss—my wife, my house, my life—to be able to insure. The buyer must have a real "insurable interest." As I pointed out in Chapter 5, there is an obvious conflict-of-interest reason for this restriction (remember "insuranburn"?), which is violated by CDSs. The owner of a naked CDS has every incentive to damage the insured entity, a classic moral hazard. CDS are also completely unregulated, so no reserve funds are required. There is no open exchange for them—they involve totally private deals. The whole market has grown to massive proportions without any regulator really being fully aware of its extent.

On the positive side, CDSs offer a way of hedging risk—against default by mortgage-backed securities, for example. But is that always a good thing? It is a pervasive myth of financial markets that shedding, selling or insuring against risk is *always* good. Remember the boy Geithner saying: "By spreading risk more broadly, providing opportunities to manage and hedge risk, and making it possible to trade and price credit risk, credit market innovation should help make markets both more efficient and more resilient."[35] It is generally unquestioned in financial markets that what's good for *me*, the financial player, is ipso facto good for all. The market is *efficient* after all, isn't it? (Well, actually, no, that's a silly idea—but never mind.) The fact is that risk and return are two sides of the same coin. Both are essential properties of any purely financial instrument. "Shedding" the risk of a bond, say, is like buying a car without knowing its maintenance cost and gas mileage. If a bond is priced at a certain amount, which accurately reflects its risk-return ratio, and it becomes possible to insure against the risk, then the price is now wrong. The bond is too cheap and too many will be bought—a bubble.

Accepting risk is essential for markets to work properly. In the recent crash, the combination of CDSs and MBSs turned out to be an infernal conjunction, with one dodgy instrument, CDSs, apparently providing cover for another, MBSs. With the fig leaf of CDSs, investment banks could borrow more money and buy more MBSs than they would have been able to without them. Given this synergy, little wonder that both spiraled up into the tens of trillions of dollars before contributing to the Lehman flameout in 2008. This kind of thing should not happen after Dodd-Frank, many assumed. But it did, on a smaller but still shocking scale than at Lehman, at J.P. Morgan Chase in May 2012. Do you feel safer now?

The world before CDSs were invented in 1997 was prosperous. What have they added? What they and other derivatives seem to have contributed is two things: A false sense of security, and the ability to evade regulations limiting leverage. Instead of having to live with the default risk of (say) a company bond, it could apparently be insured against. The apparent mitigation of risk allowed more risk to be taken on and, when all goes well, more profit made. The animating philosophy is that risk is always bad, so any kind of insurance is always good. A popular cant phrase in the markets is that "risk should be assumed by those best able to bear it" as if financial markets were some kind of redistributive welfare state. Shedding risk is often another example of the malign hand: good for the individual, but not necessarily for the community as a whole. That is to say, if you buy a risky bond, default is bad for you. But if you are able to share that risk with the community, and if that risk and others like it is spread very widely, that is good for you but may be bad for the community, especially if this risk is eventually assumed involuntarily by innocent parties. Many honest citizens who had nothing whatever to do with the sub-prime market suffered grievously at its collapse. No one should be at risk as a consequence of avoidable actions of others. But that is what the $42.6 *trillion* outstanding-CDS market managed to achieve by June 2007.[36]

Involuntary and inevitable risk, such as the chance of death (life insurance), loss of property (home insurance), or chance of accident (auto insurance) is a legitimate target for insurance. Even some purely financial transactions are legitimate.

Companies that incur costs in nondollar currencies as part of some form of regular business have a legitimate interest in exchange-rate hedging with currency swaps, for example. People cannot avoid being exposed to these risks, and, absent fraud, they have no adverse motivation for precipitating an insurable outcome. Most people will not torch their houses to collect the insurance, and suicide is explicitly excluded by life-insurance policies. Clearly insurance of this sort represents an addition to the common good. But the number of involuntary risks to which we are subject is relatively limited.

The number of *voluntary* risks that people can take on is not limited, however. Making insurance available for voluntary financial choices means that the sky is the limit. Risk voluntarily borne disciplines choice. To the extent that voluntary risk becomes insurable, that discipline is removed—the reinforcement contingencies are changed in damaging ways. Risk shed by the individual is shared by the market as a whole. But the possibility of CDS-insurance for voluntary (as opposed to involuntary) financial choices removes the limit on the assumption of risk by the financial community as a whole, so the size of the shared risk rises without limit. CDSs are the malign hand—private gain = public loss—at work. They seem to have contributed to a bloated, debt-laden and intrinsically unstable, financial market that was bound eventually to crash.

An objection to my objection is that if the insurer assesses the risk accurately and prices the CDS accordingly, no one is getting something for nothing. How likely is it, in fact, that things like market risk can be accurately assessed? The problem is that the formulas CDS insurers use are all based on assumptions of no, or low, correlation among risks; and on the stability of statistics based on experience from the recent past that break down utterly in times of crisis, when defaults skyrocket. In other words, the insurance always fails when it is most needed. No matter. The real function of CDSs and their like is not really to insure, but to allow the buyer to evade reserve requirements and take on not less but more risk—with borrowed money. The buyers don't really care how much it costs, and so long as markets are stable, the insurers may not either. For a while, everyone makes money.

The fauna in the derivatives jungle are many and varied and, I suspect, mostly malign in their collective effects. I hope this account of two of the most popular will raise suspicions sufficiently to direct the public gaze at other cages in the derivatives zoo.

Size of the Financial Sector In addition to particular practices, we can also get an idea of the real value of financial innovation by looking at the economy as a whole. Does a large financial sector go along with an increase in general prosperity or not? In recent years, the financial sector has grown to an extraordinary size: in 2002 it absorbed a staggering 45 percent of U.S. domestic corporate profits, for example, a huge increase from an average of less than 16 percent from 1973 to 1985.[37] Is this growth a good thing, a bad thing, or irrelevant? Well, from 1960 to 1980,[38] inflation-adjusted GDP per capita, the conventional measure of national wealth, grew 63.3 percent, while the financial industry grew from 3.9 percent to 4.2 percent of GDP, an increase of just 7.7 percent. In other words, over those two decades, excellent growth went along with an almost constant-proportion financial sector. In contrast, after 1980 the financial sector grew rapidly: from 1980 to 2000, for example, it grew by 85.7 percent, from 4.2 percent of the economy to 7.8 percent. At the same time, GDP per capita increased by only 59 percent—less than in the prior 20 years. So, rapid financial-sector growth went along with average overall growth. (It's interesting that the slowdown in GDP per capita growth between 1980 and 2000 is almost equal to the increase in the financial sector over that period: growth rate declined by 4.3 percent, the financial sector increased by 3.6 percent.)

The story in the UK is much the same—the title of a recent article says it all: "The Contribution of the Financial Sector: Miracle or Mirage?" *The Economist's* Buttonwood column concludes that the problem is, in effect, positive feedback not real growth: "The financial industry has done so well for itself…because it has been given the license to make a [self-reinforcing] leveraged bet on property." [39] Even mainstream financial journalists, like *The New Yorker's* John Cassidy, are now writing articles with titles like "What Good is Wall Street?"[40]

Moreover, income inequality increased substantially over the second period, the Gini coefficient going from about .38[41] in 1960 to .403 in 1980 (not much change) and then to .467 in 2000, a substantial increase in inequality. So as we saw from a slightly different angle in Chapter 2, growth in the financial industry has been accompanied by a substantial increase in income inequality.

Correlation is not causation, as everyone knows, and there are debates about how much income inequality is acceptable. Nevertheless, it is much easier to argue that financial sector growth inhibits wealth creation in the rest of the economy than the reverse.

Agricultural employment didn't shrink from 41 percent of the population in 1900 to 1.9 percent in 2000[42] because people ate less. It shrank because farmers became more efficient. If the financial industry had become more efficient over time, if computers were used to speed financial calculations and reduce the number of accountants needed, the industry should also have shrunk mightily in relation to the rest of the economy. Has it? Far from it. Instead of using technology to speed up and simplify—as happened in agriculture and many other industries—finance used technology to complexify and baffle. Finance is a utility. By itself it produces nothing. (Perhaps that's why it is now the custom to label financial instruments as "products"!) It's just supposed to allocate resources efficiently to where they are most needed. But the fact that almost half the industrial profits in the U.S. went to the financial industry in recent years is like finding that half the costs of the airline industry go to the air-traffic controllers. Given the vast increases in information-processing capacity over the past 30 years, most white-collar industries have reduced their total cost. Finance alone has not. Why? Because the new computing power has been used not to streamline but to amplify, justify and complexify. Clever computer models, profitable in the short term but useless, malign and self-canceling in the long term, have allowed the creation of, and provided justification for, a swarm of complex new financial products that contribute to systemic instability and whose social value is almost certainly negative.

Finance is less efficient, *really* efficient, and absorbs more of our national wealth, than it did 20 years ago. It also wastes human capital.

For example, in 1970 only about 5 percent of Harvard graduates went on to work in finance; by 1990 that figure had tripled, to 15 percent— that's 10 percent of Harvardies who did *not* become doctors or scientists or start new businesses or work in manufacturing or some other part of the "real" economy.[43] The situation by 2007 was worse: *47* percent of Harvard graduates entered finance or consulting (although after the crash, in 2009, the figure dropped to a still-high 20 percent).[44] Economist Raghuram Rajan has recently made a strong case for the point that growing income inequality in the U.S. is partly attributable to a shortage of skilled workers.[45] Well, we have the skilled people, they're just working in finance rather than something more generally productive like engineering or product design.

It hard to see the current crisis as anything but a gigantic, if unconscious, fraud perpetrated by the financial industry on society at large. I say "unconscious" because most of the actors are apparently devout, albeit self-serving, believers in what might be called the First Church of the Efficient Market, doing "God's work," their rectitude proved by their swelling bottom lines. "When I took over at the FSA [the Financial Services Authority, the UK's equivalent of the SEC] … It was clear to me that I had been appointed high priest of a particular religious cult," said Adair Turner at the INET conference, April 9, 2010. But it's a huge fraud nevertheless.

The malign hand, in the various forms I have described, has been allowed free rein in bloated and dangerous financial markets. Given the now-obvious perils the sector poses to the economy as a whole, there is every reason to attend to its flaws and do whatever is necessary to rectify them. If, as a consequence, the financial sector is forced to shrink, no one should shed a tear. Both liberal and conservative economists now agree that would be a good thing. Paul Krugman writes[46]: "I think there are two big structural changes that we'd want to see. One is we need to reduce the role of the financial sector in the economy. We went from an economy in which about 4 percent of GDP came from the financial sector to an economy in which 8 percent of GDP comes from the financial sector, and in which at its peak 41 percent of profits were being earned by the financial sector. And there is no reason to believe that anything productive happened as a result of all of that. These extremely highly compensated bankers were essentially just finding new ways to offload risks on to other people." One-time Republican strategist Kevin Phillips has laid out a similar thesis in several books and articles arguing against what he calls the "financialization" of America.[47] A British commentator refers to the need to "break finance's stranglehold" on the U.S. economy.[48] Everyone but its beneficiaries seems to agree that the U.S. financial sector needs to be reined in. Shrinking the financial sector will have few societal costs and will yield substantial benefits. The next two chapters look at more ways to tackle the problem.

11

Financial Markets are Different, II: Risk and Competition

What can be done to fix the financial markets? Before I get to some more answers to this question, I need to say more about a couple of remaining issues: the difficult topic of *risk* and the too-big-to-fail problem and what it can tell us about the uncompetitive nature of financial markets.

Risk Risk is usually defined in terms of the probabilities of gain and loss. The expected value of a given gamble is the probability (p) multiplied by the amount (V) of potential gain minus probability (q) multiplied by the amount (L) of potential loss: $EV = pV - qL$. For example, if you bet $10 to win 20 on a single throw of a die, your value at risk is 10, your expected gain is 1/6 times 20 = 3.33 and your expected loss 5/6 times 10 = 8.33. The expected value of this (bad) bet is therefore $3.33 - 8.33 = -5$. To p, V, q and L, must be added the time, t, at which the payoff (loss or gain) can occur. p, V, etc. are pretty straightforward, but time is much harder to incorporate in a formal way.

Real risks come in four main forms, most more complicated than this example. It's helpful to give them names and bring them all together in one place. Here is a list starting with the simplest:

- numerical risk (*N-risk*). This is the least interesting kind of risk, the kind involved in games of chance like roulette or a coin toss. The *sample space*, number of alternative outcomes (2 or 37), the chances of winning and losing ($\frac{1}{2}$ and $\frac{1}{2}$, or $\frac{1}{36}$ vs. $\frac{36}{37}$), and the time at which the payoff occurs are all exactly known. No financial product involves risk exactly like this.

- numerical risk with indefinite odds (*I-risk*). This is the risk involved in betting on horse races or sporting contests. You know the number of players, that someone will win, and when, but there is no objective way to assess the probability of a win by any particular team or horse. The bookie's odds are simply guesses, tuned by the pattern of bets—the odds shorten as more people bet on a given horse.

- *Options* are derivatives that present a sort of I-risk. In a *put* option, for example, a buyer agrees, for a fee (the price of the put), to buy a stock from the purchaser of the put at a certain "strike" price within a certain period of time. Both the amount and the exact time at which the seller might win are uncertain: if the stock price goes up throughout the period, he will not exercise the option and just loses his fee. On the other hand, if the price of the stock declines below the strike price, the put owner can sell and make the difference as profit.

- actuarial risk (*A-risk*). This is the kind of risk involved in life and property insurance. Given the individual's age, sex and perhaps lifestyle, mortality risk, for example, can be accurately assessed from mortality statistics. The underlying assumptions are: (1) That the state of the world will not change in a way that makes statistics based on the past invalid, i.e., no unusual wars, earthquakes, hurricanes, epidemics or advances in medicine will occur. And (2) that there will be no effect of insurance on the event that is insured against: your life expectancy should not depend on whether or not you have life insurance, for example. The appropriate regulatory rule is that the probability of the insured-against event should be independent of the existence and extent of insurance against it.

Or, to use slightly different language, there should be no positive feedback (more insurance → more risk) between the amount of insurance that people take out and the risk that is insured against. Negative feedback, the more insurance the less actual risk, would be OK. But in the real world positive feedback is much more likely: the more insurance the more actual risk.

- unmeasureable risk (*U-risk*). This is Knight's "uncertainty" or the "unknown unknowns" of Mr. Rumsfeld. Many of the new financial products are presented as if they involve A-risk but they really involve U-risk. Both securitization and credit default swaps, for example, assume that the risk of default on mortgages or other financial instruments can be computed in actuarial fashion. But it cannot. The risk even of a single mortgage is at best an A-risk, but often a U-risk. The best you can do in computing the risk of mortgage default is to measure the creditworthiness of the borrower and look at past default histories of people with that credit rating. But this method assumes that housing prices, employment, etc., will all continue on their historical trajectory, which of course they may not. The collective risk associated with hundreds of sub-prime mortgages, with bad or even unknown credit histories for the borrowers, is even harder to assess. Financial crises can neither be predicted nor reliably identified until after the fact—so CDSs cannot exclude them as regular property insurance can exclude natural disasters. Financial engineering tools like the Black-Scholes model take a small sample of the past and then use clever math to come up with the chance of gain or loss for a bond or company stock. The models tend to ignore "tail risk", i.e., a higher probability of extreme events than predicted by the normal distribution. Like life insurance, their key assumption is that the statistical future will be like the past. Unlike life insurance, this assumption is only true for periods of time that are usually brief and always undefined. Black-Scholes–based Long-Term Capital Management collapsed after just four years, for example.[1]

A major reason the models fail is that the very existence of instruments like credit-default swaps allows bankers to take on risk they would otherwise have avoided. In other words, the existence of "insurance" *did* have an effect on the insured risk—CDSs represent U-risk with positive feedback, not A-risk with zero feedback. Securitization and credit-default swaps both violate what should be a firm regulatory rule: that the existence of insurance and the probability of the insured-against event should be strictly independent of one another.

Voluntary and Involuntary Risk Cutting across these four categories is the distinction between voluntary and involuntary risk. *Involuntary risk* is the kind for which standard insurance was devised: mortality, accident, property, etc. Everyone is forced to assume these risks; their only choice is whether or not to insure against loss. Everyone also has to park their savings somewhere: loss of savings is therefore an involuntary risk. Hence, FDIC bank and money-market insurance is perfectly justifiable, although there is no reason it should be subsidized by government. So also, to a degree is health insurance. Cargo insurance, and derivatives such as futures used to limit exposure to price rises in commodities such as wheat, oil and gas, are an intermediate case. A producer or purchaser of wholesale goods owns them for their intrinsic value. Insurance against loss, either in a warehouse or in transit, is part of his cost of doing business but not part of the business itself. A shipment of cars, for example, is in a very different category than a financial security where the acceptance of risk is an *intrinsic part* of the business. So is a futures market designed to smooth out price fluctuations in essential commodities (to the extent that these fluctuations are not themselves a product of market instability). Insurance or hedging via derivatives for voluntarily assumed risk of the trade type poses no new problems.

But risk in the financial market is accepted *voluntarily* not as a consequence of some other line of business. You *choose* to buy a bond, stock or derivative; you are not forced to do so in the course of living or engaging in some nonfinancial enterprise. The risk associated with purchase of a security is an essential feature of a sound financial industry. It provides the discipline—the appropriate reinforcement contingency—that maintains price at a reasonable level, balancing chance of gain against risk of loss.

So what does it mean to *insure* against voluntary risk, as credit-default swaps purport to do? The naïve onlooker might well ask: if you need to insure against it, why take on the risk in the first place? There are several answers. Perhaps the most important is that by apparently offsetting some risk, the investor is free to take on more. This seems to be the main reason people go in for these things.

But there is another possibility. People buy insurance-like products as part of an investment plan that is designed to make money. So let's see whether CDSs and the like really do make money for buyers. There are two possibilities: either the seller of the CDS correctly prices the risk of the insured security (bond, stock, CDO, or whatever), or he does not. If he has it right,[2] then the buyer of the CDS must lose by the amount of profit the CDS seller makes, just as the average-risk homeowner in the long run loses by buying insurance. The homeowner's premium must match the expected value (probability times amount) of his loss, *plus* the costs and profit of the insurer. So why does the homeowner do it? Because having a place to live is essential, so that home ownership represents an involuntary risk and the loss of your home is more than most people can afford to bear—especially if there is a mortgage involved. Not so with bond ownership. You aren't forced to acquire any financial "product." If you can't afford to lose it, you shouldn't buy it in the first place; just put your money in government bonds or an FDIC-insured account.

Conclusion: If the CDS is correctly priced, it should be unprofitable for the buyer and there should be no market for it. If you are at average risk or better and can afford a loss (i.e., you're rich, or the risk was taken voluntarily) then you should self-insure, not buy insurance. Warren Buffett probably does not have home insurance on his modest house, for example. Is it possible, then, that CDSs and similar insurance-like products are *underpriced* and that's why people buy them? If they are, then of course they are a good deal for the buyer but not, by definition, for the seller. So they are probably not underpriced.

CDS are probably correctly priced, which means they should be a bad deal for a banker who is taking a voluntary risk. But CDSs nevertheless found a huge market. Why? Why would a banker buy a correctly priced CDS? There are two reasons: One is *leverage*. CDSs are used to insure securities bought with borrowed money, like a home on a mortgage. In this case, although the risk assumed is voluntary, the speculator cannot afford a loss because he is risking borrowed money. If the insurance costs less than the expected gain from the gamble, it's a good buy. The second, and possibly most important, reason for buying CDS insurance is because *it allows bankers to get round regulatory limits on leverage*. If the banker can say he has insured against some risk, then the rules will allow him to take on more. CDSs were a smash hit because they allowed the banking community to take bigger gambles.

There is another odd thing about this whole process. Investors buy CDSs to allow them to insure bonds (say) that they have bought with borrowed money: A, insured by B, borrows from C in order to lend to (buy a bond from) D. But why doesn't D borrow directly from C? What useful functions do A and B perform in all this? Does this look like an "efficient" process? The answer, of course, is that this process is efficient only in the generation of revenue for A and B.

U-risk derivatives all involve voluntary risk. Insurance against voluntary risk *should always be an exception rather than the rule* because: (1) insuring against voluntary risk relaxes the normal market discipline on buyers. (2) The existence of such insurance *does* affect the risk to the insured entity (i.e., it violates the "insuranburn" rule). And (3) the unlimited nature of voluntarily assumed risks means that the effects of insurance can grow almost without limit, affecting markets as a whole. Voluntary risk is also systemic risk.

These aspects of financial risk are so fundamental it is really quite incredible that they seem to form no part of current regulatory thinking. In Treasury Secretary Timothy Geithner's 4,700-word presentation on risk regulation to the House Financial Services Committee on March 26, 2009, for example, the word "incentive" occurs just once, in connection with executive compensation—and "feedback" occurs not at all. To be fair, he did use the word "procyclical," which implies positive feedback, but in a way that assumes that there is some kind of regular cycle, and that we know what part of the cycle we are in. But history shows that the "business cycle" is so irregular that the term "cycle" is a stretch, and that in any case we almost never know exactly where we are in it. Secretary Geithner also said that "[new regulatory] rules must...produce a more stable system...that rewards innovation..." apparently assuming, despite the markets that lay in ruins around him, that all financial innovation is beneficial. It would be more accurate to say that all recent financial innovation has been dangerous. But we can be grateful that at least he seems to care about stability.

Competition, Too Big to Fail and those Bumper Banker Bonuses In late 2009, in the middle of the recession, we learned that Citigroup, which has survived in part through direct government aid as well as general support of the financial system, may "let go" one Andrew Hall, who is owed $100 million as "his cut of [$2-billion worth of] profits from a characteristically aggressive year of bets in the oil market."[3] Citigroup is embarrassed to seem ungrateful for the benefits it has received from taxpayers, not to mention its apparent insensitivity to their fortunes, which have been less good than Mr. Hall's. They would like to renege on the deal. Mr. Hall, a forceful chap by all accounts, doubtless feels that it ain't luck, he made the buck, so what the *@#&! But the key question is, where do all these bazillions of dollars, first of profit and then in remuneration—where do they actually come from? Is the "value added" by such as Mr. Hall real value? Or is it a side-effect of some kind of conscious or unconscious market rigging?

Well, these profits come from bets made with borrowed money, of course. That's one problem—a problem that can be solved by banning certain kinds of bets, as I will show in a moment. But there is another problem with financial markets—they aren't really competitive. Nobel-winning experimental physicist Percy Bridgman in the early part of the twentieth century came up with the concept of an operational definition as a way to force scientists to be precise about their terms. The idea is that you need to define any scientific concept in terms of some empirical test. For example, weight is defined by the operation of weighing on a standard scale against a standard comparison, an inch is defined by matching with a standard ruler, and so on. A concept is just the set of operations necessary to measure it.

Operational definitions are not used in economics, probably because it has until very recently not been an experimental science. By its very nature, *macroeconomics*, the bit that deals with economies as a whole, can never be truly experimental. Nevertheless, an operational definition or two might be helpful. Take the term *competitive market*, for example. It is usually defined in terms that amount to a theory of its operation. For perfect competition, there must be an infinite number of buyers and sellers, no entry or exit barriers, perfect information (we've encountered that one before), costless transactions, homogeneous products and perfect profit maximization. By these criteria, no market is perfectly competitive. But, obviously, some markets are sort of competitive. How shall we identify them? Well, how about looking at the opposite of a competitive market, namely, *monopoly*. If a market is not monopolistic, then it must be sort of competitive, mustn't it?

Unfortunately, monopolies are not defined operationally either: "a monopoly exists when a specific individual or an enterprise has sufficient control over a particular product or service to determine significantly the terms on which other individuals shall have access to it."[4] Again, a theory of operation. And how do we know who is really controlling/causing what? The definition doesn't give an answer.

Well, here's an operational definition of competition. If a market is competitive, injury to one firm should *increase* the profitability of those that remain.

We can't go out and injure one company just to see the effect on others, of course. But once in a while there are "natural experiments" where one company is harmed for some extraneous reason that lets us look at the effect on the market as a whole. The troubles of the Toyota Motor Co. in 2010 constitute a natural experiment for the auto industry.[5] Its effects could not be clearer: Toyota's woes were a joy to its competitors. Headlines like this were the rule: "Ford sales leap 43 percent in February as Toyota's drop 9 percent amid recall woes."[6] Some pessimists predicted that Toyota's problems would have a bad effect on the industry as a whole,[7] but the main effects on Toyota's competitors were all positive. Clearly car manufacture *is* a competitive industry.

But the financial industry is not. It has also been the subject of a couple of natural experiments recently. The first was the federally enabled purchase of about-to-go-bankrupt Bear Stearns by JP Morgan Chase for a derisory $10 per share in March 2008.[8] The fear was that the failure of Bear Stearns, far from strengthening its competitors, would threaten the whole industry—even though Bear Stearns was by no means the largest investment bank at the time. The Feds were right to be concerned. The confirmation came a few months later when much larger bank Lehman Brothers filed for Chapter 11 bankruptcy protection on September 15, 2008, after the Federal government failed to engineer a similar private takeover. The result was not whoops of joy by supposed competitors Goldman Sachs or Morgan Stanley, but wails of anguish and an industry-wide crisis. The too-big-to-fail firms of the financial industry *do not* compete with one another.

Not everyone agrees that these banks were too big to fail. For example. Joseph Stiglitz writes: "I actually think that all of this discussion about too-big-to-be-restructured banks was just a ruse… based on fear mongering…a tool to extract as much as possible for the banks and the bankers that had brought the world to the brink of economic ruin."[9] If Stiglitz is right, the argument for shrinking these companies is even stronger.

But surely Wall Street is competition personified, I hear you cry? These "masters of the universe" work long hours and compete ruthlessly. A firm will give those great "retention bonuses" so as not to lose good people to its competitors. How can you possibly say that these firms are not competitive? Well, competition among *individuals* is not the same thing as a competitive *industry*. The real estate guys in David Mamet's powerful 1982 play *Glengarry Glen Ross* competed with each other alright; but they all worked for the same firm. Pontiac (when there was a Pontiac) competed with Oldsmobile (likewise) and Chevrolet. But the failure of Oldsmobile was a sign of weakness in General Motors not a source of strength. The failure of Lehman Brothers had bad effects that reverberated throughout what is in effect one large company: the investment banking industry. That's one take-home from the financial crisis.

The fact that the financial industry is in effect a monopoly also provides a clue to another kind of take-home: the obscenely large pay packets of financiers. In highly competitive, mature industries, like airlines or automobiles, profits and bonuses are relatively modest. What we should be concerned about, therefore, is not the fact that bankers make huge amounts of money, but the monopolistic, hence relatively unproductive, nature of the industry that allows them to do so. By 2011 the noncompetitive nature of the banking industry was becoming apparent at least to some observers. Philosophically inclined (he has spent some time studying theology) Paul Myners, one-time chief executive of the UK retail giant Marks and Spencer and former Financial Services Secretary, was asked about the banker-bonus problem. He responded: "It's in significant part because the banking industry is insufficiently competitive and is therefore able to earn high returns on equity [termed *rents* by economists]...The baking, grocery, hotel and engineering sectors don't have problems with bonuses because they're not generating excess returns which allow rents to be paid."[10]

The other factor, of course, is OPM—"other people's money." Only the financial industry (with the collusion of the Federal Reserve) can in effect create money through leverage. These two together—leverage and lack of real competition—make a toxic mix that allows for huge profits and equally huge losses. The problem is that the profits go to just a few players in the financial industry, but the losses are delayed and shared—shared eventually by society as a whole—the malign hand, big time.

Andrew Carnegie, Thomas Edison and Bill Gates all made tons of money. But few resent them, because they left behind productive real industries that employ thousands of people and make everyone richer. But what do we have to show for the $33.8M that Jimmy Cayne, bridge-playing CEO of dead-man-walking Bear Stearns, got in 2006, or the $40.5M that Dick Fuld, CEO of likewise-situated Lehman

Brothers, got in the same year? Not to mention "impish" Lloyd Blankfein, CEO of Goldman Sachs, who got $54.72M, Chuck O'Neal (Merrill Lynch) at $48M, John Mack (Morgan Stanley) at $41.41M, and so on through a string of eight-figure payouts to CEOs of other financial firms that would be rubble without the coerced munificence of the U.S. taxpayer in propping up tottering financial markets. Misplaced munificence, I would add, since in a properly designed financial system, these folk, rather than the rest of us, would have had to pay for their own lost bets.

Fans of the financial markets will point out that much of the financial bailout money has been repaid—and the markets were saved! True enough, but if Bernie Madoff had asked for, and received, big enough loans from the Federal government his Ponzi scheme also might have held up for a few more years. It remains to be seen whether the Federal bailout has really revived the economy (Keynes wins) or has just propped up a nationwide Ponzi scheme for a few more years (we all eventually lose).

The enormous sums paid to leading investment bankers are dwarfed by the eye-watering payouts to a handful of successful hedge funds in recent years. In 2009, not a great year for most people, the 25 top-earning hedge fund *managers* were paid a collective $25.33 *billion*,[11] an amount sufficient to take care of the 2009 budget shortfalls of California, Massachusetts, North Carolina and Idaho.[12] The *lowest* paid guy got a measly $350 million (still enough to take Louisiana out of the red).

But these big wins were not directly funded by the government, so what's your problem! True, but not relevant: these guys won by betting, with copious amounts of other people's money, that the government would in fact rescue the rest of the financial industry. So the government was indeed involved.

The U.S. financial industry has grown bloated beyond most people's imagining. In 1978, for example, all commercial banks held assets equal to 53 percent of GDP; by the end of 2007 this had risen to 84 percent. If investment banks are included, the whole financial sector by the end of 2007 held debt equal to *259* percent of GDP.[13]

Where does all this money come from? It's hard to figure out where the Brobdingnagian profits of financial firms in recent years, and the bonuses that go with them, are really coming from. No amount of "efficient resource allocation"—even supposing such a thing could be accurately measured—can possibly be worth 45 percent of all commercial profits in one year, as was the case in 2002. The answer is that the bloated profits of the financial industry actually come from the *future*—the huge losses that all suffer when the financial bubble finally bursts. In other words, what the few receive as huge payouts *now*, the many suffer as debt that must be paid in the future—paid by mortgage or credit card defaults, or via higher taxes when the system collapses or, most likely, by inflation of the dollar. Every financial boom is like a wastrel buying a mansion he can never afford—a lethal mortgage on the nation's future. The financial industry is the worst example of the malign hand in the last 50 years.

In a properly regulated, malign-hand-free, and truly competitive system, with an industry as devoid of truly productive innovation as the financial industry over the past decade or two, such huge profits would simply not be possible. Without these monopoly- and debt-fueled profits, the much-criticized bonus incentives in finance would be largely irrelevant. The profits, not the bonus formulas, are the real problem.

If the industry can be made truly competitive—and the test would be: does major firm A smile or weep when major firm B is in trouble?— no firm would be too big to fail, and gargantuan payouts would simply be impossible.

How did the Financial Industry Become a Monopoly? The International Monetary Fund spends most of its time dealing with failed economies, experience that is unfortunately very relevant to the current situation in the U.S. Economists expert in this area, such as Joseph Stiglitz, Carmen Reinhhart and Kenneth Rogoff, Raghuram Rajan, and Niall Ferguson, tend to have similar diagnoses about what is wrong with the U.S. financial system. For example, the IMF's one-time chief economist Simon Johnson, in his compelling piece *The*

Quiet Coup,[14] sees the current problem in the U.S. as largely political. The U.S., says Johnson, is in effect a financial oligarchy:

> Over the past decade, the attitude took hold that what was good for Wall Street was good for the country. The banking-and-securities industry has become one of the top contributors to political campaigns, but at the peak of its influence, it did not have to buy favors the way, for example, the tobacco companies or military contractors might have to. Instead, it benefited from the fact that *Washington insiders already believed that large financial institutions and free-flowing capital markets were crucial to America's position in the world.* [my italics]

Growth in financial firms was thought to be always good, there have always been many firms, and so antitrust objections were never raised. Johnson argues that faith in the financial markets—"what was good for Wall Street was good for the country"—became the conventional wisdom among politicians of both parties. This attitude allowed successive regulatory relaxations to increase greatly the volume of financial transactions on which money could be made.[15] The comparable transition in 1986 in the UK took place so rapidly it has come to be known as "the Big Bang." I believe that it is this increase in transactions that by itself has welded the financial markets into one large monopoly.

The reason is that financial transactions are not like transactions in normal markets. The technology industry provides a sort of parallel. In 1980, Bill Gates beat out the much more computer-savvy Gary Kildall (1942–1994), then head of Digital Research, a hugely successful pioneer in the nascent microcomputer industry, to provide the operating system for IBM's new PC, the opening act in the history of a vast new industry. Although it was less well developed than CP/M, Kildall's system (indeed, Kildall always claimed that Gates had stolen parts of his program), Gates's business acumen ensured that successive versions of Microsoft's DOS and then Windows operating system soon captured 80 percent or more of the ever-growing PC market. Despite numerous criticisms, and competition from Apple, whose system has at various times been better, or much better, than Windows,[16] Windows continues to dominate. The reason is a familiar one in the tech world: a given product gains added value as its share of the market increases. The more people who use it, the more useful it becomes. This positive feedback absolutely ensures that any industry subject to it will soon be dominated by a single firm, unless government takes steps to prevent it. But government is often deterred from doing so, because of the obvious benefits to uniformity. The U.S. is probably better off being dominated by a single set of software that allows workers to shift easily from one computer to another rather than having to buy or learn a new system every time they change jobs. So, given that the financial industry is a sort of monopoly, we can be pretty confident that some sort of positive feedback is involved.

Of course, now that computer software, and the market for new hardware, appears to be plateauing, Microsoft has a problem. Rather than buying the new version, people would just like to keep copying their old software—which would put the company out of business. In response, Microsoft (like many other software manufacturers) tries to limit copying and keeps changing its software—the Aladdin's-lamp strategy. As people learn the new, they forget how to use the old, so that eventually it becomes behaviorally, if not electronically, incompatible with the latest version. I can think of no reason other than this "behavioral obsolescence" for Microsoft's drastic menu changes to Word in 2003, for example.

But no single financial firm "ha[d] sufficient control over a particular product or service to determine significantly the terms on which other individuals shall have access to it," did it? Well, to some extent this happens. Complexification of financial products has led to specialization by different firms, each selling its own portfolio of financial tricks. Firms have thus become more like divisions of one company than true competitors. But there are stronger forces also at work.

As we have seen, competition is defined by a firm's effect on its competitors. Eliminating one large investment bank, far from strengthening the rest, weakened them. By this critical test, financial markets are not competitive. So how *do* they do it? The answer is both political and economic. The economic answer is: basically, they do it by taking in each other's washing. The buzzword is "interconnectedness." The quote from Scott and Taylor in Chapter 5 showed how thousands of residential mortgages can be repeatedly bundled, sliced and diced and rebundled many times, to diffuse risk across the financial markets of the world. As these new products were invented, ways to create debt were found to allow them to be purchased. It seems to be this interlinking that gives the financial market the character of a monopoly. Control over the market is exerted by the positive feedback between the creation of new financial products, financed by leverage, and the prices for which they can be sold. Each new product does not take away from the collective wealth but, via leverage, the ratio of debt to equity (cash), adds to it. And the growth of leverage has been staggering. On June 30, 2008, just before the crash, huge European bank ING had a leverage ratio of 48.8, Barclays Bank was 61.1, and so on for all the others. The median (middle) leverage ratio in Europe was 45, in the U.S. 35[17]—compared with historical ratios of 5 to 20. As leverage increased in recent years, the amount of money in the markets increased and, just like the housing market, everybody got richer.

So each new product is more or less self-financing: the more products, the more debt; the more debt, the more products—positive feedback. A steady flow of new financial gimmicks, CDOs, CDSs and so on, each yielding a bounty of new debt and new business, keeps everybody happy. The only competition is between individuals for bigger and bigger bonuses, all drawn from a swelling gusher of manufactured profits.

The political answer convincingly proposed by Simon Johnson is that the U.S. has a financial oligarchy rather like Russia's. There is less overt corruption because (he argues) the oligarchs—the big banks—are essentially pushing at an open door. When, in a crisis precipitated by a Fed-enabled tsunami of debt, they plead that bailouts are essential to save the country, everybody believes them. Even more usefully, judging by the memoirs of Goldman's Henry Paulson (then

Treasury Secretary), they believe it themselves. I'm reminded of the Goldwynism about acting: "Sincerity is the key; once you fake that, you've got it made." Yet Christian Scientist Paulson was surely sincere when he wrote (heartrendingly!) in his autobiography[18] that at the height of the crisis "I stood under the harsh bathroom lights, staring at the small [sleeping] pill in the palm of my hand. Then I flushed it—and the contents of the entire bottle—down the toilet. I longed for a good night's rest. For that, I decided, I would rely on prayer, placing my trust in a Higher Power."

But God helps those who help themselves. The "Higher Power" that Paulson had in mind turned out to be the U.S. government. Paulson hijacked the taxpayers of America. In a move condemned at first equally by left and right[19] (and still condemned by a majority of the American people) the government, controlled by men mostly on loan from Wall Street, like Paulson himself, was receptive. So generous were the terms of Paulson's first bailout, on October 13, 2008, signed on to by nine major banks, that Vikram Pandit, CEO of Citigroup, apparently exclaimed, "This is very cheap capital!"[20]

Though at first rejected by Congress, pretty soon the bailouts were flowing freely. Simon Johnson concludes: "Paulson, a former CEO of Goldman Sachs, was pushing free money at his former colleagues....an extraordinary gift from the government, on behalf of taxpayers, to the financial sector."[21] Happy days, if not quite here again, are at least on the horizon—or so we are led to believe. And that wasn't Henry's only gift from the taxpayers: "When Paulson joined the Bush administration in July 2006, he was exempted from paying capital-gains tax on the sale of his half-billion dollar holdings of Goldman stock, which presumably saved him (and cost the taxpayer), at least $100 million."[22]

It's impossible to say for certain whether the successive financial industry bailouts under presidents Bush and Obama were the proper response to the crisis of '07–8. On the one hand, they apparently averted a much more severe disaster—certainly for Wall Street, not-so-certainly for Main Street. Wall Street would certainly have suffered much more without the various bailouts. On the other hand, it is less certain that Main Street would have been worse off than it actually is, with unemployment figures still, in 2011, well above original estimates. Nor is it certain the recovery in the long run will be swifter after the bailouts than if more fiscally responsible measures had been taken.

What would have been the alternative? Well, at other times, other solutions seem to have worked better. For example, *The Economist* reminded its readers recently of what happened in the UK in 1981:

> Deficit hawks might point to another British parallel, the 1981 budget, in which Margaret Thatcher's government unveiled an austerity package in the middle of a recession. *A group of 364 economists (including the present governor of the Bank of England) signed a letter to the Times newspaper denouncing the government's folly.*
>
> To the economists, Mrs. Thatcher's approach was positively antediluvian. Had not the Depression taught that attempts to balance the budget would only worsen an economic downturn? Yet the British economy, far from relapsing into slump, enjoyed a prolonged boom for the rest of the 1980s. (my italics)[23]

So much for the collective wisdom of economists! Of course, Britain's situation in 1981 was different in many ways from the United States' in 2008—devaluation was then an option which may happen in the U.S., but is certainly not desired by Americans. As of May 2011, the dollar was showing signs of strain, however. If you're a "world citizen", like so many of our *bien pensants*, rather than a mindless patriot, dollar devaluation has many attractions. A real difference is that interest rates have no room to fall here as they did in the UK.

But, interestingly, the 1981 example is not unique. Thomas Woods has pointed out that another previous depression, the crash of 1920—"the crash you never heard of"—was handled very differently. Far from being stimulated, the economy was inhibited—the deficit hawks were in control—yet the depression ended swiftly.

The first year of the 1920 depression was worse than the first year of the 1929 Great Depression: production was down by 21 percent, GDP by 24 percent and unemployment went from 4 to 12 percent within a year.[24] But within two years, the depression was over. What happened? What happened was the opposite of what happened in 2008–9. First, in 1919–20 President Woodrow Wilson suffered a series of strokes that largely incapacitated him. Their effects were concealed from the public until 1923, well after the end of his term. He was able to do little in 1920. During this period his forceful wife Edith seems to have been the power behind the throne. In 1921, the new President Warren G. Harding (not many people's favorite president!) was elected and promptly cut both taxes and spending drastically, reasoning that high taxes and high spending were the source of the problem. Spending was cut 22 percent in 1921 and 36 percent in 1922. The Fed did not begin open-market operations until 1922, so it provided no "stimulus." In other words, Harding did the opposite of what was done in 1929 and what is being done even more vigorously now. Yet within two-and-a-half years, the economy was back on track.

Would a similar strategy have worked better with the recession of 2007–8? No one can say for sure. But given that all agree excessive debt creation was the source of the recession, it does seem at least questionable that the creation of yet more debt is the solution. It may in fact delay recovery, as many, including even FDR's friend and Secretary of the Treasury Henry Morgenthau, allege of Herbert Hoover's and FDR's similar response to the Great Depression. In May 1939, after ten years of depression, Morgenthau told Congress:

> We have tried spending money. We are spending more than we
> have ever spent before and it does not work. And I have just one
> interest, and if I am wrong…somebody else can have my job.
> I want to see this country prosperous. I want to see people get a job.
> I want to see people get enough to eat. We have never made good
> on our promises…I say after eight years of this Administration we
> have just as much unemployment as when we started…And an
> enormous debt to boot![25]

The conventional view of the Great Depression is that FDR cured it, through government spending. In the words of one recent commentator, he "drove unemployment down from 25 percent to 15 percent [!] during the '30s using this recipe." The alternative view—that World War II ended the Great Depression is true "only because the war required the government to raise money to build the infrastructure for war..."[26]

This is a common view of the cause and cure of the Great Depression, but it needs a little unpacking. First, the reduction in unemployment from 25 percent to 15 percent during FDR's tenure stills leaves it at ludicrously high levels. If FDR prescribed a cure, it was only slightly better than the disease. WWII did the job, though, reducing unemployment drastically, from 14.2 percent in 1940 to 4.7 percent in 1942.

But...living standards declined during the war. Even though GDP rose, personal consumption fell (see Figure 11-1)[27]. No new cars were made, few new houses and appliances, etc.—which just shows how misleading GDP can be as a measure of living standards. Government can, in a pinch, keep people employed, at least for a while. But it cannot make them richer.

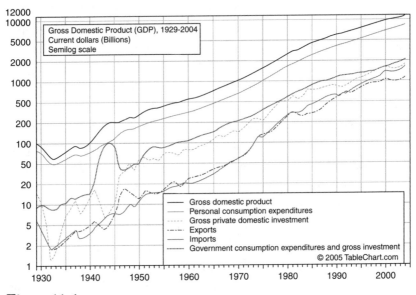

Figure 11-1

In retrospect, it is pretty clear what happened to the economy in the U.S. between the Great Crash of 1929 and 1950. From 1929 to 1941, increased government expenditure elevated GDP erratically, but put little dent in stratospheric unemployment levels. As a cure for the depression, FDR's policies were in fact a failure. But in 1942, when the U.S. declared war and military production ramped up, unemployment fell to the low single digits. Many more people were employed, and those who were not employed were drafted into the armed forces. People had more money in their pockets. But because of wartime restrictions, *they could not spend it.* Wage earners were forced to save and consumer goods and new housing were lacking. People's standard of living in fact fell during the war. After the war, many feared a return of unemployment, but the pent up demand from three years of austerity, and the plentiful savings accumulated during that time, fueled a consumer boom that maintained industrial production (though now for consumer goods rather than war materiel) and kept employment high for several decades.

Where did the money for wartime full employment come from? From taxes, yes, but mostly from government debt which, after the war, showed up as a devaluation of the currency. A measure of this devaluation is the price of gold. By government decree, gold was unavailable to individual American citizens from 1933 until 1971. Before the Depression, gold sold for around $20/oz. After people were once again allowed to buy it, the price soon rose to hundreds of dollars per ounce. The loss of value of the dollar from 1928 to 1971 represents the debt incurred by the Federal government during the Roosevelt years.

Presumably the present depression could be fixed in the same way as the Depression was fixed by WWII. But the Paul Krugman/Maynard Keynes solution—massive debt-funded government spending—is only half the story. The other half is to create enduring demand after the burst of spending by enforcing, as WWII enforced, several years of austerity to go along with the government spending spree. Without the period of austerity, unemployment will likely increase and the depression return after the spending spree comes to an end. This may be happening now.

Somehow, I don't think that several years of artificially enforced hard times would be regarded as an acceptable solution to our current problems.

But the creation of yet more debt in 2008–9 did serve the interests of Wall Street and provided some immediate goodies for many others in positions of influence. So, Devil take the long term! The malign hand rules!

Financial Markets are Different, III: Regulation by Rule

Free-market Maestro Greenspan at the height of his influence reportedly thought that even laws against fraud were unnecessary, but I doubt he believes that after the debacle of 2008. "Free" market is of course a misnomer; there cannot be any such thing as a completely unregulated market. The result of "no regulation" would not be a "free" market, but a battlefield. So there must be some rules for a market to function at all. This position is neither pro-nor anti-free market. It simply recognizes that there are many kinds of markets. Some tend to the collective good—most so-called "free" markets fall into this category. But some lead to malign-hand instabilities—almost all planned economies as well as many financial markets fall into this category. The only question, therefore, is what is the minimum set of regulatory principles necessary to ensure—not with 100 percent certainty, human ingenuity being what it is, but with high probability—that financial markets fall into the first category and not the second? I believe that reasonable solutions are much simpler than most people think.

There are two ways to regulate a market: by *rule* and by *scrutiny*. Regulation by scrutiny is what has been done previously and what is being proposed now:

First, supervisors—as we are already doing—must vigorously address the weaknesses at major financial institutions with regard to capital adequacy, liquidity management, and risk management. Firms whose failure would pose a systemic risk must receive especially close supervisory oversight and be held to the highest prudential standards.[1]

This is a promise by Fed chairman Ben Bernanke to scrutinize especially carefully firms who "pose a systemic risk." I'm sure he was sincere, but the realist might well respond: "How easy is *that?*" You should have read enough by now to know that it is well-nigh impossible, at least on a case-by-case basis. The *Wall Street Journal* was skeptical as late as September 4, 2010, heading their comment "The Diviner of System Risk: Ben Bernanke as Carnac the Magnificent."

Restructuring the financial system is basically a technical problem. We are dealing with "a delicate machine, the working of which we do not understand" as Keynes put it. The effects of anything we might propose are necessarily more or less uncertain. We should expect any measures to fix things to be fact-based, with assumptions and methods clearly explained and substantiated as carefully as possible. How do actual policies measure up?

A financial reform bill sponsored by Senator Chris Dodd (D–CT) and Representative Barney Frank (D–MA) was signed into law by President Obama on July 21, 2010. Is Dodd-Frank a serious attempt to actually solve the problems revealed by the crash of 2008? Not really. Far from being dispassionate and scientific, it is an entirely political document. The language is both obscure and bland, designed to sound good while committing the regulators to very little—and that "little" vague enough to be dangerous.

The best evidence for the bill's fundamental irresponsibility is that it was passed six months *before* completion of a thoughtful report from the National Commission set up expressly to inquire into the causes of the crisis.[2] Deleted from the final bill was a Glass-Steagall-type "Volcker Rule" that would have cleanly separated boring (retail) banking from more risky "proprietary trading." Paul Volcker, with characteristic understatement, commented: "[The bill] doesn't have the purity I was searching for."

Not in more than a thousand pages of power-grabs and lobbyist-crafted exemptions, no.

Dodd-Frank is full of empty claims to carry out regulation-by-scrutiny. Here are a couple of examples. The word "abusive" occurs many times in the bill. It is perfectly clear who the good guys are—Dodd and Frank—and who the bad—those nasty, abusive financial people. We are led to anticipate the firm smack of regulatory authority! There's a section of the bill referring to "Abusive Swaps." We can surely expect some pretty severe restraints and penalties for people dealing in *those* suckers, can't we?! Well, not exactly. Here's what we actually get:

> SEC. 714. ABUSIVE SWAPS.
>
> The Commodity Futures Trading Commission or the Securities and Exchange Commission, or both, individually may, by rule or order—
>
> (1) collect information as may be necessary concerning the markets for any types of—
>
> (A) swap (as defined in section 1a of the Commodity Exchange Act (7 U.S.C. 1a)); or
>
> (B) security-based swap (as defined in section 1a of the Commodity Exchange Act (7 U.S.C. 1a)); and
>
> (2) issue a report with respect to any types of swaps or security-based swaps that the Commodity Futures Trading Commission or the Securities and Exchange Commission determines to be detrimental to—
>
> (A) the stability of a financial market; or
>
> (B) participants in a financial market.

Wow! "collect information", "issue a report" find if these things are "detrimental to the stability of a financial market." Tough stuff! But wait, *what* "information…necessary concerning the markets"? What *is* necessary? How is "stability of a financial market" to be assessed? Who are the "participants in a financial market"? What is "detrimental" and how do you know? None of these things is defined. We really have no idea what is being proposed. This guff is typical of H. R. 4173 as a whole, all 1,616 pages of it. One more example from many I could have chosen—here is the proposed action if a threat to stability is detected by the regulators:

SEC. 121. MITIGATION OF RISKS TO FINANCIAL STABILITY.

(a) MITIGATORY ACTIONS.—If the Board of Governors determines that a bank holding company with total consolidated assets of $50,000,000,000 or more, or a nonbank financial company supervised by the Board of Governors, poses a grave threat to the financial stability of the United States, the Board of Governors, upon an affirmative vote of not fewer than 2/3 of the voting members of the Council then serving, shall—

(1) limit the ability of the company to merge with, acquire, consolidate with, or otherwise become affiliated with another company;

(2) restrict the ability of the company to offer a financial product or products;

(3) require the company to terminate one or more activities;

(4) impose conditions on the manner in which the company conducts 1 or more activities; or

(5) if the Board of Governors determines that the actions described in paragraphs (1) through (4) are inadequate to mitigate a threat to the financial stability of the United States in its recommendation, require the company to sell or otherwise transfer assets or off-balance-sheet items to unaffiliated entities.

(b) NOTICE AND HEARING.—

(1) IN GENERAL.—The Board of Governors, in consultation with the Council, shall provide to a company described in subsection (a) written notice that such company is being considered for mitigatory action pursuant to this section, including an explanation of the basis for, and description of, the proposed mitigatory action ...

I see, so, among other things, if there is a problem with a large bank holding company the regulator will "limit the ability of the company to merge." Apparently the aim is to block further growth. A few questions: How will this "limiting" be done? Is "merging" the only way growth might happen? How are limits to be imposed and what might they be? How is "threat" to be detected? How verified? How do the drafters of this vacuous prose know how "large" is large? No problem there, actually, it's anything over $50,000,000,000. Well done! The government knows just exactly how big a company needs to be before it can become dangerous! Smaller than 50 billion, no problem! Larger, a threat! How was that number arrived at? We are given no clue. (And what if the dollar inflates?) How long will the enforcement process take—and notices and hearings—and lawyers—are involved? Will all be completed before the "grave threat" has become "grave harm"?

There are many more pages of this kind of vacuity. As I said earlier, fixing financial markets is a technical problem and should have a technical solution. What is offered is politics and self-serving damage limitation crafted by financial lobbyists. And the process continues. In April 2011: "The Treasury Department said Friday that it plans to exclude foreign-exchange instruments from key portions of new derivatives rules, as being devised under last year's Dodd-Frank financial-overhaul law, in a move certain to please banks and business groups."[3] I have no idea whether the proposed change is an improvement or not. What is certain is that most of the bill is ill-considered. It is truly frightening that the financial future of the U.S. may rest on this kind of mush.

Dodd-Frank would probably be defended by conceding its vagueness and pointing out that the real work will be done later by the professional regulatory apparatus. The bill is just a set of guidelines for regulators. But its length and technical language suggest otherwise. The bill looks like an attempt, albeit an ineffectual one, to actually control the financial industry. If the regulators are to do the real work, let them come up with the rules first and let Congress then debate them. Doing it the other way round is like having a bunch of amateurs build an airplane and then letting the aeronautical engineers in afterwards and asking them to fix it.

Will Dodd-Frank help at all? Almost certainly not. The bill appears to be in effect a pre-emptive strike, something that will give the appearance of action, elicits choreographed howls from the financial industry ("Whatever you do," cried Brer Rabbit, "Don't throw me into the briar patch!"), will pacify a few naïve proponents of reform, but will leave the present structure essentially unchanged. In return for basically leaving the financial industry alone, the bill seems to create new, vaguely defined and constitutionally question-able takeover powers for the Federal Government. Without doing anything serious to stabilize and downsize the industry, it neverthe-less greatly increases the incentives for lobbyists who will seek to limit the damage posed by new and undefined powers.[4] If this is the best we can do, much more money will be made by a few, and the many will suffer, as the next crisis hits in a few years.

There is almost no chance that the Dodd-Frank bill will do anything to remedy the real systemic problems of the U.S. financial markets. What it does is add a bucketful of regulations for registra-tion, licensing, information provision (along with a list of mostly incomprehensible exemptions, exceptions and mitigations) to a set of unkeepable promises about detecting "threats" and acting to mitigate them. The bill as a whole gives the government and political class powers so large and so indefinite that the bill is in effect a gun to the head of the financial industry: play ball or else bad things will happen. The difference between this and a simple mugging is that the even-tual cost will fall not on the financiers but on the American people.

Congressional hearings after the passage of Dodd-Frank offer little hope of change. The treatment of Wall Street heavies like Robert Rubin and Chuck Prince enlarges our understanding of the term "soft-ball" and makes "How are you today?" look like the Spanish Inquisi-tion. ("Diminished interrogation," anyone?). The headline of Peggy Noonan's article sets the tone: "After the Crash, a Crashing Bore: The men behind the bailout take refuge in impenetrable jargon."[5]

So much for regulation by scrutiny, but perhaps I'm too pessimistic. Perhaps it *can* work? Well, has it worked in the past? No, not really. There were plenty of signs of trouble in the run-up to the disasters of 2008, but essentially none was acted upon. Here are three examples.

My prediction was based on my research into the residential mortgage market and mortgage-backed securities. *After studying the regulatory filings related to those securities,* I waited for the lenders to offer the most risky mortgages conceivable to the least qualified buyers. I knew that would mark the beginning of the end of the housing bubble; it would mean that prices had risen—with the expansion of easy mortgage lending—as high as they could go.[6] [my italics]

This quote is from Michael Burry, a hedge fund manager who, in the years before the 2007/8 meltdown, saw the same data the SEC saw, saw the implications of the data (disaster for the real-estate market), and made a lot of money out of it. His question, quite reasonably, is "I saw the crisis coming. Why didn't the Fed?" Good question.[7] I give some answers in a moment. Another hedge fund manager, John Paulson, also bet against the housing market and got rich. Did no one at the SEC see what these guys saw? Or, if they did, why did they do nothing about it? Has any SEC employee been fired, or at least disciplined in any way? That one we can answer: no and no.

My second example is the incredible history of financial investigator Harry Markopolos, who warned the SEC repeatedly, over a period of several years, about the Madoff fraud—a fraud so easy to detect in its later stages that even Madoff was surprised that he had escaped for so long.[8] Indeed, Madoff may have in effect given himself up (he was turned in by his two sons, but ...) because he realized that discovery was inevitable and he wanted to limit the damage. Despite Markopolos' numerous detailed warnings, the SEC failed to act. Who was responsible for this amazing failure? What has happened to them? Well, on November 12, 2011 we learned that eight SEC employees had been not fired – "disciplined." Big whoop! as the kids would say.[9] Nothing, apparently: no one in the SEC has suffered so far for its extraordinary lapse.[10]

I have already touched on my third example: how Brooksley Born, head of the Commodity Futures Trading Commission, in 1998 spotted the dangers of credit default swaps. She did not try to regulate them but just to do a study to see if regulation was needed. She was not just ignored by the *finanzmeisters* of the Clinton administration, she was told to shut up! In testimony before a Senate Committee that was part of a successful effort by the establishment to block Born, the brilliant Lawrence Summers, subsequently Treasury Secretary, then President of Harvard University, then White House economic advisor—and one-time boy-wonder of economics—had this to say about CDSs:[11]

> first, the parties to these kinds of contract are largely sophisticated financial institutions that would appear to be eminently capable of protecting themselves from fraud and counterparty insolvencies and most of which are already subject to basic safety and soundness regulation under existing banking and securities laws; second, given the nature of the underlying assets involved—namely supplies of financial exchange and other financial instruments—there would seem to be little scope for market manipulation of the kind seen in traditional agricultural commodities, the supply of which is inherently limited and changeable. .
>
> *To date there has been no clear evidence of a need for additional regulation of the institutional OTC derivatives market…* (my italics)

Oh, really? Maybe "sophisticated financial institutions" can protect themselves (in fact, they couldn't, for the most part), but who will protect the rest of us? On that point, Mr. Summers was silent. Regulation of derivatives was squashed, with the results we have all experienced.

So, just how much faith can we have in regulation by detailed scrutiny in systemic risk cases that will all, *all*, be much more difficult to detect than Madoff's blatant illegality and probably harder to see than the crazy explosion of the housing market spotted by Burry and Paulson or the systemic risk posed by derivatives? Regulation by scrutiny is an arms race, between regulators and players in the financial markets. The bankers will always win such a race: there are more of them, their incentives are stronger, and they are likely to be smarter—at least in the details of their own business—than the potential regulators. Regulation by scrutiny can work in more conventional arenas—real estate, electrical installation, environmental safety, power utilities—although even there, problems of over-regulation and rent-seeking usually emerge after a few years. But I believe regulation by scrutiny is likely to be worse than worthless in the "innovative" financial area—worse, because its very existence gives all a false sense of security.

When the best brains in the business of economics and finance, confronted with the clearest possible evidence of a potential problem, either ignore it or actively refuse to acknowledge it, how much faith should we have in regulation by scrutiny? How much faith can we have in Mr. Bernanke's "especially close supervisory oversight"? I would suggest zero to none.

Larry Summers's puzzling faith in the soundness of derivatives should make us ponder. How is it that economics, which is populated by some of the brightest people on the planet, so often gets it all wrong—and often in ways that are pretty obvious to many noneconomists? I think that part of the reason is mathematics. You have to be really good at math to succeed as an academic economist. Unfortunately, being good at math makes it easy to see the world as a sort of formal system. A handful of axioms—rules—differing slightly between contending economic schools, are accepted and success then goes to the individuals who can best play the chess game thus created. The problem is that no matter how brilliant the player, if the rules of the game are not accurate, not based on real laws of nature, the conclusions will be wrong. In other words, a reputation for "brilliance" in economics is not a reliable guide to soundness of judgment about the real world.[12] Perhaps this can explain Professor Summers's confidence in credit default swaps and other grotesque efflorescences of financial genius?

REGULATION BY RULE

There is a better and simpler way. Regulation by rule means looking at the reinforcement contingencies under which players in financial markets operate and asking a simple question: do they involve the malign hand? As I will show, the necessary rules are relatively simple, much better suited to the limits of human intelligence than the ever-lengthening list of well-meaning prescriptions required by the likes of Dodd-Frank. The reasons to prefer regulation by rule are as follows:

- Regulation by scrutiny has failed repeatedly in the past as even Treasury Secretary Geithner has admitted. During the housing boom (for example), "There were many organizations and institutions that had the authority to respond, but failed to act."[13] There is no reason to expect that regulation by scrutiny will be much more effective in the future.
- Regulation by rule is simpler and cheaper than regulation by scrutiny. Instead of numberless experts having to study a whole industry of complex firms to discover if they pose a vaguely defined "systemic risk," a smaller number of moderately skilled people can just look to see if all are following the rules—a task to which regulatory bureaucracies are much better suited.
- Keynes is still right that we really do not understand the financial organism. If we try to fix it by dealing with problems— symptoms—as they arise we will always be several steps behind. The only way to tame the market is to create an environment that allows it to evolve in a healthy way, even though we can never be *certain* that the set of rules we devise is the very best.
- The market *is* an evolutionary system. The future behavior of such systems can never be exactly predicted. Even Mr. Greenspan agrees on this point: "We cannot expect perfection in any area where forecasting is required"[14]—which is to say the prediction of "systemic risk." Greenspan's own words undercut the fundamental premise of Dodd-Frank and other like legislation, that systemic risk can be detected in advance. And as I pointed out earlier, even

if it can be detected, the pressures to "keep the music playing" are usually too strong for regulators to resist. The best we can do is create a set of rules that makes sense, that does not violate obvious principles of prudence and personal responsibility, that does not create malign-hand reinforcement contingencies.

- Many effects of new practices are long delayed. The profits are seen at once, the malign hand takes a while to show itself. Sometimes the ill effects of a new "product" take decades to play out. This is another reason why regulation by scrutiny is a bad idea. By the time the bad effects are obvious, damage has already been done—and the momentum provided by a history of phony profits makes action to rein things in almost impossible.

A bit more background. Never forget that the limitation and sharing of risk is the *fons et origo* of modern capitalism. The limited-liability company (LLC) originated with the Dutch East India Company in the seventeenth century. But until the nineteenth century the dominant form of collective business ownership was still the partnership. A number of entrepreneurs got together to pool their resources for a commercial venture such as a voyage or a factory. The benefit: more resources. The downside: partners are fully liable for all the debts of the firm. Many organizations still operate this way—legal and medical partnerships and Lloyds of London, for example. But it can be dangerous, as the "Names" of the insurance giant found out in the early 1990s when Lloyds faced unexpectedly large claims. Since each Name was fully liable for the firm's debt, many went bankrupt, the final cases being settled only in 2009.[15]

The limited-liability firm, the main business structure in the modern economy, limits risk via share ownership. Shareholders own the company, although their power is circumscribed in various ways. They share in the profits, but their losses, their "exposure," is limited to whatever they paid for their shares. But the firm itself is treated legally in many ways like a person. It can borrow money, for example. Obviously, a limited-liability firm is able, and likely, to take more risks than a partnership. Despite the obvious dangers, in practice the idea has worked very well indeed. Limited-liability companies powered the industrial and commercial revolution of the nineteenth and twentieth centuries. Overall, the LLC is a good idea.

But not, perhaps, for financial firms. Investment banks used to be partnerships. But in recent years, they have increasingly changed to shareholder-owned, limited-liability companies with most of the shares owned by outsiders. For example, Bear Stearns became public in 1985, Goldman Sachs in 1999. Lehman Brothers began as a partnership in 1850 and remained so until about 1969. After a series of mergers and restarts, it was an LLC by 1994. Although most employees of these firms retain a substantial share position in the firm, and may be remunerated by stock options, this change meant that salary and bonuses—based on fees—began to play a larger role. Dealing now largely with other people's money, with huge possibilities for leverage, and with personal liability limited to share ownership, the door was open for Wall Street and the City of London to take on almost unlimited risk. Short-term gains could be pocketed; long-term losses would hit shareholders only. Or maybe the government would step in... The contribution of the change in company structure from partnership to LLC to these destabilizing changes is hard to measure, but that there was a contribution is hard to deny.

Hedge funds are an exception that proves the rule. Most are limited-liability entities, but in most cases executives are required to own a substantial stake in the company. Sebastian Mallaby comments: "Hedge fund bosses mostly have their own money in their funds, so they are speculating with capital that is at least partly their own—a powerful incentive to avoid losses. By contrast, bank traders generally face fewer such restraints..."[16] They have a "paranoid culture" in Mallaby's words. It is no surprise, therefore, that although some hedge funds failed in 2007–8, none did so in a way that posed systemic risk. But perhaps they learned a lesson from the failure of Long-Term Capital Management in 1998? The hedge fund was failing and threatened the stability of the whole financial industry. Under pressure from the Federal Reserve Bank of New York a group of financial firms provided the necessary bailout. Perhaps the

LTCM fiasco gave rise to the necessary "paranoid culture" that helped prevent major problems with hedge funds ten years later.[17] The change from partnership to limited liability by investment banks was just the first of a long series of changes in regulation and legal arrangements, every one tending in the same direction: to reduce the risk borne by traders and increase the risks shared with others. The astonishing thing is that throughout most of this relatively recent history, regulators thought that helping traders to share risk was *always a good thing*.

Rules to Regulate By The financial system has evolved, as any evolutionary system must, by moving in any direction that signals short-term advantage. If a new product, or a relaxation of some regulation, promises an increase in profits, all efforts are bent toward ensuring that the necessary changes come to pass. Each new product is justified by any means necessary (quants, present arms!) and political forces are mustered to abolish regulations that get in its way. So, like a blind man climbing a hill by tap-tapping his stick, the system moves up an ever-growing mountain of debt and profits towards the precipice it cannot see.

At some point in the last few decades, the accelerating profits generated by these changes, combined with political shifts in Washington, pushed the whole thing to a tipping point. The persuasive power of vast sums of money became overwhelming, influencing not just those who benefited directly and indirectly, but the whole political system. Everyone looked on in amazement as profits escalated into the billions, thinking "they must be doing something right!" Regulators became increasingly reluctant to block proposals from Wall Street; the universal desirability of sharing risk was widely accepted; and financial "innovation" was venerated as an absolute good.

The result is a hideously complicated and dangerous financial system that defies orderly disassembly. Yet restructuring, indeed, reinvention, is desperately needed. How to do it? I suggest that the necessary changes are in fact straightforward, because we have arrived at the present danger by violating a handful of relatively simple principles. Financial markets have been operating under a set of reinforcement contingencies that are partly good—the invisible hand—and partly very bad—the malign hand. There is no need to tackle an impossible problem piecemeal. Just re-establish a few principles of prudent financial behavior. Here are my suggestions for rules that may postpone the next crisis:

1. Unlimited money being a major source of financial instability, the ability of the Federal Reserve to create money should be severely curtailed. Let the market decide on interest rates, as far as possible.
2. Those who choose to take financial risks should have to bear them. In other words, **voluntary** risk should usually **not** be insurable. Otherwise risks will be systematically underestimated and markets correspondingly distorted.
3. The "insuranburn" rule: The probability of an insurable event should be independent of the existence and extent of insurance against it—no positive feedback. Insurance-like products that pose a risk of positive feedback should be banned.
4. Firms that deal in financial markets should be partnerships not LLCs. Retail—community, "boring"—banks can be LLCs, so long as they are separated by Glass-Steagall-type provisions from casino banks.

My guess is that these provisions alone would make the financial industry truly competitive. If a financial firm fails, others – competitors – would cheer, not frown, as they do now. Making financial firms partnerships rather than limited-liability companies reduces their incentive to take risks with other people's money. Poisonous inventions like securitization and credit default swaps would be banned because of positive feedback effects (Point 3, *insuranburn*) and erosion of market discipline (Point 2). Both George Soros and Warren Buffett have condemned CDSs. Soros has called them "toxic," Buffett's phrase was "financial instruments of mass destruction." With these and other dangerous instruments out of the way, the volume of financial transactions would decrease a lot. With severe limits placed on its ability to diffuse risk all over the planet, the financial industry would necessarily become less interconnected, hence more stable, more competitive—and *smaller*.

Commentators worry about how to break up the big banks, but of course the simplest solution is to change the economics so that big banks are no longer profitable and so break themselves up. Reducing the amount of leverage and amount of risk that the mega-banks can take will make them less profitable; requiring them to be partnerships rather than LLCs will encourage them to shrink themselves. By appropriately modifying the environment in which this financial kudzu has sprouted, healthier, smaller plants will be favored and overweight strangling vines may go extinct. Banks too big to fail will be, finally, too big to exist.

The rules I am proposing don't deal with "products," with their names, or with categories, as does the present system. "Insurance" is highly regulated, "swaps" are not, even though both amount to the same reinforcement schedule for the people who buy and sell them. The rules I propose are aimed directly at the reinforcement schedules that these products and institutional arrangements embody, rather than just their names or the particular sub-sector of the financial industry where they reside. The idea is simply to make sure that the costs and benefits of any voluntary financial arrangement fall directly and completely on the participants and not on third parties. Many existing rules, like reserve requirements, which are cumbersome proxies for direct regulation of reinforcement schedules, could be completely abolished. The resulting system should be a great deal simpler than the ungodly mess we have now.

The political obstacles to such sweeping changes are immense. Detailed study will certainly suggest some reasonable exceptions to these rules. But I believe they provide a starting point for a kind of regulation that would in the end be easier, less intrusive, and much simpler than the kind of arms race between regulators and regulated that is implicit in current proposals. The result should be a smaller, more stable and more efficient (*really* efficient!) financial industry.

Mitigation. But what if we are stuck for a while with the flawed system we have now? What might be done to mitigate the present crisis? Tinkering with existing regulations is one approach that has already been suggested. Obviously, if banks had to maintain larger reserves, leverage would be reduced and thus the systemic risk posed by extreme debt creation would be diminished. Forcing over-the-counter derivatives on to exchanges would help regulators see what is going on, and so on. Doubtless new forms of "shadow" banking, not obviously subject to the new rules, would soon emerge. But in the meantime, stability might improve a bit.

Here's another suggestion. There are three things that everyone seems to agree on.

- The U.S. has a severe government-debt problem.
- Consequently some taxes will have to be increased, even though raising taxes in the middle of a slump may slow recovery.
- A major cause of the 2007-? crisis was the absorption of too much risk by banks.

These three things suggest a relatively simple solution. If something is thought to be injurious to the common good, as is smoking, a standard policy move is to tax it.[18] Clearly taking on too much risk contributed to the present crisis. In the present dilemma, two birds, government debt and (financial) vice, may therefore usefully be slain with one regulatory stone by imposing a *tax on financial risk*. The national debt will be alleviated by a tax that should also have beneficial rather than damaging economic effects.

A total-risk (total exposure, in the jargon) tax should be steeply progressive: zero to negligible on "small" risks, large on very large ones.

How could this be done in a way that does not impede real market efficiency? A common risk management tool is something called *value at risk* (VaR). It is defined this way:

> For a given portfolio, probability and time horizon, VaR is defined as a threshold value such that the probability that the mark-to-market loss on the portfolio over the given time horizon exceeds this value (assuming normal markets and no trading in the portfolio) is the given probability level.[19]

In other words, the firm looks at its outstanding debts and promises, then uses a history-based mathematical model to estimate the probabilities that it will actually experience different amounts of loss.

VaR is typically computed once a day, after the close of trading. It has two parts, one questionable, the other not. The OK bit is the total value at risk. The questionable bit is the "threshold," the *probability* that losses will actually occur. Just how questionable was illustrated by the illustrious J.P. Morgan in May, 2012: average daily VaR, $67M; actual loss on May 11, $2.3 billion.[19a] The threshold is usually set at 5 percent, so that a financial firm feels safe if it sets aside reserves that will be needed 5 percent or less of the time. The accuracy of the probability models used to compute the 5 percent is of course absolutely undermined by recent events. Even if they are accurate, they imply that a sound firm will be thought failing one time in twenty and a failing firm thought sound at a similar frequency.[20] But we can set the threshold probability at zero, i.e., just look at the *worst loss that can possibly occur*—no probability needed. This value, the *total value at risk* (TVR), will obviously be much greater than the old VaR, but of course it would in most cases be much closer to the losses actually suffered by financial firms during the recent crash.[21] TVR is as good, and certainly as simple, a measure of systemic risk as we can find.

Let us simply impose a steeply graduated tax of the following sort. The tax should be applied daily, to the total value at risk. On a TVR of $1M or less the daily tax is negligible, say $100, less than a tenth of one percent. But on a billion (one thousand million) it will be about $9M, just under one percent, a disproportionate increase.[22] This is just an example. The actual numbers would require some research into details of profit margins to be expected from transactions of different sizes and so forth. The aim is just to discourage very large exposures by making them unprofitable. With this kind of progressive tax, it will not pay a firm to build up its daily risk beyond a certain point. Large financial firms will be forced to divide themselves into a number of smaller ones—small enough, given the proper choice of tax rates, that none is "too big to fail." A financial industry with small "failable" firms should be truly competitive, which, as we have seen, the current industry is not. Its share of total national profits should decrease; and it should also be more efficient, in the real sense of serving the resource-allocation needs of society in an inexpensive and stable fashion.

I think of the TVR as an interim measure that could be applied relatively quickly. The rate could be "tuned" just like the Federal Funds Rate (perhaps Mr. Bernanke could advise?). It should induce changes in the financial industry that would make the more drastic proposals I made earlier much easier to implement.

DO WE HAVE THE WILL?

What has happened in the aftermath of the great crash of 2007–8? Has the financial system changed in any essential way? Shockingly, not only has it not changed, the bloated structures that led to the crisis have become even more bloated. A few big banks have departed; but the ones that remain are even bigger than before. If the sector was in effect a monopoly before the crash; it is even more so now.[23]

There are many reasons why taking really effective action is difficult. I have already mentioned the longstanding revolving door relationship between Washington and Wall Street and the mesmeric effect of the extraordinarily large sums of money flowing out of the financial system. To these we can add the role of campaign contributions which, though close to a rounding error for the wizards of finance, make a big difference to the recipients. Money plus the conventional wisdom still sees financial innovation and sharing risk as invariably good. Washington still sees nothing wrong with a huge financial sector.

But perhaps the most intransigent obstacle to change is that people, not just Wall Street, but most people, may actually *prefer* boom-and-bust to a modest stability. Although everyone suffers from the inflation that eventually follows any boom, it may also be true that more people, and certainly more people with influence, are immediately excited by a boom than immediately depressed by the bust. What this means for the economy, with its inflation and confusing statistics, is that people may only notice the occasional boom and discount the bust that follows, thinking on the whole that "well, we have our ups and downs, but basically things are getting better and better!" If this is really true, then people will be more ready to accept the self-serving mantra of the surf riders that, well, boom-and-bust are just part of the wonderful wealth-creation machine that is our favored form of capitalism. I showed in Chapter 7 that in fact Americans are little better off now than 50 years ago. Chapter 2 argued that shrinkage of the middle class—increased income inequality—can be traced in large part to debt-fueled growth of the financial sector. So if people really do like booms more than they hate busts, they are much mistaken. Whether all these obstacles to a stable, democratic and truly prosperous America can be overcome remains to be seen.

A "FAILURE OF CAPITALISM"?

The depression of 2007-? is prompting changes in long-held beliefs. Like a new husband intolerant of any imperfection in his beloved, a few free-market fundamentalists are ready for divorce at the first sight of dirty underwear. Referring to "a once-in-a-century credit tsunami," Maestro Greenspan, for example, in 2009 famously commented "Yes, I've found a flaw. I don't know how significant or permanent it is. But I've been very distressed by that fact [that].... [t]his modern risk-management paradigm.... collapsed in the summer of last year."[24] Pro-market Judge Richard Posner has explicitly renounced at least some of his faith: "Some conservatives believe that the [current] depression is the result of unwise government policies. I believe it is a market failure"[25]—as if the two are incompatible. Coming to this conclusion, and not blaming the failure on government, is a big step for free-market fans. But is it accurate? Is it necessary to abandon faith in free-market capitalism? Can government be let off the hook?

I hope the arguments in this book have persuaded you that government is indeed massively implicated in the present crisis: in favoring housing over other kinds of "investment"; in loosening the money supply to make this possible; in acquiescing to numerous self-serving calls to deregulate the financial industry; and by its misguided faith in regulation-by-scrutiny. So also is the financial industry itself, but mainly in its capacity as an industry largely populated by competitive, ingenious and money-obsessed people. (But what other kind of person would you expect to do well in such an industry?) The government's fault was that it failed to see what these guys could achieve in the absence of proper controls.

Of course markets can "fail," but of course that doesn't mean markets are a bad idea. The disappointed husband is upset not because his bride has behaved badly, but because he had an unrealistic vision of her. You need to give up on markets in general only if you believe in a sort of Platonic perfect market which real markets must match.

The standard definition is that a free market is "without economic intervention and regulation by government except to regulate against force or fraud," but this restriction is of course totally arbitrary. Every market exists within a set of constraints—legal, customary, formal and informal. There are many other constraints that society might impose in addition to the prohibition of force and fraud. Yet, as we have seen, free-market fundamentalist Greenspan didn't even think sanctions against fraud were necessary. Many constraints will make markets worse. But some will make markets, especially financial markets, work better, for the common good rather than just for private benefit—the invisible hand rather than the malign hand.

Markets deal in products, but the standard free-market definition makes no distinction between different kinds of "product." Yet, as we've seen, financial "products" are not really products at all. They are very different in their properties from products of a more conventional kind—"end-use" products (consumption goods) or products used to manufacture other kinds of good (capital goods). Financial products are not "products" but reinforcement schedules of a very special and often inscrutable kind. The kind of faith in markets that is challenged by "market failure" is a naïve view that believes all markets are essentially the same, and all operate according to the benign invisible hand. But financial markets, even when free of "force or fraud," involve both benign and malign processes. As we have seen, some "innovative" products and practices introduce destabilizing positive feedback or impair the discipline, the reinforcement contingencies, necessary for any market to work for the common good.. The unlimited expansion of complex debt and industry-wide sharing of risk can imbue the whole financial industry with the inefficiencies and excessive profits of a monopoly. Under these conditions, a change in the rules is totally reasonable. Intervention is not at variance with the idea that markets are uniquely capable of allocating resources efficiently. If properly done, regulation just ensures that markets work as Adam Smith said they could.

Notes

PREFACE

1. *A Tract on Monetary Reform* (1923) Ch. 3.

INTRODUCTION

1. There are many ways to show that the self-interested optimal strategy in the Prisoner's Dilemma is to defect. Here is one. Suppose we denote by Ab, aB, AB and ab, the cases where A defects and b does not, B defects and a does not, both A and B defect, or neither a nor b defects. In the prisoner's dilemma, typical values to each prisoner of the outcomes in these four cases are as follows (I've made them positive values, rather than costs, for simplicity): Reward to A if: Ab 10, aB 0, AB 1, ab 5.
In other words, A wins big if he defects and B does not, but loses big in the reverse case, etc. The expected payoff to A is just the sum of these four possible outcomes, weighted by the probability that B will defect. Suppose we denote that probability by p. Then the expected value to A of defecting is: $10.(1-p)+p.1 = 9p$ (the weighted values of Ab and AB); and to A of not-defecting $= 0.p+(1-p).5 = (1-p).5$ (the weighted values of aB and ab).
Since p is between zero and one, $(1-p).5$ is always less that $9p$, so defecting always wins. The same analysis applies, of course, to B, so both parties, behaving 'rationally' defect and the total value of the game is just 2 rather than the possible 10 if neither defect. People do better if the game is played repeatedly, because the history of outcomes allows them to learn the rules and thus settle on a mutually beneficial strategy.

2. http://www.sciencemag.org/content/162/3859/1243.full.pdf

3. I'm ignoring transaction costs – closing costs, fees, sales taxes etc. *These costs just* mean the owner has to wait for a bit larger rise in price before selling.

4. See The Association for Behavior Analysis Internationalž: http://www. abainternational.org/

5. http://www.time.com/time/covers/0,16641,19710920,00.html

6. See William D. Cohan's *Money and Power: How Goldman Sachs Came to Rule the World*. Doubleday, 2011 for the full history.

7. See Michael Lewis's highly readable books *Liar's Poker* and *The Big Short: Inside the Doomsday Machine* (W. W. Norton, 1989, 2010) for some vivid character studies of Wall Street types.

8. http://www.taxfoundation.org/news/show/250.html Tax Reform Act of 1986 changed the definition of AGI, so data these comparison cannot be absolutely precise.

CHAPTER 1

1. http://en.wikipedia.org/wiki/Parkinson%27s_Law

2. L. von Mises, *Bureaucracy* (1944); summary of public choice at http://www.dallasfed.org/research/ei/ei0302.pdf and http://en.wikipedia.org/wiki/Public_choice_theory

3. http://www.businessweek.com/news/2010–06–30/u-k-to-lose–610–000-government-jobs-by–2016-watchdog-says.html

4. http://www.marketwatch.com/story/north-carolina-wont-quit-on-microsoft–2011–03–10

5. Octogenarian Stevens died in a small-plane crash in August 2010.

6. http://councilfor.cagw.org/site/PageServer?pagename=PorkerProfile_Stevens

7. *WSJ*, May 28, 2011

8. http://www.trygve.com/taxcode.html

9. *WSJ*, June 11, 2011.

10. http://www.washingtonpost.com/wp-dyn/content/article/2010/12/22/AR2010122203771.html

11. http://reason.com/blog/2010/03/09/nancy-pelosi-on-health-care-we

12. Gillian Tett provides a trenchant summary of these grotesqueries in Dodd-Frank Takes Paper Chase Complexity to New Heights, *FT*, October 28, 2011.

13. Joseph Stiglitz (2006) *Making globalization work*. Penguin, p. 4.

14. For example, http://knol.google.com/k/a-limit-to-globalization-fuzzy-chaos-modelling-in-ecology-and-economics#

15. Staddon, J. (2008) Distracting Miss Daisy. *The Atlantic*, July-August, 102–104. http://www.theatlantic.com/doc/200807/traffic/1

16. Terence Kealey *The Economic Laws of Scientific Research* (St. Martin's Press, 1996) and *Science Sex and Profits* (Heinemann. 2008). In the summer of 2011, a bunch of high-profile academics proposed to start a second private university in Britain.

17. For an encomium in favor of Bush's report and the strengthened government-university links that followed, see distinguished biologist and Stanford University ex-president Donald Kennedy's Clark Kerr lectures, e.g., http://podcast.uctv.tv/mp3/13556.mp3

18. http://en.wikipedia.org/wiki/Bell-Boeing_V-22_Osprey

19. Full disclosure: I had one of these awards for many years.

20. See for example, distinguished economist Raghuram Rajan's comments on this problem in economics in his book *Fault Lines: How Hidden Fractures Still Threaten the World Economy* (Princeton UP, 2010).

CHAPTER 2

1. No one seems sure of the true origin of this perceptive comment. See, for example, http://www.lorencollins.net/tytler.html

2. Historical Trends in Executive Compensation 1936–2003. Carola Frydman and Raven E. Saks

   November 15, 2005.

3. http://www.taxfoundation.org/news/show/250.html Tax Reform Act of 1986 changed the definition of AGI, so data these comparison cannot be absolutely precise.

4. http://en.wikipedia.org/wiki/Gini_coefficient

5. For this example, rank, order, r, and salary, S are related by $S_{r+1} = S_r^{1.005}$, yielding an accelerating income distribution with a Gini (inequality) score of 0.42.

6. http://www.taxfoundation.org/research/show/1410.html

7. http://www.telegraph.co.UK/news/newstopics/politics/liberaldemocrats/7952539/The-middle-classes-can-thank-Vince-Cable-for-their-double-whammy.html

8. http://www.usatoday.com/news/nation/2010–03–04-federal-pay_N.htm

9. Why bonuses, one might ask? These don't sound like bonus-type jobs . . .

10 http://en.wikipedia.org/wiki/Tax_per_head

11. Thatcher's poll tax was supposed to pay for community services, but other poll taxes have made payment a condition for voting.

12. *The Economist,* Jan 30, 2010

13. http://www.csmonitor.com/2005/0614/p01s03-usec.html

14. See, for example, Warren Buffett Is Wrong On Taxes: Millionaires and billionaires pay a higher share of their income in taxes than the middle class, by Stephen Moore. *WSJ,* July 28, 2011. Buffet's businesses make use of every legal tax loophole.

15. http://en.wikipedia.org/wiki/Gini_coefficient

16. http://img.slate.com/media/3/100914_NoahT_GreatDivergence.pdf

17. J. Stiglitz, Of the 1%, by the 1%, for the 1%. *Vanity Fair,* May 2011.

18. The Rise of the New Global Elite. *The Atlantic,* January/February 2011.

19. The evolution of top incomes: a historical and international perspective. Thomas Piketty & Emmanuel Saez http://www.nber.org/papers/w12404

20. Difficult enough that Thomas J. Sargent of New York University and Christopher A. Sims of Princeton University were in 2011 awarded the Nobel Prize in Economics for their research on causation in macroeconomics. Unfortunately, much of their work is based on the idea of rational expectations, which has some serious conceptual problems (see Chapter 3). And nothing that they or anyone else can do via clever statistical manipulation can overcome the impossibility of doing real experiments – which are essential to identify real causes – in macroeconomics.

21. http://img.slate.com/media/3/100914_NoahT_GreatDivergence.pdf

CHAPTER 3

1. Alan Greenspan, *The Age of Turbulence: Adventures in a New World,* Penguin Books, 2007, pp.489–90. Greenspan was Chairman of the Federal Reserve Board from 1987 to 2006.

2. Justin Fox, *The Myth of the Rational Market,* Kindle Edition, 2009.

3. The LEX column, *Financial Times,* August 26, 2011. Further embarrassing comments from financial big shots about the wonderfulness of Alan G came to light early in 2012 when transcripts from 2006 Federal Reserve meetings became public. Treasury Secretary Tim Geithner, then president of the Federal Reserve Bank of New York, for example, fawningly (or perhaps playfully) observed about Mr. Greenspan's legacy: "I'd like the record to show that I think you're pretty terrific. [Laughter] And thinking in terms of probabilities, I think the risk that we decide in the future that you're even better than we think is higher than the alternative."

4. Testimony of Dr. Alan Greenspan, Committee of Government Oversight and Reform, October 23, 2008.

5. Address to America's community bankers, November 2, 199.

6. THE FINANCIAL CRISIS INQUIRY REPORT: Final Report of the National Commission on the Causes of the Financial and Economic Crisis in the United States. January 2011.

7. Burton Malkiel *A Random Walk Down Wall Street: The time-tested strategy for successful investing.* New York: W. W. Norton, 1973/2007.

8. 'What's in a Name: If It's 'China,' a Pick-Me-Up. *WSJ,* March 20, 2010.

9. http://en.wikipedia.org/wiki/Tulip_mania

10. London *Sunday Times,* June 19, 2011.

11. Smith, Adam (1776). "Book I, Chapter V Of the Real and Nominal Price of Commodities, or of their Price in Labour, and their Price in Money" in *An Inquiry into the Nature and Causes of the Wealth of Nations.*

12. Accounts of the various types of reinforcement schedules, including response-based or *ratio* schedules (N lever presses or key pecks for one bit of food, analogous to piece-work) and time-based or *interval* schedules (a bit of food for the first key peck after a specified period of time has elapsed, analogous to a weekly wage) are widely available. An internet source is my book *Adaptive Behavior and Learning* (2010) http://dukespace.lib.duke.edu/dspace/handle/10161/2878 Chapter 5.

13. Oxygen-motivated behavior in the goldfish, *Carassius auratus.* Peter Van Sommers, *Science 31* August 1962, Vol. 137. no. 3531, pp. 678 – 679.

14. See, for example, the Special Issue on Behavioral Economics of *The Journal of the Experimental Analysis of Behavior,* 1995, or, for early work, see chapters in Staddon, J. E. R. (Ed.) (1980). *Limits to action: The allocation of individual behavior.* New York: Academic Press.

15. The term 'operant' was coined by influential behavioral psychologist B. F. Skinner to replace terms like 'voluntary' which he considered to be mentalistic. Terminological innovation played a large role in Skinner's rhetoric. See Staddon, J. (2001)

The new behaviorism: Mind, mechanism and society. Philadelphia, PA: Psychology Press for a critical evaluation of Skinner's approach.

16. Probabilistic choice: a simple invariance. *Behavioural Processes*, 15 (1987) 59–92. Horner, J & Staddon, J. E. R. http://dukespace.lib.duke.edu/dspace/handle/10161/3231

17. Simon, H. A., 1956. Rational choice and the structure of the environment. *Psychol. Rev.*, 63: 129–138.

18. Simon, H. A. (1957). *Models of man: Social and rational.* New York: Wiley

19. For a collection of important papers, see *Preference, Belief, and Similarity: Selected Writings of Amos Tversky* edited by Eldar Shafir. MIT/Bradford, 2004. Available on the web at http://www.blutner.de/MOL%20project/Tversky_texts.pdf

20. For details of these strange rites see http://en.wikipedia.org/wiki/Endowment_effect, and for an entertaining account of many other studies in behavioral economics see Ariely's *Predictably Irrational: The Hidden Forces that Shape our Decisions.* HarperCollins, 2008.

21. Which may itself be a by-product of linear waiting, which I discuss in a moment: Staddon, J. E. R. & Cerutti, D. T. (2003) Operant behavior. *Annual Review of Psychology*, 54:115–144, pp. 137–9.

22. See, for example, Gigerenzer, G., & Selten, R. (Eds.). (2001). *Bounded rationality: The adaptive toolbox.* Cambridge, Mass.: MIT Press for a related set of arguments.

23. CBS News program *60 Minutes*, January 13, 2012; and check out http://en.wikipedia.org/wiki/New_Caledonian_Crow for an account and videos.

24. J. R. Krebs & N. B. Davies *Behavioural Ecology*, Oxford U. P. (1984)

25. As paraphrased in a biographical article by Larissa MacFarqhar, *New Yorker*, March 1. 2010.

26. Maynard Smith, J. Theory in evolution. *Annual Review of Ecology and Systematics,*1978, 9, 31–56; Oster, J. F., & Wilson, E. 0. *Caste and ecology in the social insects.* Princeton: Princeton University Press, 1978; Staddon *Adaptive Behavior and Learning* (2010/1983) http://dukespace.lib.duke.edu/dspace/handle/10161/2878, Chapters 7–9. See for example Glaister, S. (1972) *Mathematical methods for economists.* London: Gray-Mills. For psychological commentary on the issue see J. E. R. Staddon, J. E. R. (1991) Selective choice: A commentary on Herrnstein (1990). *American Psychologist*, 793–797 http://dukespace.lib.duke.edu/dspace/handle/10161/3395

Staddon, J. E. R. (1992) Rationality, melioration and law-of-effect models for choice. *Psychological Science, 3,* 136–141. http://dukespace.lib.duke.edu/dspace/handle/10161/3895

27. On a fixed-interval reinforcement schedule, the subject typically waits a fixed fraction *d* of the scheduled time *I* between rewards. In this new situation where the timer is started by the first response, he will wait the same fraction of the new interreward time *wait+I*. For example, if the organism typically waits half the time to reward, i.e., 15 seconds when the scheduled interval is 30 seconds, then he

will wait 30 seconds on a 30-s response-initiated–30-s schedule, thus unnecessarily delaying each food delivery by 30 seconds.

28. There seem to be limitations on memory processes that cause memory for the time of *reward* to overshadow memory for the time of the clock-starting *response*, which is the real temporal cue – because valuable events, like reward, are better remembered than neutral events, like a key-peck. These effects show up in other experiments also – on the so-called 'frustration' effect, for example (see, for example, Chapter 13 in *Adaptive Behavior and Learning* http://dukespace.lib.duke.edu/dspace/handle/10161/2878, or a paper Staddon, J. E. R. (1970). Temporal effects of reinforcement: A negative "frustration" effect. *Learning and Motivation, 1*, 227–247. http://dukespace.lib.duke.edu/dspace/handle/10161/3230)

29. Ludvig, E. A., & Staddon, J. E. R. (2004) The conditions for temporal tracking on interval schedules of reinforcement. *Journal of Experimental Psychology: Animal Behavior Processes*, 30(4), 299–316.

30. Here's a worked example. On a response-initiated fixed-interval schedule, suppose the animal typically waits for half the programmed interval (wait-time-ratio = .5), i.e., 10 s for a 20-s interval. Suppose the next interval is set (by the experimenter) to always be 1.5 times the wait time, i.e., to 15 s. Well, the next wait will be just 7.5, the interval after that just 11.25 s, the succeeding wait just 5.625 and so on until the wait time and the interval approaches zero. This is 'rational' behavior: the animal behaves in a such a way as to set the interfood interval as short as possible. On other hand, suppose the experimenter-set multiplier is 3 rather than 1.5. Now the same process that produced 'rational' behavior produces highly 'irrational' behavior. Starting with a 20-s interval and a succeeding pause of 10 s, the program sets the next interval to 30 s with a pause of 15 s, the next to 45 s, and so on so that the time between food deliveries gets longer and longer. Reference: Typical delay determines waiting time on periodic-food schedules: static and dynamic tests C. D. L. Wynne and J. E. R. Staddon http://dukespace.lib.duke.edu/dspace/handle/10161/3387

CHAPTER 4

1. I will use EMT rather than EMH.

2. http://en.wikipedia.org/wiki/Efficient-market_hypothesis. Notice that according to strong EMT, there is no real 'insider information' and according to all versions, making insider trading illegal (as it is in the U.S. and many other countries) should make markets *in*efficient.

3. E. Fama, Efficient capital markets: A review of theory and empirical work. *The Journal of Finance*, 25, no. 2, 1970. See also The Efficient market theory and Its Critics by Burton G. Malkiel, Princeton University, CEPS Working Paper No. 91, April 2003.

4. John Cassidy, *How Markets Fail*. Kindle Ed. 2010.

5. Malkiel, *A Random Walk Down Wall Street*, 10th Ed. Kindle Edition, 2010.

6. *60 Minutes*, November 14, 2011. In response to this program, the Stop Trading on Congressional Knowledge (STOCK) Act, banning insider trading on Capitol Hill was signed into law on April 4, 2012, a rare victory for the citizenry.

7. Justin Fox, *The myth of the rational market.*

8. Carl Gauss (1777–1855) being the brilliant German mathematician who worked out the theory behind the bell curve.

9. In general stock prices random-walk 'normally' only over the shortest time period. Over realistic periods, the distribution has much 'longer tails' – more extreme values – than predicted by the normal distribution. Nevertheless, the convenience of the normal distribution, and the optimistic assessment of risk that it provides, has made it overwhelmingly popular among risk-modeling 'quants.'

10. Tversky, A., and Gilovich, T. (1989). The hot hand: Statistical reality or cognitive illusion? *Chance*, 2(4), 31–34.

11. There are also problems with scaling according to the initial value of a stock. A low-valued stock is obviously more likely to random-walk through zero than a high-valued one with the same variability (volatility), for example. This may not be realistic.

12. There are obvious exceptions to this too: so-called penny stocks tend to be more volatile than higher-valued ones. This assumption, if it is generally true at all, is true only for variation in the price of a given stock, not for comparisons between stocks.

13. Fischer Black and Myron Scholes, The pricing of options and corporate liabilities. *The Journal of Political Economy*, Vol. 81, No. 3 (May – Jun., 1973), pp. 637–654.

14. For recent work on Weber-Fechner representation of number see Stanislas Dehaene: The neural basis of the Weber–Fechner law: a logarithmic mental number line, *TRENDS in Cognitive Sciences* Vol.7 No.4 April 2003.

15. Maureen Dowd, All the Way to the Bank, *NYT*, 11/12/09. Mr. Blankfein may well smile as he planned to trouser a rumored $100M in 2010 – until tragedy (public outrage) struck and he received in the end only a meager $9M.

16. See, for example, http://mises.org/. The target article is Hayek's The Use of Knowledge in Society. *American Economic Review*, 1945. http://www.econlib.org/library/Essays/hykKnw1.html

CHAPTER 5

1. For fuller accounts of bubble history see Niall Ferguson's *The ascent of money.* New York: Penguin, 2008 and the standard work *Manias, Panics, and Crashes: A History of Financial Crises*. Charles P. Kindleberger John Wiley & Sons, New York, 1978/2000 (4ᵗʰ edition). A definitive account of the 1929 crash is Milton Friedman & Anna Schwartz *The great contraction 1929–1933*. NBER, Princeton U. P., 1963, although Keynes in his *General Theory* has a rather different view, now in the ascendant (all agree that more money is the solution to depression, however). A lighter, and lazier, disaster-by-disaster account is J. K. Galbraith, *The great crash 1929*, Penguin, 1954/1992.

2. See Martin Wolf's speech (*FT* November 27, 2008), Richard Posner's *Failure of Capitalism*, Harvard U.P., 2009, Nouriel Roubini & Stephen Mihm *Crisis Economics* (2010, Penguin) and Bezemer, D. J. (2009) 'No one saw this coming': Understanding financial crisis through accounting models. *Accounting, Organizations and Society*, 35(7), 678–88. for longer lists of prescient critics. Richard

Bookstaber warned early on about the dangers of derivatives in *A demon of our own design: Markets, Hedge Funds, and the Perils of Financial Innovation* (2007). One or two Cassandras did time the crash pretty accurately, as I point out in Chapter 12.

3. Just how well paid, and at what cost to the public, is ably documented in *Reckless Endangerment: How Outsized Ambition, Greed. and Corruption Led to Economic Armageddon* by NYT reporters Gretchen Morgenson and Joshua Rosner. Time Books/Henry Holt & Co., 2011.

4. The U.S. mortgage market is complex. The intertwining of quasi-government, but private-profit-making, agencies – Fannie, Freddie et al. – with private mortgage origination and the evolution of securitization, all justified by their supposed contribution to the 'American' dream' of home ownership has created a Frankenstein monster that is proving impossible to slay. The U.S. system has is now much more costly, and no more effective in its avowed aim, than home-loan arrangements in other countries. A good summary of the problem has been put together by NPR's 'Planet Money' program. Podcasts are available at:

http://www.npr.org/blogs/money/2011/01/14/132940442/the-friday-podcast-the-frankenstein-mortgage

http://www.npr.org/blogs/money/2011/03/29/134957774/the-tuesday-podcast-fannie-and-freddies-rise-and-fall

http://www.npr.org/blogs/money/2011/04/01/135044094/the-friday-podcast-what-comes-after-fannie-and-freddie

5. http://en.wikipedia.org/wiki/Freddie_Mac

6. Thomas Sowell, *Economic facts and fallacies*, Basic Books, 2008.

7. Peter Schweizer, *Architects of Ruin*, Harper-Collins, 2009, Kindle edition.

8. Joseph E. Stiglitz, *Freefall: America, Free Markets and the Sinking of the World Economy.* New York: W. W. Norton, 2010.)

9. For the definitive English account of the problem of confidence-inducing names ('market efficiency', q.v.), check out http://www.youtube.com/watch?v=mzJmTCYmo9g

10. William D. Cohan, *House of cards: A tale of hubris and wretched excess on Wall Street*, New York: Doubleday, 2009. For a fascinating history of Ranieri's rise see *Liar's Poker: Rising Through the Wreckage on Wall Street*, by Michael Lewis. Penguin, 1990.

11. Why Toxic Assets Are So Hard to Clean Up, By Kenneth E. Scott and John B. Taylor, WSJ, July, 20, 2009.

12. The obsessive press interest in Greenspan's interest-rate manipulations during the 1990s reminds me irresistibly of the hysterical deadpan scene in the movie *This is Spinal Tap* where past-it rocker Christopher Guest proudly shows us that his new amp "goes up to 11." See if you detect the resemblance: http://www.youtube.com/watch?v=EbVKWCpNFhY

13. *Crisis Economics: A crash course in the future of finance,* by Nouriel Roubini & Stephen Mihm. Allen Lane, London, 2010.

14. Morgenson & Rosner *Reckless Endangerment.* Times Books, 2011.

15. *The Big Short* Michael Lewis, 2010, Kindle ed.

16. Matt Taibbi in *Griftopia, Bubble Machines, Vampire Squids, and the Long Con that is Breaking America*, 2010, Kindle ed.

17. *Griftopia,*

18. For example, the failed British bank Northern Rock, during the peak of the UK housing boom, offered loans of up to 125% of the assessed value of a house. Many others followed suit.

19. "No income, no job, no assets"

20. *Newsweek*, 9/27/2008

21. Rumsfeld was mocked for his perfectly sensible statement simply because he was the bad guy of choice for much of the media at that time. The same fate has befallen Glenn Beck, Sarah Palin and even President Obama, in recent years. None of these folk is without flaw; but because of their unpopularity they are likely to get clobbered even if they announce that the sun will rise on the morrow.

22. See Frank Knight (1885–1972) in his *Risk, Uncertainty and Profit* (1921). There are in fact more than two types of risk, as I point out in Chapter 11.

23. http://en.wikipedia.org/wiki/Credit_default_swap#Systemic_risk

24. *Crisis Economics: A crash course in the future of finance,* by Nouriel Roubini & Stephen Mihm. Allen Lane, London, 2010. P. 35.

25. International Swaps and Derivatives Association, "ISDA Mid-year 2008 Market Survey," news release, September 24, 2008, available at www.isda.org/press/ press092508.html

29. Live long and prosper. *The Economist*, Feb. 6, 2010.

27. *NYT* Published: June 21, 2011.

CHAPTER 6

1. J. K. Galbraith, *The great crash 1929*, Penguin, 1954/1992. P. 210.

2. For math lovers: $\Delta M = k_1 \Delta H - k_2 D$, and $D = k_3 H^c$, where $\Delta =$ "change in", $M =$ total mortgages, $D =$ total defaults, $H =$ average house price and k_i and c are positive constants. This process can be stable or periodic, depending on the value of the constants.

3. See, for example *Economics* (18th edition) By Paul A. Samuelson & William D. Nordhaus, McGraw Hill, 2009; *Money, information and uncertainty.* 2nd ed. C. A. E. Goodhart, 1989.

4. E.g., Richard Posner's acerbic *Public intellectuals.* Harvard U.P., 2000, p. 69. Posner brilliantly skewers a whole flock of academic would-be opinion makers, but even he buys into static supply-and-demand analysis.

5. A pioneer of this approach is W. Brian Arthur, see, for example, his Complexity and the Economy. *Science*, 2 April 1999, 284, 107–109. See Steve Keen's website http://www.debunkingeconomics.com/ for an accessible review and more criticism of neoclassical theory, and various talks at the April 8–11, 2010, George

Soros-sponsored conference: http://ineteconomics.org/ at the new Institute for New Economic Thinking.

6. For math lovers: $x(t+1) = x(t).(k_1P(t)-k_2)+x(t)$, and $P(t+1) = k_3(x(t)-x(t+1))+P(t)$, where P = price, $x(t)$ is supply at time-step t and k_i are constants.

7. For beautiful illustrations of chaotic behavior in a system like the one I used for these graphs, see the *logistic map*, at http://en.wikipedia.org/wiki/Logistic_map

8. *The economy needs agent-based modelling.* The leaders of the world are flying the economy by the seat of their pants, say J. Doyne Farmer and Duncan Foley. There is, however, a better way to help guide financial policies. *Nature*, Vol 460|6 August 2009.

9. WSJ, MAY 7, 2009.

10. Henry Blodget, Why Wall Street Always Blows It. *The Atlantic*, 2008: http://www.theatlantic.com/doc/200812/blodget-wall-street

11. Misleadingly populist (the book is more nuanced than this) subtitle of Gillian Tett's excellent *Fool's Gold* (London: Little, Brown, 2009).

12. William D. Cohan, *House of cards: A tale of hubris and wretched excess on Wall Street*, New York: Doubleday, 2009.

13. Math lovers: $V(t+1) = (.5-rand).s.V(t)+V(t)+w.\Delta V_{avg}(t)$, if Δ>threshold, s = standard deviation, w = weighting. In fact, random walk is so unstable, that even if there is no systematic change day-by-say, adding only positive changes in the average is often sufficient to cause a runaway boom in this model.

14. http://dealbook.blogs.nytimes.com/2010/02/04/uk-studying-high-frequency-trading/

15. http://online.wsj.com/article/SB10001424052748704370704575227754131412596.html The current view is that this crash, like all others, was a product of positive feedback – in this case, automatic trades triggered by an increase in trade volume.

16. Alan Greenspan's famously guarded note of caution in 1996.

17. Cited in Justin Fox, *The myth of the rational market.*

CHAPTER 7

1. See, for example, Symmetry and conservation laws. Eugene P. Wigner *Proc Natl. Acad. Sci. U. S. A.* 1964 May; 51(5): 956–965.

2. Harvard's Harvey Mansfield in "The Legacy of the Late Sixties," in Stephen Macedo, ed., *Reassessing the Sixties.* New York: W. W. Norton, 1997. Pp. 21–45. Recent law suits, in the UK and elsewhere, claiming immunity from (for example) firing because environmentalism should be treated like a religion, show that Mansfield's witticism is no joke. Academics are now in on the idea, e.g., Green guilt, by Stephen Asma, *Chronicle of Higher Education, Chronicle Review,* 2010, January 15, p. B11–12.

3. http://www.theatlantic.com/magazine/archive/2008/07/distracting-miss-daisy/6873/

4. In a deflationary world, of course $1000 now will be worth more in a year, but if we get the money now we will still have it in a year, so npv can never be *more* than current value.

5. http://en.wikipedia.org/wiki/Black_Monday_%281987%29

6. Math: $V(t+1) = (.5\text{-rand}).s.V(t)+V(t)+w.\Delta V_{avg}(t)$, if $\Delta>$threshold, s = standard deviation; weighting $w = (K - Vavg)$, where K is the fixed average (conserved) market price. Thus when $Vavg$ is greater or less than K, each stock price is reduced or incremented so that the average never deviates by much from K.

7. Much has been written on the meaning, and morality, of economic growth. For a brief introduction see The Capitalist Manifesto, a review by Gregg Easterbrook of *The Moral Consequences of Economic Growth*, by Benjamin M. Friedman, *New York Times*, November 27, 2005. The December 19, 2009, issue of *The Economist* was entirely devoted to the idea of progress. Megan McCardle, in the November, 2009, *The Atlantic* reviews the history and problems with GDP as a measure of national well-being.

8. http://www.telegraph.co.uk/news/worldnews/europe/france/6189530/Nicolas-Sarkozy-wants-to-measure-economic-success-in-happiness.html

9. See, for example, the excellent discussion of Maynard Keynes's sophisticated moral philosophy in Robert Skidelsky's *Keynes: The Return of the Master*. New York: PublicAffairs, 2009. Some still argue that virtue is more important than happiness: see, for example, Megan McArdle at http://www.theatlantic.com/national/archive/2010/06/the-case-against-happiness/58719/

10. Joseph Stiglitz, *Freefall*, Chapter 10.

11. Princeton, 2010

12. Will Wilkinson: In pursuit of happiness research: Is it reliable? What does it imply for policy? *Policy Research* No. 590 April 11, 2007.

13. Jean-Jacques Rousseau, *Discourse on Inequality*, 1754.

14. Levitt and Dubner in their best-seller *Superfreakonomics* dispute Smith and point to a recent study with rhesus monkeys that purports to show the development of a money economy. This study, apparently a reprise of much older operant conditioning work on so-called token economies, nevertheless fails to show that ape traders would make it in a bazaar much less the stock exchange.

15. Ted R. Schultz (2000) In search of ant ancestors. *PNAS* December 19, vol. 97 no. 26 14028–14029

16. http://en.wikipedia.org/wiki/Biomass_%28ecology%29#Terrestrial_biomass

17. Robert Reich, Preface to *The Spirit Level: Why Greater Equality Makes Societies Stronger* by Richard Wilkinson & Kate Pickett; UK: Allen Lane, 2009.

18. http://inflationdata.com/inflation/Consumer_Price_Index/HistoricalCPI.aspx?rsCPI_currentPage=0.

19. http://en.wikipedia.org/wiki/Gini_coefficient#US_income_Gini_indices_over_time

20. http://www.infoplease.com/ipa/A0104670.html See also Elizabeth Warren's *The two-income trap* (2003, Basic Books) for other problems for two-income families.

21. http://www.lifesitenews.com/news/archive/ldn/2007/jan/07011703

22. These sociological changes are ably reviewed by Charles Murray in *Coming Apart: The State of White America, 1960–2010*. Crown Forum, 2012.

23. Life expectancy at birth: http://earthtrends.wri.org/text/population-health/variable–379.html

24. 60 Minutes, CBS News, November 22, 2009.

25. Atul Gawande provides a vivid account of modern medicine and the end-of-life problem in *The New Yorker* http://www.newyorker.com/reporting/2010/08/02/100802fa_fact_gaw

26. Newsflash: In late 2010 plans to introduce new hop-on-hop-off buses in London were announced. http://www.bbc.co.UK/news/UK-england-london–11734064

CHAPTER 8

1. For a clear historical review, see Niall Ferguson's *The Ascent of Money* (2008).

2. Richard Sylla, Political economy of supplying money to a growing economy: Monetary regimes and the search for an anchor to stabilize the value of money. *Theoretical Inquiries in Law*, Volume 11, Number 1 January 2010.

3. Guido Hülsmann, *The Ethics of Money Production* (Auburn, Ala.: Ludwig von Mises Institute, 2008, p. 55). Cited in Thomas E. Woods Jr. *Meltdown: A Free-Market Look at Why the Stock Market Collapsed, the Economy Tanked, and Government Bailouts Will Make Things Worse.* Washington, DC: Regnery, 2009.

4. http://www.bbc.co.uk/news/world-europe–17680904

5. http://www.wral.com/news/state/story/9379107/

6. http://en.wikipedia.org/wiki/Liberty_Dollar

7. See, for example, Crazy as a gold bug. Tom Bethell, *New York*, Feb. 4, 1980.

8. http://seekingalpha.com/article/262205-utah-s-gold-law-challenging-the-supremacy-of-the-dollar

9. http://en.wikipedia.org/wiki/Legal_Tender_Cases

10. Ferguson, *Ascent of Money*, p. 96–7.

11. http://www.cato.org/zimbabwe

12. See, for example, the historical review in *This time is different: Eight centuries of financial folly*, by Carmen Reinhart and Kenneth Rogoff, Princeton U. P., 2009.

13. J. Maynard Keynes (1919) *The Economic Consequences of the Peace*. p. 235.

14. Phillips, A. W. H. "The Relation between Unemployment and the Rate of Change of Money Wage Rates in the United Kingdom, 1861–1957." *Economica* NS 25, no. 2 (1958): 283–99. Phillips dealt primarily with wage inflation, but the inverse argument was soon extended to price inflation.

15. *Paper Money* by "Adam Smith," (George J.W. Goodman), 1981.

16. For a reasoned critique of the idea see Fe*deral Reserve Bank of Minneapolis Quarterly Review*, Vol. 25, No. 1, Winter 2001, pp. 2–11. Are Phillips Curves Useful for Forecasting Inflation? by Andrew Atkeson and Lee E. Ohanian

17. George A. Akerloff and Robert J. Shiller, see *Animal spirits: How human psychology drives the economy and why it matters for global capitalism*. Princeton U. P., 2009.

18. http://www.slate.com/id/1937/#

19. Richard Posner (2009) *A Failure of Capitalism*. Cambridge, MA: Harvard U.P. pp. 185–6.

20. Paul Krugman, *NYT* Magazine, September 6, 2009.

21. Eric Lonergan, *Money*, Durham, UK, Acumen, 2009, p. 11.

22. See a comment by Juan Ramón Rallo at http://blog.mises.org/archives/009699. asp that criticizes Krugman's analysis in detail.

23. http://en.wikipedia.org/wiki/Paradox_of_thrift

24. Ron Paul *End the Fed*, Kindle edition, 2009.

25. Quoted in Ron Paul *End the Fed*, Kindle edition, 2009.

26. *The Economist*, December 340, 2009: http://www.economist.com/opinion/displaystory.cfm?story_id=15174533

27. http://www.wilmott.com/blogs/paul/index.cfm/2009/9/1/Hoping-For-One-L-Of-A-Recovery

28. Op ed by Tyler Cowen, *NYT* September 18, 2010.

29. Wikipedia has a good account: http://en.wikipedia.org/wiki/Money_supply

30. Larry J. Sechrest *Free banking: History, and a laissez faire model*. Auburn AL: Mises Institute, *2008*.

31. "An ounce of prevention.", David Moss http://harvardmagazine.com/2009/09/financial-risk-management-plan?page=all

32. Monetary National Income Analogue Computer, so named by a U.S. economist A. P. Lerner. My account is based on the summary at the site of the New Zealand Institute of Economic Research Inc (NZIER).

33. P. A. Samuelson *Economics: An Introductory Analysis*. 3ʳᵈ Ed. McGraw-Hill, 1955, p. 262.

34. BIS Working Papers, No 35. Central banking post-crisis: What compass for uncharted waters? by Claudio Borio

35. See books by William Cohan, Gillian Tett, Simon Johnson and many others.

36. See, for example *Secrets of the Temple* by William Greider, Simon & Schuster, 1987. An entertaining, highly critical, well-documented, but alarmingly conspiratorial, account is *The Creature from Jekyll Island: A Second Look at the Federal Reserve*, by G. Edward Griffin, American Media, 2010.

37. http://en.wikipedia.org/wiki/Federal_Reserve_System

38. There is also something called the *discount window* which is similar in effect to open-market operations, but targeted to specific beneficiaries (banks).

39. http://en.wikipedia.org/wiki/Federal_Reserve_System

40. Thomas E. Woods Jr. *Meltdown*, Washington, DC: Regnery, 2009

41. http://www.federalreserve.gov/monetarypolicy/openmarket.htm

42. Quantitative easing is explained more fully at http://www.youtube.com/watch?v=PTUY16CkS-k

43. Ben Bernanke, Congressional testimony.

44. John Maynard Keynes, The Great Slump of 1930, http://www.gutenberg.ca/ebooks/keynes-slump/keynes-slump–00-h.html

45. This suggestion is less ridiculous than it may appears. John Kay ("Money, like hat-wearing, depends on convention, not laws" *FT* Feb. 8, 2012) recently pointed out that multiple currencies already exist in the UK. "The Scottish pound already exists....The only legal tender for the settlement of a debt in Scotland is coins from the Royal Mint. But if you try to buy a house in Scotland with pound coins, your offer will not be well received. Legal tender is a concept with no practical relevance. The currency that is accepted is the currency people are willing to accept." Scottish pound notes are accepted by London cabbies and Marks and Spencer stores as well as by Scottish merchants.

CHAPTER 9

1. For light relief, and a simplified version of their differences, check out the Keynes-Hayek rap video: http://cafehayek.com/2010/01/keynes-vs-hayek-rap-video.html

2. http://www.newstatesman.com/200012250058

3. Bloomsbury is the area in central London, around the British Museum and University College, where the Bloomsburys lived.

4. Michael Holroyd, *Lytton Strachey: A Critical Biography*, volume 2: The Years of Achievement (1910–1932), Heinemann, 1968.

5. Roy Harrod, The Life of John Maynard Keynes (London: Macmillan, 1951). Robert Skidelsky, Maynard Keynes: Hopes Betrayed, 1883–1920 v.1; John Maynard Keynes: The Economist as Saviour, 1920–37 v.2: John Maynard Keynes: Fighting for Britain, 1937–1946 v.3. A fine short summary of Keynes' life, philosophy and important books about him, is John Cassidy's "The Demand Doctor: What Would John Maynard Keys tell us to do now – and Should We listen?" in the October 10, 2011 *New Yorker*.

6. *General Theory*, Ch. 24.

7. *General Theory*, Chapter 16.

8. Introduction to a new edition of *The General Theory of Employment, Interest, and Money*. Basingstoke, UK: Palgrave Macmillan, 2007.

9. Not everyone agrees. There is a burgeoning hot new field of *neuroeconomics* that basically tries to identify the elements of standard economic decision models in parts of the human brain. Despite the number of very smart researchers who are engaged in this endeavor, it is probably doomed to disappoint, for two reasons. First, wherever decision-making has been studied experimentally (particularly with animals, where it is simpler), the process fails to conform to the standard economic model. Thus, neuroeconomics imposes on brain function a functional template that is probably false. Second, we have no well-developed body of data showing how the brain functions, and how it looks (under fMRI and other imaging methods), during a wide variety of reward-based tasks. Yet such an inductive data base is necessary to make an informed guess at how the brain actually solves these problems.

It seems to me a very long shot indeed to assume that we already know, and just need to find out where the bits of our model reside in the gray matter.

10. This account is much simplified. The set of heuristics can itself evolve through time as the animal learns more and more, for example. But the basic process seems to be as I describe it.

11. See discussion of feature effects in Chapter 11 of *Adaptive Behavior and Learning* (2003) http://dukespace.lib.duke.edu/dspace/handle/10161/2878

12. Yerkes, R. M., & Dodson, J. D. (1908) The relation of strength of stimulus to rapidity of habit-formation. *Journal of Comparative Neurology and Psychology, 18*, 459–482

13. John Maynard Keynes, The great slump of 1930. http://www.gutenberg.ca/ebooks/keynes-slump/keynes-slump–00-h.html. Despite his brilliance and many memorable passages, Keynes' frequent neologisms ('wage-goods' for 'consumer goods,' etc.), many of which have failed to gain currency, grand abstract claims, and complex sentence structure often make his writing obscure to the point of impenetrability. Economic journalist Henry Hazlitt wrote a whole book *The Failure Of The "New Economics": An Analysis Of The Keynesian Fallacies* (New York: Van Nostrand, 1959) dissecting *The General Theory* chapter by chapter. Many of his criticisms make sense and he clarifies much of what Keynes had to say.

14. State, not Federal – Federal Government jobs are usually immune from these shocks because the Feds, unlike most of the states, are not bound to balance their budget.

15. Most notably Joseph E. Stiglitz, *Freefall: America, Free Markets and the Sinking of the World Economy*. New York: W. W. Norton, 2010, and several publications by George A. Akerloff and Robert J. Shiller, most recently *Animal spirits: How human psychology drives the economy and why it matters for global capitalism.*, Princeton U. P., 2009.

16. Akerloff & Shiller, 2009.

17. Akerloff & Shiller, 2009.

18. Keynes, simplified to the point of parody, still has influential fans, though. As late as October 2011, Lawrence Summers (yes, it's him again), had this to say: "The central irony of financial crisis is that while it is caused by too much confidence, too much borrowing and lending and too much spending, it can only be resolved with more confidence, more borrowing and lending, and more spending. *Most policy failures in the U.S. stem from a failure to appreciate this truism* and therefore to take steps that would have been productive pre-crisis but are counterproductive now with the economy severely constrained by lack of confidence and demand." [*Financial Times*, October 24, 2011. My emphasis] To advocate 'hair of the dog' as a cure for the macroeconomy is bold; to affirm it as a truism borders on the deranged.

CHAPTER 10

1. http://ineteconomics.org/video/andrew-sheng-sustainability-requires-caging-godzillas

2. For example, Stimulus by Fed Is Disappointing, Economists Say. By Binyamin Appelbaum, *NYT* April 24, 2011. The Keynesian Growth Discount: The results

of our three-year economic experiment are in. *WSJ* REVIEW & OUTLOOK, APRIL 29, 2011

3. Stiglitz, 2010.

4. Gold in form of bullion or coins. Jewelry was OK.

5. John Cassidy, *Why markets fail*, 2010., Figure 17.1.

6. See for, example, The Poor Are Better Off Renting: Why have we encouraged people to put all their savings in one asset? *WSJ*, Feb. 10, 2010.

7. http://www.nytimes.com/2010/04/25/magazine/25fob-wwln-t.html

8. http://www.timesonline.co.UK/tol/news/politics/article1567419.ece

9. http://en.wikipedia.org/wiki/Homeownership_in_the_United_States

10. http://online.wsj.com/article/SB1000142405274870435350457559687206396791 4.html?mod=WSJ_Opinion_LEFTTopOpinion

11. Roger Lowenstein *NYT,* March 5, 2006 Who Needs the Mortgage-Interest Deduction?

12. Sarah Quinn, *Securitization and the State.* U. C. Berkeley: http://sarahquinnsociology.com/documents/SecuritizationandtheStateASA2008.pdf

13. http://online.wsj.com/article/SB123876318076986497.html.

14. The sorry tale of political influence and government collusion that lay behind the rise of Fannie (and, to a lesser extent Freddie), beginning in the 1990s, is chronicled in great detail by *New York Times* reporter Gretchen Morgenson and her co-author Joshua Rosner in *Reckless Endangerment: How outsized ambition, greed, and corruption led to economic Armageddon,* Times Books, 2011.

15. The FTC discovers HUD. *WSJ* March 21, 1979, p. 22.

16. http://www.cbo.gov/doc.cfm?index=13&type=0

17. http://en.wikipedia.org/wiki/Fannie_Mae

18. Only if the homeowner is more interested in his children, who will inherit the home, than in himself does a house constitute a real investment. But few first-time home buyers are in this position, I suspect.

19. News flash: Not any more, apparently: "I used to feel proud of my role, but I don't feel that way anymore." *Parade* magazine, May 23, 2010.

20. Quoted in Chrystia Freeland's 2011 article The Rise of the New Global Elite. http://www.theatlantic.com/magazine/archive/2011/01/the-rise-of-the-new-global-elite/8343/

21. http://www.jparsons.net/housingbubble/

22. State of the Union address, January 27, 2010.

23. http://www.prospectmagazine.co.UK/2009/08/how-to-tame-global-finance/

24. *General Theory...,* Book 4, Chapter 12, Section 6, p. 142.

25. *The Guardian* Sept. 3, 2009.

26. Remarks by Mr Timothy F Geithner, President and Chief Executive Officer of the Federal Reserve Bank of New York, at the 2007 Credit Markets Symposium

hosted by the Federal Reserve Bank of Richmond, Charlotte, North Carolina, 23 March 2007.

27. *WSJ*, AUGUST 4, 2010.

28. Interview January 13, 2010, http://www.newyorker.com/online/blogs/johncassidy/2010/01/interview-with-eugene-fama.html

29. Greenspan's comment was reported in a PBS FRONTLINE program on Oct. 20, 2009.

30. For an early (June, 2007) good account of this magic before all its disastrous consequences had become apparent see http://www.youtube.com/watch?v=0YNyn1XGyWg&feature=related. For all the gory details, check out *Reckless Endangerment: How outsized ambition, greed, and corruption led to economic Armageddon*, by Gretchen Morgenson and Joshua Rosner. Times books, 2011.

31. J. Stiglitz, *Freefall*, 2010.

32. See also Testimony of Richard Bookstaber Submitted to the Senate of the United States, Committee on Agriculture, Nutrition, and Forestry For the Hearing: "Regulatory Reform and the Derivatives Markets" June 4, 2009.

33. …in a nonlinear way, e.g., if a $1000 agreement has 10-min limit, $1M agreement might be allowed 100 minutes: T = A.

34. J. Stiglitz, *Freefall*, Kindle Edition, 2010.

35. Remarks by Mr Timothy F Geithner, President and Chief Executive Officer of the Federal Reserve Bank of New York, at the 2007 Credit Markets Symposium hosted by the Federal Reserve Bank of Richmond, Charlotte, North Carolina, 23 March 2007.

36. Bank for International Settlements; other estimates are even higher.

37. http://chartingtheeconomy.com/?p=665, and Simon Johnson The Quite Coup, *The Atlantic*, 2009: http://www.theatlantic.com/doc/200905/imf-advice

38. The Evolution of the U.S. Financial Industry from 1860 to 2007: Theory and Evidence. Thomas Philippon, New York University, *NBER*, *CEPR* November 2008

39. http://www.bis.org/review/r100716g.pdf; and *The Economist* July 17, 2010.

40. *The New Yorker*, November 29, 2010.

41. Estimated; appropriate income statistics were not routinely gathered until 1967.

42. http://ddr.nal.usda.gov/bitstream/10113/22832/1/CAT30948096.pdf

43. Claudia Goldin & Lawrence F. Katz (2008) Transitions: Career and family life cycles of the educational elite. *American Economic Review: Papers and Proceedings*, 98, 363–69.

44. *The Economist* April 3, 2010.

45. See for example Rajan's book *Fault Lines: How Hidden Fractures Still Threaten the World Economy.*, or the INET interview at http://ineteconomics.org/rajan-interview

46. Paul Krugman: http://www.nybooks.com/articles/archives/2009/jun/11/the-crisis-and-how-to-deal-with-it/?page=4

47. See *Bad Money* (Penguin, 2009) and earlier books and articles by Kevin Phillips.

48. Larry Elliot "The decline and fall of the American empire," *The Guardian*, June 6, 2011.

CHAPTER 11

1. See Nicholas Dunbar's *Inventing money: The story of Long-Term Capital Management and the legends behind it.* (2000, Kindle Edition)

2. *How* he might get it right, how he can accurately asses the risk of default of as financial instrument, is also problematic, but we don't need to worry about that for the moment because there are other, larger problems with CDSs.

3. *New York Times*, August 1, 2009

4. http://en.wikipedia.org/wiki/Monopoly

5. The problem is still unfolding but it seems likely that these rare brake 'failures' may in fact have more to do with the machine behind the wheel than the one on front of it. But the rapid change in public perception of the safety of Toyotas nevertheless had a devastating effect. I'm told by a colleague involved in the trial-lawyer tort business that some 28,000 Toyota-targeted lawsuits had been initiated by the middle of March 2010.

6. *LA Times*, March 3, 2010

7. "Toyota's woes drag down entire industry," *CNN*, February 4, 2010 2:05 p.m. EST

8. For a blow-by-blow see William D. Cohan's *House of Cards.*

9. (Freefall)

10. *Sunday Telegraph*, June 5, 2011.

11. http://www.nytimes.com/2010/04/01/business/01hedge.html?hp

12. http://sunshinereview.org/index.php/State_budget_issues,_2009–2010

13. Data from Federal sources cited by Simon Johnson and James Kwak, 2010, in *13 Bankers: The Wall Street Takeover and the Next Financial Meltdown* (Kindle Edition)

14. Simon Johnson The Quiet Coup, *The Atlantic*, 2009: http://www.theatlantic.com/doc/200905/imf-advice

15. Johnson and Kwak's book has a mesmerizing detailed history of the regulatory collapse since the end of WW2.

16. By the time of Windows 7, the two systems were pretty similar.

17. http://www.voxeu.org/index.php?q=node/1669

18. *On the Brink.* Henry Paulson, New York: Hachette, 2010.

19. Check out William Greider in *The Nation* and Newt Gingrich on ABC News: http://www.thenation.com/doc/20081006/greider and http://blogs.abcnews.com/politicalradar/2008/09/un-american-pla.html in September 2008.

20. Quoted in David Wessel, *In Fed we trust: Ben Bernanke's war on the great panic.* New York: Crown, 239.

21. *13 Bankers.*

22. Johnson's review of Paulson's 2010 book: http://www.tnr.com/book/review/inside-man?page=0,1

23. *The Economist*, print edition, May 8, 2010.

24. Thomas Woods, *Meltdown*, 2009; see also Woods' excellent talk at http://www.youtube.com/watch?v=czcUmnsprQI .

25. Burton Folsom, *New Deal or Raw Deal?* (Simon & Schuster, 2008), p. 2; see also Amity Shlaes *The forgotten man: A new history of the Great Depression*. New York: HarperCollins, 2007, and Lee E. Ohanian "What – or Who – Started the Great Depression?", forthcoming, *Journal of Economic Theory*.

26. Frank Hyman, Raleigh *News & Observer*, December 2011

27. http://www.economics-charts.com/gdp/gdp-1929–2004.html#semilog See also http://www.infoplease.com/ipa/A0104719.html

CHAPTER 12

1. Speech by Fed Chairman Ben Bernanke at the Independent Community Bankers of America's National Convention and Tech-world, Phoenix, Arizona. March 20, 2009

2. THE FINANCIAL CRISIS INQUIRY REPORT: Final Report of the National Commission on the Causes of the Financial and Economic Crisis in the United States. January 2011.

3. *WSJ*, APRIL 29, 2011, 4:07 P.M. ET.

4. http://thehill.com/opinion/columnists/dick-morris/92019-obamas-terrible-powers

5. *WSJ*, April 8, 2010.

6. I Saw the Crisis Coming. Why Didn't the Fed? By Michael J. Burry, *NYT*, April 4, 2010

7. Michael Lewis gives a detailed account of Burry's activities in his book *The Big Short: Inside the Doomsday Machine*, Kindle Edition, 2010.

8. For a quickie summary see: http://www.thedailyshow.com/watch/mon-march–8–2010/harry-markopolos

9. http://online.wsj.com/article/SB10001424052970204358004577032280966055886.html?mod=WSJ_hp_LEFTTopStories

10. Breaking news: on November 11, 2011, it was reported that eight SEC employees were 'disciplined' (not fired) over the Madoff affair. http://online.wsj.com/article/SB10001424052970204358004577032280966055886.html?mod=WSJ_hp_LEFTTopStories

11. http://www.ustreas.gov/press/releases/rr2616.htm

12. For a thoughtful account of the weaknesses of mathematical economics and the need for a broader approach see John Kay: The Map is Not the Territory: An Essay on the State of Economics. http://ineteconomics.org/blog/inet/john-kay-map-not-territory-essay-state-economics. Steve Keen in *Debunking Economics*, London: Zed Books, 2011, argues the problem is not math per se, but that mainstream economists use the wrong mathematics.

13. http://www.financialstability.gov/latest/tg_03232010b.htmln

14. Testimony before Congress, October 23, 2009: http://www.bloomberg.com/apps/news?pid=20601087&sid=ah5qh9Up4rIg

15. http://www.telegraph.co.uk/finance/newsbysector/banksandfinance/insurance/5446813/Lloyds-Names-face-bankruptcy-as-court-battle-ends.html

16. Sebastian Mallaby *More money than God*, Kindle edition, 2010

17. See, for example, *Inventing Money: The story of Long-Term Capital Management and the legends behind it*, by Nicholas Dunbar (Wiley, 2000).

18. The evidence is that smoking does not in fact have a collective cost, but no matter…

19. http://en.wikipedia.org/wiki/Value_at_risk; see Testimony of Richard Bookstaber Submitted to the U. S. House of Representatives, Committee on Science and Technology Subcommittee on Investigations and Oversight For the Hearing: "The Risks of Financial Modeling: VaR and the Economic Meltdown" September 10, 2009 for a clear account.

19a. *Financial Times*, 5/14/12, front page.

20. Since this statistic is computed daily, with a 5% false-positive rate, it is easy to see that over a period of a year the chance of a false-positive – judging incorrectly that a firm is sound – approaches one. Mistakes will certainly be made.

21. In practice, even this will be quite tricky—should the total risk of a bond be equal to it whole value? 70% of its value? Should it be different for different types of bond?—but fewer questionable assumptions are required than for VaR. As long as the rules are simple, arriving at a meaningful total risk value should be workable.

22. Math: The formula here is $y = ax^2/(x+b)$, where y = tax, x = total risk and a and b are constants (a = .01, b = 100,000 for the example). The idea is that when x is small the tax is close to zero; when x is very large, the tax approaches a (in the example: 1%). This or a similar formula would set up for the financial industry what biologists call *frequency-dependent selection*, whereby rare forms (small firms) have a fitness advantage over common forms (large firms).

23. For a vituperative, biased, insulting, but still shocking account of perennial crash-survivor Goldman Sachs' market manipulations check out Gonzo journalist Matt Taibbi's article. Famous line: "The world's most powerful investment bank is a great vampire squid wrapped around the face of humanity, relentlessly jamming its blood funnel into anything that smells like money." (!) http://www.rollingstone.com/politics/news/;kw=[3351,11459] .

24. Testimony before Congressman Waxman's committee: October 23, 2009: http://www.bloomberg.com/apps/news?pid=20601087&sid=ah5qh9Up4rIg

25. Richard Posner (2009) *A failure of capitalism: The crisis of '08 and the descent into depression*. Cambridge, Harvard U. P.

Index

Page numbers in *italic* refer to figures.